The *Power!* To Be Your Best!

Creating and Maintaining the Life You Deserve

Todd Duncan

PUBLISHING, INC.

What Leaders Are Saying about
The *Power!* to Be Your Best!

"The *Power!* to Be Your Best! *touches all the bases. It's informative, inspiring, well thought out, solid-a "how to," "why you should," and "how you can" book that will help you to discover and use your God-given abilities. The examples, stories, and illustrations make it easy and fun to read."*

Zig Ziglar, *author*

"The *Power!* to Be Your Best! *will captivate your heart and imagination. Read it and do what Todd Duncan says. You'll thank him for believing in you."*

Ken Blanchard, *co-author of* The One Minute Manager®

"Todd Duncan is passionate about the subject of excellence and being the best we can possibly be. He entertains the reader while he underlines the importance of on-purpose living. The *Power!* to Be Your Best! *is a great book, and I highly recommend it."*

Ted Engstrom, *President Emeritus, World Vision*

"In The *Power!* to Be Your Best! *Todd Duncan addresses the full spectrum of successful living...and delivers the goods. You can find lots of books that can help you make a better living, but this book does that and more: If you take it seriously and apply its principles, it will make you a better life. I've known Todd for 25 years, and I've watched him put these truths to work in his own life. If you're ready to go to the next level of meaningful experience, in pursuit of your God-given potential, you've got the right manual in your hands to help you get there!"*

Bob Shank, *President, Priority Living, Inc.*
Author of Total Life Management

"Inspired! That's how I felt after a brief review of The *Power!* to Be Your Best! Todd has truly earned his wings with this book. You won't be the same person after you read it and apply his strategies. You'll be a better you!"*

Tom Hopkins, *Master Sales Trainer*
Author of How to Master the Art of Selling

"Today's fast-moving, competitive world places tremendous demands on all who seek to nourish the needs of body, mind, and spirit. In The *Power!* to Be Your Best!, Todd Duncan gives the reader a step-by-step plan for living an on-purpose, productive, fulfilling life. Read this book and tap in to your potential."*

Denis Waitley
Author of Empires of the Mind

"The *Power!* to Be Your Best! *is pure Todd Duncan... energetic, passionate, chock-full of lessons learned and being learned, optimistic, and practical. Todd weaves his experiences and the lessons of others to stimulate your thinking, to raise your sights, and to touch your heart."*

Kevin W. McCarthy, *Author of* The On-Purpose Person

"Todd's words will both touch and transform you at your very core... and life will spring up in you."

Glenna Salsbury, *CSP, CPAE. Author of* The Art of the Fresh Start *and 1997–98 President of the National Speakers Association*

"Todd Duncan is a powerful speaker and motivator. More important, he is a man who has his priorities straight and is an expert in helping others to figure out what's important in life and to assist them in achieving lasting success. His new book is invaluable for someone who is failing, even a person whose life is a shambles. But I predict The Power! to Be Your Best! *will be even more significant for those who are already successful and now wish to go beyond success to true significance and achieve everything God intended for them. It's a great book which I heartily recommend."*

William Armstrong
U. S. Senator 1971–1991

"Give yourself The Power! *to Be Your Best! Todd has sat at the feet of the masters and has become one himself. Read this book and put it to work and you can live a more purposeful and rewarding life."*

W Mitchell, CPAE
Author of It's Not What Happens to You, It's What You Do about It

"Walt Disney used to tell us 'Use the power to be your best.' He would like the deep spirit in Todd's new book because conventional things are raised to unconventional heights."

Mike Vance
Former Dean, Disney University

"Todd Duncan has captured in this great book the essence of what makes him so powerful as a leader and a speaker. He comes from a depth of character and knowledge that is truly inspiring. It's clear that he lives his message, and those who follow his suggestions will live more abundantly as well. I was touched and inspired by the work. You will be also."

Jim Cathcart
CEO and Founder, Cathcart Institute
Author of The Acorn Principle

"Todd Duncan has long been a leader in inspiring and coaching others to win in life. In fact, his impact on our business has helped shape our success by giving people the right tools to order their life and achieve the measure of success they desire. Once again, Todd has opened a new door to understanding how to gain success in all areas of your life through his new book, The *Power!* to Be Your Best! His principle-centered approach and thought-provoking insights helped me see and understand my own life in new ways. The *Power!* to Be Your Best! *is a refreshing, enlightening, and practical approach on becoming just that...your best!"*

William L. (Wil) Armstrong, III
Partner, Director, Vice President, Cherry Creek Mortgage Company

"Read this book and catch the spirit...it will change your life. 4 stars. ★★★★! This is not just a book, it's an island of inspiration that you will want to return to again and again. When my son and daughter leave the nest in a few years, this is the book I'll place in their hands."

Dan Zadra, *CEO, Compendium, Inc.*
Best-selling author of the Gift of Inspiration *series*

"At the core of all our beings rests the desire to live an authentic life...to be our best. In this finely crafted book, Todd Duncan gives us not only the enthusiasm, he gives us a workable, doable action plan for being our best. Todd will take you by both the hands and the heart. You will be led to new heights of success and personal happiness."

Gregory L. Jantz, Ph.D.
Radio personality and best-selling author

"Todd Duncan's book, The *Power!* to Be Your Best!, *is an incredible blueprint for living your life by design. It has become my new "bible for success." You should make it yours too!"*

Dr. Tony Alessandra
Author of Charisma *and* The Platinum Rule

"Todd Duncan writes from his heart and his experiences. A deeply spiritual man, he understands what's really important in life. Learn from this true and decent human being, and follow the principles in The *Power!* to Be Your Best!"

Danielle Kennedy
Author of Balancing Acts, *lecturer, actress*

"Some of us never went to the popular course on winning friends and influencing people. Here, Todd Duncan offers us a new look at finding the power to be the best we can be. It often involves tough choices. What habits and distractions must we give up to be our best for God? What attitudes must we hold on to? Whether you are early in life's course, or an accomplished leader, the tools offered in The *Power!* to Be Your Best! *can help you finish life's race with excellence."*

Bishop Phillip H. Porter, *Chairman of the Board, Promise Keepers*
All Nations Pentecostal Center

This book is dedicated to

Sheryl, my wife,

for shaping my vision and centering my purpose.

Jonathan and Matthew, my sons,

for being my inspiration and my hope.

My mother and father,

for giving me the compass to navigate through life.

First printing, October, 1998
Published by Dove Publishing
7590 Fay Avenue, Suite 402, San Diego, CA 92037

Unless otherwise indicated, Scripture quotations used in this book are from the
New King James Version (NKJV). Copyright©1979, 1980, 1982, 1990,
Thomas Nelson, Inc., Publisher.
Scripture quotations marked NASB are from the *New American Standard Bible*
©1960, 1977 by the Lockman Foundation.
Scripture quotations marked TEV are from The *Good News Bible*, Today's English
Version—Old Testament: Copyright©American Bible Society 1976;
New Testament: Copyright©American Bible Society, 1966, 1971, 1976.
Scripture quotations marked TLB are from *The Living Bible* ©1971 by Tyndale
House Publishers, Wheaton, Ill. Used by permission.

Library of Congress Cataloging-in-Publication Data
Duncan, Todd 1957
[The power to be your best]
Includes biographical references
ISBN 0-9665134-0-1
1. Success. 2. Motivation. 3. Life Conduct. 4. Self-Help.

For more information on Todd Duncan's books, seminars,
and video and audio materials, write:
Todd Duncan—7590 Fay Avenue, Suite 402, La Jolla, CA 92037
e-mail: tdg@toddduncan.com
Website: www.toddduncan.com
Call: 1-877-833-3683

Printed in the United States of America

Special Thanks

This book would not have been possible had it not been for the contributions of many people. It is these people to whom I offer my most sincere thanks. Thank you for making a difference in the finished product.

Sheryl Duncan—Thank you for your coaching over the years. Your guidance early on helped me to know that waiting to write the right book was far more important than hurrying to write just any book. Thank you for being my lifemate. I know that our future is bright.

John Ross—Thank you for your incredible efforts in getting this manuscript into the hands of the right leaders in our country for their endorsements. Your follow-through and positioning has led to some of the best minds in America giving this work a "thumbs up."

Robert C. Larson—Thank you for helping to shape my vision and my manuscript into the final product. You are a master at the fine art of "point making." As an author, I cannot imagine working with a finer writer. Thanks!

Ed Curtis—Thank you for your mastery when it comes to editing. You have molded this story into a fun-to-read book that is simple and nonthreatening.

Nancy Norris—Thank you for catching everything. Your proofreading skills are unmatched and the final product is better because of you.

Sally Gavin—Thank you for your creativity in our jacket design and in the layout of the book. The final product is more appealing and potent because of your awesome effort.

The Team—Thank you, *Amy Dickens*, for your relentless management of the permissions necessary for publishing, along with the constant copying, collating, and delivery of the manuscript to wherever I may have been in the world. Thank you, *Julia Gordon* and *Vicky Way*, for your input during the process and for lending your impressions and counsel as we arrived at the finish line. To all of you I simply say that I could not have done it without you.

Contents

Read This First

Dr. Viktor E. Frankl, survivor of three horrendous years at the hands of less-than-human tormentors and murderers at Auschwitz and other Nazi places of terror, records these observations on life in Hitler's prisons:

We who lived in concentration camps can remember the men who walked through the huts comforting others, giving away their last piece of bread. They may have been few in number, but they offer sufficient proof that everything can be taken from a man but one thing; the last of the human freedoms—to choose one's attitude in any given set of circumstances, to choose one's own way.

And there are always choices to make. Every day, every hour, offered the opportunity to make a decision, a decision which determined whether you would or would not submit to those powers which threatened to rob you of your very self, your inner freedom; which determined whether or not you would become the plaything of circumstance, renouncing freedom and dignity to become molded into the form of the typical inmate.

. . . Even though conditions such as lack of sleep, insufficient food and various mental stresses may suggest that the inmates were bound to react in certain ways, in the final analysis it becomes clear that the sort of person the prisoner became was the result of an inner decision, and not the result of camp influences alone. Fundamentally, therefore, any man can, even under such circumstances, decide what shall become of him— mentally and spiritually.[1]

Chills run down my spine whenever I read those words. What must it have been like to live in such conditions? How did Frankl survive? How could he have maintained such a positive outlook given the torment and suffering of his daily life? I hope you have never had to endure—even remotely—the kinds of hardships Frankl experienced during those grim years in the Nazi prison camps. But what if it *had* been you. How would you have handled the anger, the fear, the mental and physical trauma that assaulted you day after day as you saw your friends enter the "showers" never to return? Would you—would I—have been able to tap an inner resolve to catapult us beyond the horrors of our immediate circumstances and custom-make our attitudes regardless of these circumstances . . . to choose our own way? Perhaps you and I will never know. Rather than speculate about the past, let's fast-forward to your life today. You may not have been reduced to the status of an animal in a fetid prison camp, not knowing if you would ever see another sunrise, but it's conceivable, at times, you may feel that you're a prisoner of your worst fears—lashed to a mast of discouragement; handcuffed, immobilized by a feeling of powerlessness to do what you want to do or become the person you know God created you to be.

If you've ever been there—or if you find yourself mired in this condition as you read this—then I've written this book for you. Because these pages are about hope, courage, faith, and love. They are filled with workable ideas, models, road maps, blueprints, and encouragements to help you tap the resources you need to live a life of mastery. Just in case you think this is only a theoretical treatise on success, I'll be flat-out honest. It was not long ago that I had the competition beat hands down when it came to feeling powerless, afraid, immobilized, discouraged, and unable to live out the values I knew lay lodged deep in my heart. I simply could not and did not grasp the wisdom to make the right decisions, to be realistic about my limitations, or to believe in a God who loved me more than I loved myself. Of course, an eighty-thousand-dollar cocaine habit didn't help much either.

If you are...

already successful and want more out of life

a single mother or father

a homemaker trying to cope with challenges
on the home front

a downsized, middle-aged executive looking for
a new direction

a generation X'er getting ready to launch

a baby boomer looking for significance after success

a parent in a blended/step family

addicted to behaviors that are destroying you

trapped in a going-nowhere career and you want out

one who simply wants to harness the power to be your best

Then I have written this book is for you.

My Promises to You as You Read This Book

1. To help you know the difference between where you are and where you want to be.

2. To assist you in creating a *bulletproof* road map for your life. To help you maximize your strengths and develop new habits to help you get what you want in life.

3. To demonstrate how to stay motivated by incorporating into your life a daily checklist of *top behaviors for effective living*.

4. To encourage you to believe in yourself. Plans and checklists are not enough; they must be undergirded with a strong self-concept and a belief system that works for you when the chips are down.

5. To show by example the importance of practice, practice, practice. To help you remember for the rest of your life that *the highest paid performers in the world practice more than they play*.

6. To persuade you to believe that when you do what you love, the money, influence, respect, and the power to become your best will follow.

7. To help you realize that you don't need more time to get the job done. Twenty-four hours is all you're ever going to get, but *taming* your time is the key to *mastering* you time—something that goes well beyond the traditional *to do* list.

8. To show you that your greatest teachers surround you: your children, spouse, coworkers, grandparents, friends. One of the major keys to becoming your best is to learn to be an *on-purpose* parent, mate, and friend.

9. To share with you the *real bottom line* and to help you determine your true net worth. You'll discover—and learn to apply—time-tested strategies for success in managing your business and your life.

10. To demonstrate the extraordinary power of repetition, especially as it relates to being and having a model, a mentor, and a motivator.

11. To encourage you to make a commitment to be the best you can be by making ten promises that will lead you to significant rewards.

12. To remind you that as important as money, fame, and success may be, in the end, the accumulated toys and things won't matter much. It's your legacy that will count. To develop and nourish the power to be your best means you will want to know where you are going once the race has been won.

Do all the good you can
By all the means you can
In all the ways you can
In all the places you can
At all the times you can
To all the people you can
As long as ever you can

— John Wesley

These seven lines of wisdom
will push you
further than anything else to develop
The *Power!* to Be Your Best!

Building the Platform for the Life You Deserve

WHERE DO YOU WANT TO GO TODAY?
Microsoft Ad Slogan, 1997

POWER: THE ABILITY TO DO,
ACT, OR PRODUCE
Webster's New World Dictionary

This book is about power . . . The Power! to Be Your Best! It's about receiving and capturing that power so you can be the person you have always wanted to be. It can help you do those things today that will make a difference in your life tomorrow and throughout the years to come. Here's an equation that, when followed with conviction and discipline, will equip you with the high-octane power that will produce what you want for your life:

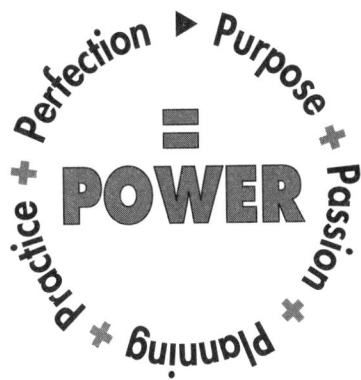

These five key ingredients are the internal molecules that can provide you with the physical and spiritual fuel to accomplish virtually anything you choose to do. It may be a desire for the power to change careers or to advance in the one you currently pursue. You may be looking for the power to lose weight, stop drinking, kick a drug habit, earn more money, enjoy better relationships, add vitality to your marriage, or create a legacy for your kids. There are no limits to what this power can and will do for you. The bottom line is: This power can secure your future.

There are no limits to what this power can and will do for you. The bottom line is: This power can secure your future.

How do I know this? With this power, I started a company that has created millions of dollars in revenue, impacted hundreds of thousands of lives, and created wealth for my family and me. With this power, I was able to avoid almost-certain bankruptcy and personal financial ruin. With this power, I was able to control negative behaviors with alcohol and quit my addiction to cocaine more than ten years ago. With this power, I'm now able to delight in a rich, rewarding relationship with my wife, Sheryl, and my sons Jonathan and Matthew. With this power, I have secured my future and made myself *bulletproof* for the challenges that continue to come my way every day. With my present secure, my past behind me, and a future that is brighter than I once ever could have imagined, I now have the energy, focus, passion, and power to be my best—and so can you.

Much of this power has come through my relationship with God. This has not always been the case. For years I ignored the potential power that a relationship with my Creator had to offer. For the first thirty years of my life, while I knew there was a God, I considered Him little more than a convenience. Like the ancient Greek actors, I would lower a *deus ex machina* ("God in the machine") onto the stage of my life to help get me out of my latest jam. Like those Greeks, when their god had done his good deed, I too would reel Him back into the ceiling of my mind. I lived for years with my own *deus ex machina*. When I needed God, I called on Him—hoping against hope that He was still there, ready and willing to come down and bail me out. Then, through an amazing human gift called selective memory, when things would begin to turn around, I'd forget about God and His assistance to me, and I was off on my own again. I would live life my own way, thank you.

Then it happened. I went through a dramatic transformation at the age of thirty in Phoenix, Arizona, when I had the honor of spending fifteen minutes one-on-one with Zig Ziglar, one of the greatest authors and motivators of our time. He told me that I did not have a part-time God, and therefore I should not serve Him on a part-time basis. Zig's straight talk set my heart in a new direction, and from that moment I have tried to follow the wisdom of King Solomon who, three thousand years ago, wrote in the Book of Proverbs, "Commit your works to the LORD, and your thoughts will be established. . . . A man's heart plans his way, But the LORD directs his steps" (16:3, 9).

The Spiritual Track

The principles in this book follow two tracks. The first is the *spiritual track*. It's my hope that your life will be impacted by a personal relationship with your Creator. Whether you do this is up to you. I can only share my beliefs and what is deep in my own heart. If, however, what you read in these pages touches your spirit and leads you to some new conclusions, I'm confident you will undergo a transformation that will have far-reaching implications for the rest of your life.

The Success Track

The second track is the *success track*. Simply, this book contains practical principles, laws, blueprints, and road maps to help you get what you want out of life. Many of these principles have biblical roots. That means they are timeless—some of the best, most workable success strategies you'll find anywhere. Whether your needs are spiritual, relational, physical, financial, or professional, what you will read in these pages will help you advance confidently in those areas of your dreams and help you to become *now* what you've always wanted to be.

One final note: As you turn these pages, you'll encounter a steady flow of ideas that are not necessarily a part of this book but rather thoughts stimulated by what you read. These musings are critical to your future success. Please take them seriously. When you bump up against these new, sometimes off-the-wall thoughts, grab a pen or pencil and move immediately to the Action Planner at the end of the chapter you are reading. This "homework" page is designed for you to record your thoughts as you think them and then use them for a disciplined plan of action. When you complete each chapter, I have designed a one-page action worksheet for you and a follow-through plan at my website.

Thank you for your investment of time and energy. Together let's now explore how you can tap in to…The *Power!* to Be Your Best!

Part I

The Future
Is You

Where Do You Want to Go Today?

---

*The chains of habit are too weak to be felt
until they are too strong to be broken.*
Anonymous

---

*We are what we repeatedly do; excellence
then, is not an act, but a habit.* **Aristotle**

I was beginning a fourteen-day international speaking tour that was to start and end in Sydney, Australia. We were at thirty-five thousand feet, and the captain of United Airlines Flight 815 came on the intercom system and said, "Folks, our computers have informed us that we do not have enough fuel to reach Sydney. We are going to have to make a emergency landing in Brisbane to get more fuel to reach our final destination." He went on to say that there was nothing to fear, that this was simply a precautionary step as the weather in Sydney was threatening and we might have to circle for up to one hour prior to landing.

As we sat on the ground in Brisbane, it occurred to me that this is what many people experience in their lives every day: They run out of fuel on the way to their destination. Sadder yet, many don't know where or how to get refueled so they can continue their journey. There are many reasons for this. Primary among them is the failure to pay attention to their "fuel" supply gauge, which would have provided ample warning of imminent disaster. But whatever the reason, the result is the same: Without fuel, none of us gets to where we say we want to go.

After refueling, we left Brisbane en route for Sydney. As predicted, the weather was terrible, and we were forced to move into a forty-minute holding pattern consisting of several 360-degree turns that allowed the backed-up air traffic in front of us to clear. As we turned toward the south, the morning sun was beginning to rise above the horizon, casting a shadow of our 747 jetliner on the clouds below. As I gazed at this huge, lumbering shadow, the most amazing sight met my eyes. There, surrounding the cockpit of the airplane, was a beautiful yellow, white, and blue halo. I breathed a sigh of relief; aware that God was in charge of our craft and that all was safe. I was overwhelmed by what I saw and felt and wrote these words on a yellow pad:

To get anywhere safely, you need a path that is illuminated, a vehicle that is protected, and enough fuel to make sure you'll reach your destination.

The path is life. The vehicle is you. The fuel supply is your belief system, which is supported by the principles on which you build your life.

You need a path that is illuminated.

Denis Waitley, one of my favorite authors and speakers writes, "Most people spend more time planning Christmas and holidays then they spend planning their life." Ouch! Denis knows how to hurt a guy! Increasing numbers of people seem just to take life as it comes, careening from wall to wall, hoping for the best, yet bracing for the worst. The concept of life design seldom occurs to them. Somehow, they hope it'll all work out. I'm still baffled why so many intelligent people continue to buy into this plan of inaction. When we are not clear about what kind of life we want, we will generally accept anything that comes our way.

"Most people spend more time planning Christmas and holidays than they spend planning their life."
Denis Waitley

As you design your life, what is the light that illuminates your path? Somewhere between my conversations and study with colleagues Glenna Salsbury, author of *The Art of the Fresh Start*, and Kevin McCarthy, author of *The On-Purpose Person*, I developed the "light" for my life by answering the following four questions. Now, I would like you to jot down your answers.

1. What is my purpose and why am I here?

_____

_____

2. What is my vision and where am I going?

_____

_____

3. What is my mission and how will I get there?

_____

_____

4. What are my values and how will I experience them en route?

_____

_____

You need a vehicle that is protected.

In 1900 the city of Galveston, Texas, was inundated by a tidal wave that caused great loss of life and property. Soon afterward, an engineer was hired to design a seawall that would withstand any future storm. Safety, not cost, was to be the primary consideration. The project was completed in 1904. It consisted of a massive barricade five miles long that towered seventeen feet above the tide. The engineer insisted that the fiercest gale would not affect it. Years later, while he was at work on a project in Alaska, he received a telegram saying that a tidal wave had again swept over Galveston and demolished the breakwater. Turning to an associate, he said with confidence, "I built that wall to stand; there must be some mistake!" And he was right. The telegram proved to be in error. Today that seawall still stands as firm as the Rock of Gibraltar—protecting the city of Galveston.

Just as this indestructible seawall continues to protect an entire community, the flesh-and-blood, sinew-and-muscle vehicle called *you* must also be protected so you can go the distance. The human body is an amazing machine. It can accomplish unbelievable things, tunnel through seemingly impenetrable obstacles, and produce results that may have once seemed impossible. Happily, once we've tasted the positive results of our labor, we will never be the same again. The eminent jurist Oliver Wendell Holmes said, "Man's mind once stretched by a new idea will never regain its original dimensions." Once we have stretched ourselves in new directions by forming new habits and have disciplined our efforts, we'll then be in position to move assertively in the direction we want to go. What is the source of your protection? What seawalls and "heat shields" surround you to give you the refuge you need during the time of a storm?

THE *POWER!* TO BE YOUR BEST!

You need enough fuel to make sure you'll reach your destination.

There are two critical components to the "fuel" analogy. First, that you fill up with the right fuel. Second, that you have adequate fuel for the trip. Plenty of people have put the wrong brand of fuel into their "vehicle" and then suffered an unnecessary breakdown. There are still others who, while having the right fuel, pay little or no attention to the gauge. They keep pushing to get where they want to go, only to come up short because their tank ran dry. As you read on, you will learn how to keep your focus on the "gauges" and your eye on an ever-diminishing "fuel supply" so that the possibility of breaking down or stopping short of your goal is eliminated.

Close the gap!

Fact: Most people are not where they want to be. They live lives of frustration and quiet desperation because their plans are short-circuited, their goals unmet, and their relationships are at a virtual standstill. They either run out of fuel, or once they arrive, discover they've parked in front of the wrong address. After repeating this course of action over time, they tend to settle for less and less because changing their behavior, they fear, would come at too great a price.

The simple truth is you are where you are because of the choices you have made, are making, or choose not to make.

Now that we know the problem, what is the solution to getting what you want out of life? The good news is this: There is really nothing that stands in your way to keep you from becoming the person you want to be now! The simple truth is that you are where you are because of the choices you have made, are making, or choose not to make. If you want to see different results in your life, you will be wise to develop a different set of choices. If those choices are based on a proven plan, powered by the right "fuel" with your destination clearly in mind, then taking the right action will lead to habits that, when repeated, will give you consistently right results. That fuel is understanding your purpose and living your values.

What's in the box?

In his books, *Halftime* and *Game Plan*, author and successful businessman Bob Buford comments on the purpose issue in the following manner:

> *Mike Kiami is a strategic planning consultant. He is brilliant. He is intuitive. He is demanding. He slices through all the pretense and posturing, and hones in on the core. He does not believe in God but I can testify that—at least in my life—God worked unmistakably through Mike Kiami.*
>
> *I went to Mike because I wanted him to do for my life what he does so well for business: Draw up a strategic plan. I needed him to show me how to live so I was not plagued by a growing sense that I was missing out. I was not sure what I was missing, and I wanted him to tell me.*
>
> *I went to Mike with tons of questions: What should I do with my life? How could I be more useful? Where should I invest my time, talents and treasures? What is the overarching vision that shapes me? Who am I? Where am I? Where am I going? How do I get there?*
>
> *In this blizzard of wonderment, Mike asked me a simple, penetrating question: "What's in the box?" This from a high paid strategic planner? I didn't have a clue as to what he was getting at and asked him to fill me in.*
>
> *"I can't put together an honest plan for your life until I identify the mainspring. I've been listening to you for a couple of hours, trying to figure out what's in your box. It's either money or*

Jesus Christ. If you can tell me which one it is, I can tell you the strategic planning implications of that choice. If you can't tell me, you're going to bounce between those two values and be confused."

No one had ever put such a significant question to me so directly. And he was right. I was highly motivated to serve Jesus, but I also was driven to be financially successful. I believed the two went hand in hand, and in a way they do. But the reason I had such an unsettled feeling deep within was that I had tried to put two things in my box.[1]

The Secret of a Winning Life

As we explore *The* Power! *to Be Your Best!*, there are three specific things I want you to consider. Each of these will become a recurring theme to help you discover the secrets to winning in life.

1: Success has many definitions.

Ask twenty people what it means to be a success, and you'll get twenty different answers. Some will say success is having all the money you can count. Others might say it's living an incredible lifestyle, or going to Europe every year, or having a loving family, or maintaining optimum health. All of these are good answers. Here are a few more thoughts on success and the attitudes that define success:

1. Success is simply a matter of luck. Ask any failure. (Earl Wilson)
2. Remember that Ginger Rogers did everything that Fred Astaire did, but she did it backwards and in high heels. (Faith Whittlesey)
3. Listen to counsel and receive instruction, That you may be wise in your latter days. (Proverbs 19:20).
4. Success is a journey, not a destination. (Ben Sweetland)

5. Success consists of getting up just one more time than you fall. (Oliver Goldsmith)
6. Now here, you see, it takes all the running you can do to keep in the same place. If you want to get somewhere else, you must run at least twice as fast as that! (Lewis Carroll)
7. "Incline your ear and hear the words of the wise, and apply your heart to my knowledge; for it is a pleasant thing if you keep them within you; let them all be fixed upon your lips, so that your trust may be in the LORD; I have instructed you today, even you" (Proverbs 22:17–19).

2: As your values change, so does your definition of success.

Whether you are eighteen years old or eighty, your values will change. As they do, so will your desire to become more significant. The time will come when you begin to do things based on their contribution to others rather than for your benefit alone. This will look something like the transition between acquiring money for yourself and your family, which has signaled success for you in the past, and using your money and time for others, which speaks of significance. Wherever you find yourself on this *success-significant* continuum, to know what is important to you today is paramount because your *second half* will be predicated on those values.

What is in *your* box may not become clear to you for months or even years. Still, the premise of *Halftime* is to help you evaluate whether the results you enjoy today are paving the way—and providing the resources—for your second half of significance, a period that generally kicks into gear between the ages of thirty-five and forty-five. If you are in this age range, then this message is especially for you.

3: The behaviors that pull you or push you away from what you want are enabled or disabled by the congruency of your values.

As you explore your success path, you will serve yourself best by developing your powers of observation. One of the defining elements in capturing the power to be your best is found in the ongoing development of your character. Character comes from being authentic. Therefore, activity management, integrated with your most cherished values, creates the authenticity that gives you power. *This is the seed of habit productive behavior.* Short of having lapses on some days, this principle will always bring you back into alignment.

Your progress in getting the life you want and deserve is tied to your personal character. These principles of character are integrity, honesty, contribution, human dignity, faith, repetition, patience, quality, excellence, effort, and service. While represented as principles, they must demonstrate themselves in your daily actions. When put into action, they have the power to direct your life. The more you experience the positive feedback of living these principles, the more consistent you will become in applying them. One central theme to your character is the issue of personal integrity—of not only making but also keeping the promises you make to yourself and others. This is the platform from which your real power is derived. The single greatest motivator is one that harnesses the momentum created when you walk your talk, when what you do every day is based on your values, and when what you do reflects who you are. Katharine Hepburn, speaking on the subject of character, said, "To keep your character intact you cannot stoop to filthy acts. It makes it easier to stoop the next time."

> *The single greatest motivator is one that harnesses the momentum created when you walk your talk, when what you do every day is based on your values, and when what you do reflects who you are.*

Class Is Always in Session

Also it is not good for a soul to be without knowledge, and he sins who hastens with his feet. **Proverbs 19:2**

This message is a time-tested recipe for true accomplishment. Over the centuries, many have tried to change the recipe, all without success. They have messed with the cake. They've removed some of the ingredients, have not followed the proper steps, have accelerated the process, and have suggested short-cuts that they promised would make a better cake. The results have never been award winning. To have a good cake—and a good life coupled with great success—there are requirements we cannot ignore.

When I was a young boy, my dad bought me a model toy that required some assembly. It was a Chevrolet Corvette. I'll never forget the beautiful color picture of the car on the cover of the box. I couldn't wait to build the model so I could put it on display in my room. I ripped open the box, fingered through all the parts, and with a quick look at the instructions, I decided to speed up the process of building my pride and joy. Mistake number one! I have two memorable recollections of that first model car: One, the pieces would not stay together because I had not let the glue dry long enough for the parts to bond. Two, my paint job looked worse than a $49.95 special. Again, a simple reason: I failed to paint the individual parts and let them dry. Instead, I built the model and then attempted to paint the whole car—details and all. Hey, I was a young boy in hurry. I knew what to do—or so I thought.

Does my story bring to mind a story of your own? The cliché "haste makes waste" is true. We say we don't have time to do something right the first time, but somehow we find the time, energy, and patience to do it over. That's the problem with short-cuts. We still try to go fast, only to be stopped and given a ticket. We still go on crash diets, only to gain back all our weight—plus a few extra pounds. We still try to pass tests by cramming and refusing to learn the curriculum. We still try to make elevators go faster by pushing the button over and over. We still try to keep marriages on track with an occasional card, box of candy, or expensive gift. We still try to make flowers grow faster by watering them too much. I say "we" because I'm confident these are experiences you and I have struggled through together. So consider the following.

The best way to go fast is to go slow.

In the Book of Galatians, the apostle Paul took the time to communicate some profound truths to the churches in an area of ancient Greece known as Galatia. He'd observed behaviors that were not in concert with their professed faith in God. Specifically, he addressed a group of "agitators"—those who tried to mislead the church and its followers regarding the requirements of their faith. Of all his counsel, the apostle's ten most profound words are "For whatever a man sows, that he will also reap." What he said then is still true today. Since life is a result of our collective experience, it's important we sow seeds that produce crops we'll enjoy harvesting. We've all got some sowing going. The first question is, Are you and I sowing seeds that will bring us the life, success, fulfillment, and power we say we want? Question number two is, Are we willing to be patient in our sowing, recognizing that planting and harvest are two different seasons?

Since life is a result of our collective experience, it's important we sow seeds that produce crops we'll enjoy harvesting.

Jeffrey Meyer writes in his book by the same title, *If You Can't Find the Time to Do It Right, When Will You Find the Time to Do It Over?* While it is emotionally unhealthy to expect perfection of ourselves, it is realistic to choose excellence in all we do. Here's a worthy goal: Starting today, I want you to do the hard work demanded to lock in to something that will help you avoid the unnecessary detours that keep you from getting what you want and will ensure that you will become all that you were designed to be.

Shortcuts That Kill Authenticity

For many centuries genuine pearls commanded a high price because of their scarcity. Great quantities of oysters had to be examined before a few could be found that contained the coveted treasures. Then suddenly the market became flooded with them. After some investigation, the mystery of the abundant supply was revealed. Enterprising individuals had discovered that if a foreign object is lodged in an oyster's tender flesh, the oyster would form a glistening pearl around the source of discomfort. Deciding to help nature along, these people artificially induced the process by inserting irritants such as tiny beads and buckshot into the shells. When the pearls had formed, they were carefully harvested. Wealthy patrons became suspicious, however, and insisted that the lustrous jewels be subjected to special tests. Although outwardly they seemed perfect, the x-ray showed their impurity, for they had "false hearts" of lead or glass.

Authenticity versus what is false. What does it mean to you to be authentic? Do you, on occasion, succumb to having a "false heart"? One sure way to subvert the process of developing the power to be your best is to engage in shortcuts—those little actions that, in fact, will always keep you from getting what you really want. Take a few moments to think through the following categories. Then write down some of the shortcuts you are taking in each that you feel may be keeping you from becoming the person you want to be.

Spiritual

_____

_____

_____

Relational

_____

_____

_____

Physical

_____

_____

_____

Professional

_____

_____

_____

Financial

_____

_____

_____

How My Life Might Look without Shortcuts

What are you prepared to do in each of these areas now that you recognize your shortcuts may not be giving you the results you want?

Spiritual

_____

_____

_____

Relational

_____

_____

_____

Physical

_____

_____

_____

Professional

_____

_____

_____

Financial

_____

_____

_____

The Knowledge Platform

You've heard it said that knowledge is power. That's a half-truth. Knowledge is power only when it's applied. Here's what some well-known people have said about the pursuit of knowledge: Coach John Wooden: "It's what you learn after you know it all that counts." The philosopher Friedrich Nietzsche: "Better know nothing than half-know many things." King Solomon: "The fear of the LORD is the beginning of knowledge." Anthologies are filled with quotes and statements and illustrations about knowledge. Here's the step-by-step sequence that will strengthen your knowledge platform:

1. accumulate knowledge
2. apply knowledge
3. evaluate the results of that knowledge
4. improve the use of knowledge

Coach John Wooden: "It's what you learn after you know it all that counts." The philosopher Friedrich Nietzsche: "Better know nothing than half-know many things." King Solomon: "The fear of the LORD is the beginning of knowledge."

Enough's Enough, Socrates

A devoted follower of Socrates asked him the best way to acquire knowledge. Socrates responded by leading him to a river and plunging him beneath the surface. The man struggled to free himself, but Socrates continued to hold him under water. Finally, after much effort, the man was able to break loose and emerge from the water. Socrates then asked, "When you thought you were drowning, what one thing did you want most of all?" Still gasping for breath, the man exclaimed, "I wanted air!" The philosopher wisely responded, "When you want knowledge as much as you wanted air, then you will get it."

As you read the following chapters, I hope your desire for knowledge will increase as you encounter a flow of ideas based on your personal experience that, hopefully, will be

15

further stimulated by what you read here. These *personal thoughts* are critical to your future success. As you engage in this beyond-the-book thinking, I encourage you to turn to the Action Planner segment at the end of each chapter and follow-through plan at my website. This is your *knowledge platform* to help you move your thoughts and ideas into a plan of action.

Three Fundamental Laws for Success

If I were to give you a football, how far could you throw it? Thirty yards? Maybe fifty? Perhaps you could manage sixty or more. What if the football I gave you had no air in it? How far could you throw it now? Perhaps ten, possibly twenty yards. What's the difference? What's a "little air" got to do with it? Simply put, without the right amount of air, the ball loses its aerodynamics, its lift, its balance, and its propulsion. It's useless.

If you are going to gain *The* Power! *to Be Your Best!,* you must have the right amount of "air" in you. Without it, you won't be able to go the distance. You will simply find that you're another example of an out-of-air, flat football that was intended for high velocity, productive living, but fell short, incapable of meeting life's demands. Enter the three fundamental laws for success. Just as a seed planted by a child or an adult will grow to its limits, these three laws will work for anyone. They require no special circumstances and certainly no astronomical IQ. The only requirement is that you understand how the laws work and then put them to work for you. As you review each one, ask yourself, How might my life be different if I were to obey these laws and make them part of my life?

Law Number 1: The Law of Responsibility

One way to gain and maintain the life you deserve is to accept full responsibility for where you are in relation to where you want to be, to realize your most common behavior is a function of choices and decisions, not external conditions. Your success is an inside job. All movement toward the life you want comes from managing your responses to past and present situations. Those who get what they want from life don't blame their circumstances. We all have circumstances, and they're all pretty much the same. We've all had conditions, backgrounds, childhoods, parents, schoolteachers, divorces, marriages, people who have done us wrong, and every other possible excuse for failing with good reason. A friend keeps reminding me that a good memory is one trained to forget past events over which I have no control. No matter how bad circumstances may have been or are in your life, you can move beyond them and become a person with unlimited power because you have the capability of achieving a level of thinking that pushes you beyond your circumstances to a higher plane of becoming. Once there, your new thinking will drive different behaviors based on what's important to you. Let me illustrate.

> *All movement toward the life you want comes from managing your responses to past and present situations. Those who get what they want from life don't blame their circumstances.*

Mitchell is my friend—a man who personifies responsibility. On June 19, 1971, Mitchell was riding his brand-new motorcycle in downtown San Francisco. He was in great spirits as he reveled in the accomplishment of a lifelong dream. That morning he'd soloed in an airplane for the first time. His reverie, however, was short-lived. He was driving on Van Ness Avenue when a truck turned right, cutting him off. He smashed into the truck at a 90-degree angle and suffered a crushed pelvis and broken left elbow. The nightmare continued as the gas cap on his motorcycle popped open, spilling two and a half gallons of gasoline on his body and the hot engine. Mitchell and his bike went up in flames.

Later, at the hospital, Mitchell was given the grade of "low end survivability." With burns over 65 percent of his body, his chances of making it were fifty-fifty. As he tells the story, "The first two weeks are a blank since I'd slipped into a coma. Virtually every part of me except for my scalp—which was protected by my helmet and my torso, which was shielded by my

WHERE DO YOU WANT TO GO TODAY?

leather jacket—was red-and-black charred meat."

After extensive hospitalization, surgeries, and physical therapy, Mitchell survived. Now he faced a new set of conditions. Let me fast-forward four years. Mitchell became a pilot who had to learn to fly again with his new conditions. On November 11, 1975, he offered to fly four other guys to San Francisco in his Cessna 206 from Gunnison Airport just outside Crested Butte, Colorado.

> To change your life, you must engage in new choices and make different decisions.

After de-icing his wings and letting the rising sun melt any remaining ice, he and his friends took off. At one hundred feet, Mitchell knew the plane wasn't handling right, so with the runway still left, he made the critical decision to reduce power and land the aircraft. Yet when he made his maneuver, the plane stalled. Simply, the wings could not provide adequate lift, so the plane came to an in-air standstill, then plummeted to the ground.

Mitchell and his four passengers hit with enormous impact. Since the landing gear had not retracted, it was the first to absorb the shock. One of the wheels was crushed, and the plane rested on the ground and tilted to the right. This caused the gasoline to seep over the wings. Fearing fire, Mitchell yelled to his friends, "Get out! Everyone out now!" Mitchell tried to join his friends, but his legs would not move. Later he learned he'd crushed his T-12 vertebra. When the doctor finally made his diagnosis, he told Mitchell: "Sir, it appears you will never walk again. You'll have to use a wheelchair for the rest of your life."

Those are two significant conditions that probably would challenge anyone's application of the law of responsibility. Mitchell, however, has never been one to allow conditions to dictate his outcomes. Now, twenty years later, he is still in a wheelchair, unable to walk, confined to a body that lacks fingers and toes and remains afflicted with facial distortions. Yet he has gone on to become a happy person, earning millions of dollars in business and using his conditions to help others make better decisions and choices. As I write of his experiences and my relationship with him, I find myself choking up. Then I turn in my chair and look back at my credenza on which is an acrylic stand that holds Mitchell's signature life philosophy,

---

*It's not what happens to you,
it's what you do about it.*

Control your choices and your decisions, and you will control your destiny. Whatever is not happening in your life that you want to have happen, or whatever is happening in your life that you don't want to happen any longer is not rooted in external situations. To change your life, you must engage in new choices and make different decisions.

"To see a world in a grain of sand, and heaven in a wild flower, to hold infinity in the palm of your hand, and Eternity in an hour. That's the power and wisdom that comes from the cultivation of observation."

Law Number 2: The Law of Cause and Effect

Cause-and-effect thinking helps you become intentional about getting what you want—a process that begins with developing the power to make astute observations. Benjamin Franklin said, "The eye of the master will do more work than both his hands." William Blake wrote, "To see a world in a grain of sand, and heaven in a wild flower, to hold infinity in the palm of your hand, and Eternity in an hour. That's the power and wisdom that comes from the cultivation of observation." The habit of making intentional observations forces you to evaluate all your behaviors, and where your behaviors are productive and positive, you have clarified your values. Everything you do is tied to a values-based lifestyle. You always reap what you sow. If you find your crop disappointing, you'd best have a heart-to-heart talk with the one who planted the seed.

Consider these examples of some cause-and-effect scenarios.

You eat too much food, yet you wonder why you weigh so much.

You drink too much alcohol, yet you wonder why you feel tired and plagued with headaches.

You don't save any money, yet you wonder why you're broke.

You don't spend enough time with your spouse or children, yet you wonder why they feel distant.

You don't call on prospects, yet you wonder why you don't have enough business.

You don't coach your employees to the highest degree of success possible, yet you wonder why they leave you.

You don't spend time in God's Word, yet you wonder why you don't feel God's presence.

When your values are clear, your decisions become easy, and you consistently make better choices.

WOW! It's so simple. We work so hard, but not always in the direction of our dreams. When we recognize the negative effects of some of our best-laid plans, we often try to correct our behavior with a stiff upper lip and the sheer determination to do better next time. While this may produce short-term results, before long we find it easy to settle into previous negative behavior patterns. Solution? One of the most productive ways to improve the results you get in life is to link all your actions to a clarification of your values. When your values are clear, your decisions become easy, and you consistently make better choices.

Often we get into habits, which are not producing the effects or outcomes we desire. It's not that we do this intentionally. Rather, we have settled into a comfort zone where we are not aware of our values and, therefore, are less conscientious about the decisions we make.

In their book, *Breaking Outside of the Box*, authors Mike Vance and Diane Deacon call this phenomenon, "Nonthinking". It is the taking of an action without first of all thinking of the consequences, either positive or negative. By becoming more intentional about the outcomes in advance of the action, we can insure a higher level of success. This applies to every area of our lives.

Let me make sure you understand what I mean by abuse. We were in a full-blown habit where for four days out of seven we were high, not on one or the other, but both—alcohol and cocaine.

Law Number 3: The Law of Repetition

Nothing becomes a habit without the first two laws of responsibility and cause and effect, but they are not enough. Habits become habits only with the application of the law of repetition. When you act in accordance with your goals and values, and realize the power that comes from their interaction, the easier it will be for you to repeat whatever behavior you choose. Let me illustrate from an example in my own life.

One year before I was to be married, I decided I wanted to be in the best shape of my life. Sheryl, my wife to be, and I had just emerged from a time in our lives where our priorities got a little, no, a lot messed up. Our financial success combined with a racehorse-fast '80s lifestyle had led us both down a long, treacherous road of cocaine and alcohol abuse. Let me make sure you understand what I mean by abuse. We were in a full-blown habit where for four days out of seven we were high, not on one or the other, but both—alcohol and cocaine. When we were in that state, we also smoked twenty to thirty cigarettes a night. It didn't take long until our addiction led to several all-nighters.

I'll never forget the moment that all changed. It was midnight, and I remember feeling invincible—bigger than life itself—when I decided to go out for a jog. Even though my heart was still racing from the cocaine coursing through my body, I left for my run. Upon returning home, I felt a massive pain in my heart. I didn't suffer a heart attack, but my heart rate had accelerated to a level where it actually hurt when it beat. The next day I read a story you may remember: Maryland basketball star Len Bias, who had just been selected by the Boston Celtics in the first round of the NBA draft, had died of cocaine intoxication.

Wake-up call for Todd Duncan...the man who thought he was invincible. I now had something think about, but what would I do with the information? Would I make any life changes? Or would this just be a wave of panic that would soon pass? What were my options? Where would I go for the support I needed? Sheryl and I had always talked about our faith in God, but the Almighty never played much of an active role in our lives. We were too busy making money, making love, and getting high. Suddenly, our worlds crashed. Within two weeks I was fired from my high-paying job. While it was never said, I'm convinced it was because of my drug use and the negative effects it had on my performance in the workplace. I had been out of control for almost twelve months, and now, more than ever, I felt hopeless, powerless, and helpless in my battle to stop using drugs. When I finally decided to take full responsibility for my actions, I was able to short-circuit the negative cause-and-effect circumstances of my life. I decided the only way for me to grasp the power to deal with these behaviors was to ask God to give me the strength. The Bible promises that He will send us a Helper, and that He will guide us into all truth. I chose to believe those words literally and accepted God's generous offer of divine power. I believed He could change my behavior and that I could give up my habit immediately.

It was the most difficult thing I have ever done in my life. I learned through discussions with others that to see positive results I would need an accountability partner. Thankfully, Sheryl also decided to quit; I would not be alone in my struggle. We had to shift from enabling each other to disabling each other. We knew it would be tough, but we were determined to give it a try. We began with a resolve and made it through the first day, the first week, the first month, and finally the first year. When I was weak, Sheryl was strong; when she was weak, I was strong. The more we repeated our new, positive behaviors, the easier they became. We were driven by what became our core value: survival. Each day we linked one new behavior after another to the idea that we wanted to live.

Months later we mobilized our new power to put our bodies back in shape. Our old lifestyle had drained our energy, atrophied our muscles, and made us physical and emotional weaklings. With no active physical-fitness program, I had gained almost forty pounds. Since we knew the law of repetition was designed to work in every situation, we decided to link it to a disciplined workout program. Again, accountability played a key role in our success. When Sheryl started to drop away from the program, I would provide the encouragement to continue and vice versa. Soon a quarter-mile run turned into a half-mile, a half-mile became a mile, one mile became two, and within three months, we were running five miles a day, five days a week. Within six months I had lost forty-three pounds of blubber and Sheryl was in the best shape of her life.

Those experiences, now more than a decade old, have formed such subsequent strong habits that neither Sheryl nor I have repeated our previous destructive behaviors. We have gone on to use the law of repetition to become debt-free, create a wealth plan, avoid alcohol and drug abuse, and develop a closer walk with God.

The Bottom Line

Everything you say you want in your life hangs in a delicate balance between the three laws of responsibility, cause and effect, and repetition. As you become more responsible, make more astute observations about the implications of your daily decisions, and repeat positive behaviors linked to your innermost values, you will move confidently in the direction of your dreams. Nothing—no circumstance in the world—is strong enough to keep you from receiving and harnessing the power to be your best.

Rewards Today and Tomorrow

Yet if you refuse to do what you know you should do, you will still be where you are now and in the less-than-bright future that lies ahead. If you do not make the necessary changes today to develop the power to be your best, you will sentence yourself to a life of mediocrity and untapped potential. Denis Waitley says these are the people who "put their plans on Some Day Island." Someday I will lose weight. Someday I will start saving. Someday I will call on that prospect. Someday I will stop drinking. Someday I will come home early enough to be with my family.

My friend, that day is now. There is no better time than the present to start moving in the direction of your dreams. I don't care how old you are, what mistakes you've made, the nature of your pedigree, or any other of the myriad of excuses we often mention for not doing well. Your tomorrows will be great if you make today great. If, however, you ignore the possibilities of today, then your tomorrows will never change.

Emerson says, "Finish every day and be done with it. You have done what you could. Some blunders and absurdities no doubt crept in; forget them as fast as you can. Tomorrow is a new day; begin it well and serenely and with too high a spirit to be cumbered with your old nonsense. This day is all that is good and fair. It is too dear with hopes and invitations to waste a moment on the yesterdays."

Plan of Action for Living Your Life with Purpose

1. What's in your "box?" What is the one purpose around which you are prepared to center the rest of your life?
2. This relates to the Law of Responsibility. List those areas of your life where you feel you are *not* taking full responsibility. Now rank these in the order of *most serious to least important*. When you come to chapter 2, I will show you how to take these areas of your life and make them work for you.

*   _____
*   _____
*   _____
*   _____
*   _____

3. This relates to the Law of Cause and Effect. Look at what you've written for number 2 above. Using those as your guide, list the top *one to three* actions that—when taken—you're confident will produce different and better results for you.

*   _____
*   _____
*   _____

4. This relates to the Law of Repetition. Look at what you've written for number 3. List five benefits you feel you'll receive when your new actions become daily habits.

*   _____
*   _____
*   _____
*   _____
*   _____

When you've completed
these four assignments,
go to my website at
www.toddduncan.com
for a fifteen-minute
motivational message to help
you move one step closer to
your quest for the life you
desire. *See you on-line.* —*TD*

www.toddduncan.com

Action Planner Notes

_____

_____

_____

_____

_____

_____

_____

_____

_____

_____

_____

_____

_____

_____

_____

_____

_____

_____

_____

_____

_____

_____

_____

_____

WHERE DO YOU WANT TO GO TODAY?

LifeQuest:
The Blueprint
for Total Life
Management

Man is the only animal that laughs and
weeps, for he is the only animal that is
struck with the difference between what
things are and what they ought to be.
William Hazlitt

Faith is the assurance of things hoped for,
the conviction of things not yet seen.
Hebrews 11:1, NASB

*I*n 1988, while attending a seminar featuring Tom Hopkins, a well-known international sales trainer, I learned one of the most important lessons in life: the value of this life. Tom captured the attention of nearly two thousand participants when he encouraged us to think about what this life was prepared to offer us if we were only willing to pay the price. In an early morning session he said, "There are not many things you need to acquire to get the life you deserve. In fact, each of you in this room possesses all the ingredients necessary for success. But, more than any one thing, you must have a plan." He then made the transition to a powerful series of questions.

Five Questions That Changed My Life

How valuable is your life to you?

How important is the time that your life gives to you?

What has more value, this building in which you are seated or your life?

How long do you think it took to "plan" this building?

Then what is your conclusion?

There were my answers:

How valuable is your life to you? **Very**

How important is the time that your life gives to you? **Very**

What has more value, this building in which you are seated or your life? **My life!**

How long do you think it took to "plan" this building? **Eighteen months**

Then what is your conclusion? **That if my life is more important than this building, why have I not spent eighteen months planning it? Why have I not even spent eighteen days? Or eighteen hours?**

My conclusions were clear. If I were to make progress in my life with intent and purpose, I needed a plan. I had been successful, but I knew I'd barely tapped my potential. I wanted so much more. After hearing Tom, I made the commitment to take concrete steps to develop a plan for my life. For me it was choosing to believe in the laws of responsibility, cause and effect, and repetition; laws I've shared with you in chapter 1. Now I want to coach you to take your own understanding of these laws a step further. You have already grasped the importance of these three laws, but now I want you to look at them in the form of affirmations—statements that are personal, powerful, and present tense.

The Law of Responsibility— An Affirmation

I am responsible for my life. Whatever is not happening in my life that I want to happen—and over which I have an element of control—is my responsibility. Today I am responsible for all areas of my life, and I am making the right choices, thereby controlling my direction and my destiny.

> *Today I am responsible for all areas of my life, and I am making the right choices, thereby controlling my direction and my destiny.*

The Law of Cause and Effect—An Affirmation

I alone am responsible to choose my outcomes. Whatever negative situations exist in my life, I am now changing them. I am doing this by changing what I do and/or do not do. I am now making my outcomes positive and profitable.

The Law of Repetition—An Affirmation

All that I attempt to accomplish is becoming easier day by day. My positive behaviors, when repeated, are consistently leading to more positive behaviors. By repeating my positive behaviors and attitudes today, I am building my character. This gives me the confidence I need for tomorrow. With confidence for tomorrow, my life is becoming a series of better choices.

Here's the Formula

Just as Tom Hopkins's questions helped me draw a believable blueprint for my life, the ability to ask yourself clarifying questions can also put you on a road to personal power and fulfillment. These questions are designed to cut through to the innermost part of your spirit and desires. They will challenge you to think about your life in fresh, new ways. The answers to these questions will help you know why you are here, where you are going, how you'll know when you reach your goal, and how to discover what you truly want to experience along the way. Additionally, these questions can help you identify your unique gifts and provide you with key insights that will help you to maximize your gifts.

The Power of Clarification

Clarifying Question Number 1: What Is My Purpose in Life?

As a living, breathing creature, God has given you a purpose for being on planet Earth. As you begin to understand and articulate that purpose, you will begin to take another look at how you evaluate your work, your relationships, your money, your body, and everything else that is important to you. As I mentioned earlier, I will often use biblical examples to work through the principles I'm sharing with you. With that in mind, please be reminded of the two tracks that we'll work with throughout this book: the spiritual and the success tracks. I have decided to include the spiritual track because the Bible—the number-one best-selling book of all time—contains wisdom for living that cannot be found elsewhere. Its principles work. If they did not, people would stop buying it. In fact it has been referred to as **B**asic **I**nstruction **B**efore **L**eaving **E**arth. Among the many life-management thoughts contained in this book for effective living are two primary messages that sum up much of what I am attempting to say in this book. Observe the words of the apostle Paul in the New Testament Book of Ephesians.

And He gave some as apostles, and some as prophets, and some as evangelists, and some as pastors and teachers,… As a result, we are no longer to be children, tossed here and there by waves, and carried about by every wind of doctrine, by the trickery of men, by craftiness in deceitful scheming.
Ephesians 4:11, 14, NASB

Message Number 1

Paul's message is the central platform on which you need to build your life. The first part of the verse says that God has given you the ability to be, the capacity to learn, and the where-withal to do. Simply put, God has filled you with purpose. It's the why behind your existence. As you intentionally peel away the layers of life's onion and discover your underlying purpose, you will use your purpose to make your most important deci-sions. Before long, this force of purpose will become so powerful it will drive everything you do.

Message Number 2

When an unnamed captive POW from the Korean War was led to believe that he would soon be shot, he sent a letter to his wife with some instructions for their son. He wrote, "Tell Bill the word is integrity."

Once you know your purpose, you'll discover you will no longer be tossed about by the waves or carried away by every ill wind that blows. When you follow your purpose, you will be less likely to get sidetracked. You will stay focused. When an unnamed captive POW from the Korean War was led to believe that he would soon be shot, he sent a letter to his wife with some instructions for their son. He wrote, "Tell Bill the word is *integrity*." The general knew that character and purpose mattered most in life and that a life of integrity would win the day—even if that was to cost him his life. He knew that integrity is always the first step to greatness. It was a sense of purpose that kept him alive, sane, and motivated while suffering at the hands of his captors.

My friend Bill Bachrach, author of *Values Based Selling*, says that you and I must spend whatever time it takes to discover our purpose in life. He asks us to frame the question like this: What's important about success to me?

Bill uses the word *success* because this is where most people begin their quest for their life's purpose. Unfortunately, most people have no answer to this question except that they want to make a lot of money. I hope you already know that to earn money just for earning it is a dead-end street. Ask yourself: Why do I want to earn this money? What contribution am I prepared to make? Do I own this money or does this money own me? If your earnings and contributions are in sync, then money, for you, is a good thing. If these are not in sync, then you could be heading for trouble. The Bible throws out two warning signs about the misuse of money:

THE *POWER!* TO BE YOUR BEST!

He who loves silver will not be satisfied with silver; nor he who loves abundance, with increase. This also is vanity. When goods increase, they increase who eat them.
Ecclesiastes 5:10–11

But those who desire to be rich fall into temptation and a snare, and into many foolish and harmful lusts which drown men in destruction and perdition. For the love of money is a root of all kinds of evil, for which some have strayed from the faith [truth] in their greediness, and pierced themselves through with many sorrows.
1 Timothy 6:9–10

If you use your money to contribute to the well-being of others, then it is one of the most powerful tools available for you and those to whom you give it. In his best-selling book, *See You at the Top,* author Zig Ziglar describes his perspective on money:

On many occasions I have mentioned earnings as a mark of success primarily because money is a familiar yardstick by which we can measure a contribution. Regardless of what your occupation might be, there are others with the same opportunity who earn considerably less money and still others who earn a great deal more. In the final analysis, opportunity for growth and service lies with the individual. Almost without exception, you can measure a person's contribution to society in terms of dollars. The more he contributes, the more he earns. The oft-repeated philosophy, "You can have everything in life you want, if you will just help enough other people get what they want," is another way of saying if you serve more, you earn more.

From time to time some of my Christian friends ask me how I reconcile my Christian beliefs with my view on money. I always smile and tell them that I believe God made the diamonds for His folks and not Satan's crowd. All you've got to do to verify this is check the record. Read what God said in Malachi 3:10, Psalms 1:3 and III John 2, and I believe you will see that money is scripturally okay. Solomon was the richest man who ever lived. Abraham had cattle on a thousand hills, and Job would not have qualified for food stamps. The only admonition God gives us is that we must not make money or anything else our god because when we do, we will never be happy—regardless of how much we have.[1]

In your quest for a life of significance, money must be used, not loved; it must be leveraged, not lusted after. With that fundamental principle in place, you will now see by the dialog that follows how success and money can become the platform to help give you the life you want and deserve. As we walk through this scenario together, I will give you several practical illustrations to demonstrate how wealth-building and service must go hand in hand for you to develop the power to be your best.

Purpose: Important "Values" Questions

Here is how Bill Bachrach used a series of questions to help me understand my purpose for living:

BB: *Todd, what's important about success to you?*

TD: *One of the reasons I do what I do, Bill, is to earn a good living.*

BB: *Earning a good living is important to a lot of people for a lot of different reasons, Todd. What's important about earning a good living to you?*

TD: *If my earnings are good, it gives me a great deal of freedom. The better my earnings, the less I have to work.*

BB: *Freedom is a good thing, and having more of it is important. Todd, tell me, what's important about freedom to you?*

TD: *It gives me the chance to spend more time with my family. It also provides an opportunity for me to speak to church groups.*

BB: *I appreciate the nature of what you want to do with your freedom. Just out of curiosity, what's important about spending time with your family and speaking to church groups to you?*

TD: *It gives me a feeling that I am making a difference in their lives.*

BB: *Making a difference is something you do that impacts other people. What's important about making a difference to you?*

TD: *When I am making a difference, I feel I am accomplishing God's plan for my life and living His will.*

BB: *Is there anything more important to you than to know that you are living life according to God's plan for you?*

TD: *No.*

Wow! What a great series of questions. I encourage you to go back, reread them, and then ask them to yourself. How do you answer his final question? Obviously, by my answers, my purpose is to make a difference in my life and in the lives of others. Money is simply a powerful vehicle that allows me to do this more consistently. I think I already knew this, but only when I was led through this question-and-answer process did the penny finally drop. Perhaps it will be the same with you as you ask yourself, What's important about success to you? When you become clear on your purpose, you will know your direction and you'll begin to live out your most cherished dreams.

Rickey, Keller, and Rochefoucauld on Purpose

> *Rochefoucauld said, "Few things are impracticable in themselves, and it is for want of application rather than of means, that people fail of success."*

Baseball legend Branch Rickey said, "The greatest single thing in the qualification of a great player, a great team, or a great person, is a desire to reach the objective that admits of no interference anywhere." Helen Keller reminded us, "We can do anything we want to do if we stick to it long enough." Rochefoucauld said, "Few things are impracticable in themselves, and it is for want of application rather than of means, that people fail of success." Purpose! It's what makes life worth living. It adds power, depth, direction, and compassion to your daily life. Let me illustrate this principle by sharing something that happened to me on a recent flight.

My Name Is Sanford, and I Am Strong!

I had left San Diego en route to Dallas and was seated in the first-class section about two rows from the rest room. Midway through the flight, I heard some commotion behind me, and as I turned I saw one of the attendants struggling to help an elderly passenger to the rest room. As she passed me, my purpose kicked in. Without thinking, I stood up and offered my assistance. The elderly gentleman put his frail arm around my shoulder as I guided him into the rest room. I'm six foot five and weigh two hundred pounds, so getting my new friend into the rest room was no small maneuver. This, however, was only the beginning of the story. He not only had a need to be guided into the rest room, but he also needed further assistance. Now the walls seemed to close in on both of us—if you can imagine the scene. Since he was immobilized, I realized it was up to me to help him in any way I could. I pulled down his pants and underwear and carefully helped him get seated so he could do what he needed to do.

I looked at him and said loudly, "Sir, you be sure to knock on the door when you are done, and I'll help you back to your seat." He reached out his hand to shake mine as he said, "My name is Sanford. I'm eighty-seven years old, and I'm strong." Then, with all his might he squeezed my hand. I was overwhelmed by his frailty. A few minutes later, he knocked on the door. I opened it, and he was sitting there just as I'd left him. I asked him to put his arms around my neck. I hoisted Sanford from the toilet seat, pulled up his underwear and pants, somehow extricated ourselves from the rest room, and began the slow journey back to his seat.

I returned to my seat with a sense of fulfillment that brought tears to my eyes. To this day, I can remember how I consciously translated my "general" purpose to make a difference into a simple act of helping an elderly man go to the bathroom at thirty-five thousand feet. It was one of the most powerful moments in my life. The flight attendants expressed their gratitude. The captain came out of the cockpit later and also thanked me. The airline even sent me a letter thanking me for what I'd done—all of which gave me a sense of satisfaction. The real blessing, however, was yet to come. A woman who was traveling with Sanford sent me a note a few weeks later, thanking me for my help. Her closing line was, "Thanks for making a difference." I couldn't hold back the tears. Purpose. It makes all the difference in the world.

I Drove the Car . . . but My Purpose Drove Me

On another occasion, I was forced to cool my heels at Chicago's O'Hare Airport while waiting for a flight to Salt Lake City. No new departure time had yet been announced. I had been scheduled to arrive in Salt Lake and then catch a commuter flight to Sun Valley, where I was to give a seminar the following morning at 8:30. The airline had no idea when the flight would eventually depart, but the gate attendant informed me that there was a flight on another airline leaving in eight minutes. That was the bad news. The good news was there was still one seat available. If there were no further delays, I'd be able to make my connection.

It was purpose that got me through this travel ordeal. I could easily have called the client and explained why I could not make it, but purpose wouldn't let me do it.

Wishing I were wearing tennis shoes rather than wingtips, I made a mad dash from Terminal H to Terminal L. Upon arriving at the gate I could see the plane pulling away from the Jetway. Sweating and about to die, I pleaded for mercy, asking the gate attendants to let me board the plane. They said the flight had closed and I would have to catch another one. The only other flight that evening was my original flight that still had no departure time.

So, I trekked back to the original gate and approached the counter. Again, good news. A plane would be leaving in half an hour. The bad news was I would miss my connection to Sun Valley. Worse yet, the first flight out in the morning would get me in forty minutes after my speech was to start. I quickly calculated that I would rent a car and drive to my seminar. No problem. I asked the agent how far Sun Valley was from Salt Lake. Without even looking it up she said it was 163 miles. I figured if I were to land at 11:30 P.M. I could be in my rental car by midnight and, with a little luck, I might even be in my bed by

4:00 A.M., in plenty of time for a quick three-hour nap and a shower, with time to spare prior to my presentation.

I arrived in Salt Lake at 11:30 P.M. and was in my rental car by midnight. So far, so good. About three hours into my trip, however, I sensed something was terribly wrong. I was still more than a hundred miles from Sun Valley. So I stopped and asked directions (which proves that some men do) only to discover I had to negotiate one more mountain range. I then asked calmly, "By the way, how far is Sun Valley from Salt Lake City?" The reply threw me, "About 280 miles," the man said. What! 280 miles! I didn't realize the estimated mileage given to me by the airline representative was the mileage the airplane would fly— or a crow perhaps.

I pulled in to Sun Valley at 6:00 A.M., ate breakfast, showered, and delivered my speech without a moment's sleep. Only those close enough to see the bags forming under my eyes and my drooping eyelids would be able to guess that I'd done an all-nighter.

Here's my point: It was purpose that got me through this ordeal. I could easily have called the client and explained why I could not make it, but purpose wouldn't let me do it. Each time I felt like stopping on that long drive and throwing my hands up in frustration, purpose kept me going. Once I got to the seminar, my purpose kept me focused. That was one of the most powerful days of my life because I did what was right, and I made a difference by being there. Your purpose lived with passion, commitment, and inner resolve will also give you the power to be your best!

Here's a model to help you understand how these life-enhancing, clarifying questions can become your platform to achieve and maintain the life you deserve.

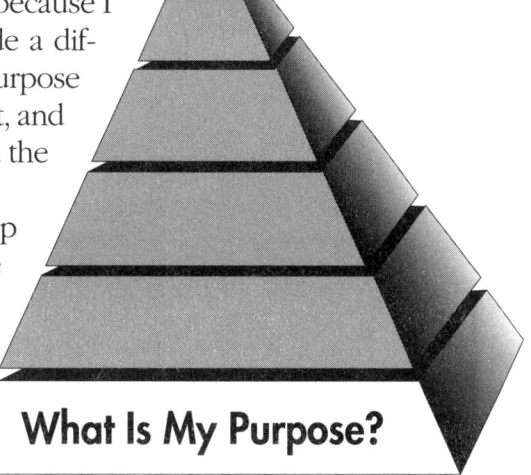

What Is My Purpose?

Clarifying Question Number 2: What Things Do You Value and What Do You Need to Do to Fulfill Them?

Once you've defined your purpose, you can then begin to apply it to the key areas of your life—to those things you value most. If it's still a challenge to unearth your most treasured value areas, let me help you accelerate the process. A great way to determine your values is to engage in a special time that I call "My Day on My Rock." I live in La Jolla, California, and every year I go down to the Cove, where I'm surrounded by the crystal blue waters of the ocean, and sit on a rock. Not just any rock, mind you, but the same rock, year after year. For three to five hours I sit and reflect and reaffirm my values, probe for new ones, explore those that are changing, determine which need more attention, and discard those that are no longer important. Some of the questions I use to foster my thoughts are:

What do I value most in life?

What important areas of my life are not getting the attention they deserve?

Where do I sense I need to add fulfillment to my life?

What have I valued in the past that I no longer value, and therefore need to review…and possibly de-emphasize?

What do I do that gives others pleasure? How can I do more of that?

The singular thread that goes through each question is What do I value? What's important to me? What needs my attention? As you approach your life by continually asking yourself these questions, you'll discover that values-based living becomes your platform for gaining and maintaining the life you deserve. Over the years, I've discovered no more effective method for coaching people to higher levels of performance than this. As you work through your value areas and combine them with your vision (long-term goals), mission (shorter term actions), and your daily tasks (immediate actions), you'll begin to accomplish amazing things that will create meaning and value for you, your family, and for your business.

With this foundation, I can now ask, How can I make a difference in my relationship with my spouse? How can I make a bigger difference in the life of my children? How can I make a bigger difference with my money? What can I do with my body to keep it in shape as I can make a difference for a longer period of time in other people's lives? The answers to these questions are bedrock to harnessing the power that is unleashed when you know your values.

Your Values Are in Constant Flux

What's important about life to you?

This is one of the most important core-value questions you'll ever ask yourself. We noted in chapter 1 that your values represent, at their deepest levels, what is of uncompromising importance to you. What many people fail to realize, however, is that this list of values is constantly changing as we develop and mature physically, spiritually, and emotionally. You are not static. You're dynamic. You're moving in some direction at all times. Therefore, you will make many adjustments as you hit different benchmarks in your life. What was important to you five years ago may not be as vital to you today. Conversely, what wasn't so critical five years ago may be of great significance to you now. Let me illustrate. As a twenty-three-year-old salesperson, money was very important to me. As a forty-year-old successful business owner, it's important but less so. At twenty-three, I was unmarried, and therefore time with spouse and children was not important. Now, as a forty-year-old husband with two children, my wife, Sheryl, and my kids are extremely important to me. As my values change, the dynamics of my life also change—as does how I allocate my time and resources to them. The same holds true for you—whether you are conscious of the process or not.

When you discipline yourself to clarify your values, you will continually ask yourself this question: What's important about life to me? Some people never ask themselves this question. Think of this: From now on you are going to ask yourself this exciting, motivating, provocative question again and again—and your answers will never be precisely the same. To help you get started, I want you to write down eight of your primary values on the lines below. I have given you several of my own to help you get started. These values are in no particular order or rank, but are simply eight things I consider valuable in my life.

1. Family
2. Health
3. Giving to others
4. Spiritual vitality and my relationship with God
5. Financial security
6. Personal development/intellectual growth
7. Integrity
8. Professional success

Now list your values randomly as they come to your mind:

1. _____

2. _____

3. _____

4. _____

5. _____

6. _____

7. _____

8. _____

THE *POWER!* TO BE YOUR BEST!

Now that you have written down what you say is important to you, your next step is to rank and restate them. To gain and maintain the life you deserve demands that you create momentum and that energy begins to manifest itself when you focus on your most important values first. When they are in the right order, the rest become easier to implement. As you work through this process, you'll discover the emergence of a remarkable quality known as synergy—that special combination of separate, even disparate ideas and values that, when working together, prove the truth of the axiom that the whole is greater than the sum of its parts. This is the foundation from which your momentum gets its power to move you toward being your best.

Every time I go to my "rock," I discover some remarkable things about my values and myself. Here is how my values appear to me today in the order of their importance:

1. Spiritual vitality and my relationship with God
2. Health
3. Family
4. Integrity
5. Intellectual growth
6. Giving to others
7. Professional success
8. Financial security

Now list your values in order of their priority. The best way to do this is start with the first one on your list and then compare it with all the rest. When another one becomes more important, compare it with the remaining ones until you have arrived at number one. Cross it off and move to the second one you've written down and compare it with the others. When another value becomes more important, compare it with the remaining ones until you have arrived at number two. Cross it off and continue until all eight have been ranked. If when starting with one and comparing it with all the rest no other value emerges as more important, place it in the order of the spot you are trying to fill. Use the list you created on the previous page.

1. _____

2. _____

3. _____

4. _____

5. _____

6. _____

7. _____

8. _____

You have now determined the second level in your pyramid to success. From this level up, each of your value areas will lead to its own separate vision—long-term, mission—short-term and immediate actions—today. While you are building your pyramid, your foundation—purpose—will not change.

What Do I Value?

What Is My Purpose?

Clarifying Question Number 3: What Is My Vision and Where Am I Going?

Walt Disney once said, "If you can dream it, you can do it." Read that statement again and let it resonate in your heart, only this time read it personally and with passion: If I can dream it, I can do it. Do you think Walt Disney had purpose? Did Disneyland, Disney World, Disney Animal Kingdom, and everything else Disney just happen? Of course not. His corps of imagineers was told to think outside the box, to do things that had never been done before, to never say never. Are you willing to be your own imagineer? The important thing for you is to be so firmly grounded in your purpose that you're willing to do what it takes for you to become the person God designed you to be. George Bernard Shaw once said, "People are always blaming their circumstances for where they are. I don't believe in circumstances. The people who get on in this world are the people who look for the circumstances they want, and if they can't find them, they make them."

"If you can dream it, you can do it."
Walt Disney

Circumstances. We all have circumstances. When our lives come to an end, we all will have encountered most of the same circumstances. Therefore, success has virtually nothing to do with our circumstances. While Shaw's quote brings us back to the Law of Responsibility, there is an even larger message: All movement toward anything requires first knowing what that thing is. Microsoft's advertising campaign keeps asking the question, "Where do you want to go today?" What does this imply? That as soon as you know the answer to the question, Microsoft is ready to take you there. When you combine the implication of the Law of Responsibility with the Microsoft inquiry it sounds like this:

*Only when you know where you want to go
in all the areas of your life will you have
any chance of getting there.*

Your purpose is your North Star, your guiding light. Let's confirm the importance of this statement with a question that's probably forming in your mind: Okay, Todd, how do I discover my overall vision in life? Answer: Stay on your rock. When you pursue clarity in your thinking, you'll need to do it quietly and alone. No television. No phones. No pagers. No e-mail. No interruptions. It's just you and your rock. I've had thousands of students go through this exercise, and they report it to be one of the most significant experiences of their lives. Okay, you've already asked the question, What's important about life to me? Now it's your life's assignment to determine where you want to be in each of those areas. At the core of this thought process is the discovery of what you want to be, have, or do in the five to eight major areas of your life and in what time frame you become, have, or do them. I call these time frames "windows." The metaphor is simple—to see through to the possibilities of what is outside, you must be on the inside looking out. The clearer your window, the better the picture. I'd suggest you make your "windows" time frames of five to ten years. Visions that take longer may be useful, but outside of ten years you will go through some significant shifts in your values, level two of the pyramid. As those shift, so will your long-term visions.

The metaphor is simple—to see through to the possibilities of what is outside, you must be on the inside looking out. The clearer your window, the better the picture.

Those Little "Bumps" in the Center of Your Road

As the visions for your primary values become clear to you, move them into clarifying vision statements. These statements, one for each of your value areas, now become centering mechanisms to help you focus your direction and maintain your course. Clarifying statements act as those little "bumps" that divide the highway of life. When you veer off course, you feel the bumps in the center of the road that wake you up, alert you to oncoming danger, and provide you with the necessary feedback to put you back on course. The bumps keep you safe. They keep you on the road on which you've decided to travel. While initially jarring, you will find them instructive because they prohibit you from drifting away from your values.

Destination Inner Peace

In 1993 I had the pleasure of flying to Salt Lake City to meet with Hyrum Smith, chief executive officer of the Franklin Quest Company—the largest producer of personal productivity systems and software in the world. I had flown to Utah to interview Hyrum as I had done with many other CEOs, authors, and people of influence. I asked Hyrum to tell me about his company—what made it tick, and why it was so successful. Most important, I asked him, What is your core purpose? Hyrum told me, "We teach people how to organize their lives and their businesses around events that, when completed, will make the biggest difference in their lives. When people are able to match activities with what's important to them, they create inner peace." That reminder was worth the trip and the interview. How many people do you know who have no inner peace because they have no "road" to follow, let alone any "warning bumps" in the road to keep them on course. Perhaps that person is you—up until now!

Hyrum continued, "People don't expose themselves often enough to what's important to them, and they end up settling for whatever comes their way." When your values are clear, your vision becomes clear. When your values and visions are clear, your daily decisions become more manageable. What and how you allocate your time become the small bumps in the road that keep you headed in the right direction and along the right path.

Installing the Bumps

The bumps get attached to the center of your "road" when you spend time on your rock to clarify your values. You've probably heard what I'm about to say many times. It's been the subject of many books, tapes, and motivational talks. As Mae West said, "Too much of a good thing is wonderful." So here it is again. When you create your clarifying vision statement, you must speak and write it boldly, confidently, and in the present tense, as if what you desire is already in your possession. Your subconscious mind is a powerful machine that takes present-tense information and stores it as true. It's a fact that your mind cannot differentiate truth from a strong desire. Your mind is a slave. It acts unthinkingly on whatever you give it. The old computer term says GIGO—garbage in, garbage out. It's the same with WSIWSO—wonderful stuff in, wonderful stuff out. When you feed your mind with clarifying visions of where you want to go, your corresponding actions, over time, will provide you with the drive to stay the course and develop those positive habits to help you achieve and maintain the power to be your best.

Your Blueprint for Life

Here's your next assignment: Write a clarifying vision statement for each of your value areas. Once you've done this, you'll need to build two more levels on your pyramid: "mission: short-term" and "daily actions: immediate activities." This is where it

What Is My Vision?

What Do I Value?

What Is My Purpose?

really gets exciting, because you now have in your grasp the power of a process to give you the blueprint you need to achieve anything you want in any area of your life forever. There's no magic, no smoke and mirrors, no mind-altering process to make this happen. What you do have, however, is a readable map to help you arrive at your destination with a minimum of stress.

Here are some examples of my own clarifying-vision statements (CVS). I've listed them in the order of my values, stated earlier. As you read these, be thinking of how you will determine your own CVS. Pay particular attention to the present tense and positive affirmation of each statement.

> *Value: Spiritual vitality and my relationship with God*
> *CVS: My life is devoted to energizing people's passion and commitment to Jesus Christ through active teaching and by sharing my faith to help build God's kingdom and to make an eternal difference.*

> *Value: Health*
> *CVS: My life is vibrant. I focus on my body and its*

fine-tuning because this helps me enjoy an energy-rich life, giving me the experience and the power to go the distance. By preserving my "temple," I fulfill my other values more consistently.

Value: Family

CVS: *I have a vital marriage that is committed to the vow "until death do us part." I transfer my Judeo-Christian values to my wife and children and do what I can to help them grow in God's light and love. By my example, I live out the qualities of joy, hope, respect, and healthy esteem. I do this by being a spiritual model of compassion in our home by giving my greatest gift: my time.*

Clarifying Question Number 4: What Is My Mission and What Activities Will Help Me Get There?

The next two levels of the pyramid lead to action—both long and short term. Actions always produce results. That's simple stimulus-response, cause and effect, but only right actions produce right results. You will take the right actions more often if you link them to your clarifying vision statements. These statements give birth to your actions. While these actions are short term, they've not yet necessarily become habitual. This is why you need to take your "windows"—those five- to ten-year periods and break them into shorter "missions." This more manageable approach will help you fulfill your larger vision. With that determined, you can then proceed to your short-term actions. Here's an example from my own model. Note the critical difference between my overall mission and my daily activities:

Value: *Spiritual vitality and my relationship with God*

CVS: *My life is devoted to energizing people's passion and commitment to Jesus Christ through active teaching and by sharing my*

	faith to help build His kingdom and to make an eternal difference.
Mission:	*I am an evangelist. I bring my faith into my work and will write a minimum of five Christian books by the time I reach the age of fifty-five. I will speak at least twenty times each year for Christian conferences. I will be active in helping my local church in its Christian education needs.*
Daily Activities:	*1. Study the Bible daily. Select, catalog, and store scriptures in my mind that will have application to my work.* *2. Read at least one Christian book each month to help expand my spiritual knowledge.* *3. Build and fill folders with research on the twenty main topics of interest that will fill my books.* *4. Engage in an active prayer life each day where I seek and attempt to follow God's will for my life.*
Value:	*Health*
CVS:	*My life is vibrant. I focus on my body and its fine-tuning because this helps me enjoy an energy-rich life, giving me the experience and the power to go the distance. By preserving my "temple," I fulfill my other values more consistently.*
Mission:	*I have a lifestyle that supports this vision, which includes maintaining a weight of two hundred pounds, a cholesterol level less than 160, and the proper workout and maintenance programs to maintain these outcomes.*

Daily
Activities:

1. *Work out three times this week for at least thirty minutes. I will make sure my heart rate elevates to a minimum of 130 beats per minute.*

2. *Avoid high-fat foods that will deplete my energy and alter my mission.*

3. *Avoid any behavior or substance abuse that takes away from my mental clarity.*

When you put it all together, here's the way it looks as a model:

The Blueprint for Success Pyramid

What will I do today in each value area?

What are my short-term goals in my value areas?

Develop clarifying vision statements.

What do I value in life?

What's important about success to me?

Daily Activities

What Is My Mission?

What Is My Vision?

What Do I Value?

What Is My Purpose?

The Iceberg Principle

As you look at the pyramid that has been evolving in this chapter and its various levels, you must continually focus on the power of a strong base, namely, your purpose. Most people start and end their day stuck at the top of the pyramid. Trying, trying, trying, but never really doing much of significance with their lives. Sadly, as people grow older, most get no closer to the land of their dreams. They never realize their full potential. Take another look at the pyramid and imagine that a line extends from the left of the page all the way to the right margin directly beneath the top section, "What are my activities today?" Ask yourself: How does my day and my life end up if all I do is do? Ninety percent of the mass that gives an iceberg its strength is below the surface. Unseen, yet so powerful. The same is true for you: 90 percent of your strength comes from below the surface—the first four levels of the pyramid. Your life will gain momentum and power and you will begin to achieve the results you desire as you follow this model for success. This is best summed up in this principle for action:

"If one advances confidently in the direction of his dreams and endeavors to live the life which he has imagined, he will meet with success unexpected in common hours. He will pass an invisible boundary; new universal and more liberal laws will begin to establish themselves around and within him; and he will live with the licenses of a higher order of being."

Henry David Thoreau

Plan of Action for Living Your Life by Design

To implement the principles in this chapter:

1. Go to your "Rock."
2. Ask the purpose question and work the dialog:
    What's important about success to me?
    What is my purpose?
3. Ask the values question and arrive at five to eight value areas. Rank them. Why are they important to me?
4. For each of your value areas, develop a clarifying vision statement (CVS) written in a positive, affirming, and present tense.
5. For each CVS, develop a mission statement.
6. For each mission statement, develop three to five activities that, when accomplished, you feel will move you intentionally in the direction of fulfilling your mission and vision in each important area of your life.

Now develop the habit of spending a minimum of fifteen minutes each morning or evening reviewing your "map." Schedule your activities to allow you to develop a success routine. You will discover great power to act when you live your life with values-based commitments. As your coach, I also want you to be realistic. You will have good and bad days. Some days you will forget to review your map. At other times, you'll be so tuned in to your values that you'll be unstoppable. The key to your greater success is to promise yourself, as much as possible, to stay focused on the map. Because whenever you are lost, your map will bring you home.

When you've completed
this assignment, go to
my website at
www.toddduncan.com and
upload your action plan.
Upon receipt, I will send you
a laminated wallet *LifeQuest*
card to help you on your journey. *See you on-line.* —*TD*

www.toddduncan.com

Action Planner Notes

_____

_____

_____

_____

_____

_____

_____

_____

_____

_____

_____

_____

_____

_____

_____

_____

_____

_____

_____

_____

_____

_____

_____

_____

THE _POWER!_ TO BE YOUR BEST!

Seven Top Behaviors for Effective Living

Security is mostly superstition. It does not exist in nature, nor do children or men as a whole experience it. Avoiding danger is no safer in the long run than outright exposure. Life is either a daring adventure or nothing. **Helen Keller**

What lies behind us and what lies before us are tiny matters compared to what lies within us. **Ralph Waldo Emerson**

---

o enjoy your life based on your values is the only way to live. That's the good news. The more challenging thought is that as you live your values and work through your purpose for living, you will hit roadblocks, jump hurdles, and tunnel through obstacles you'd rather not even think about. There are seven specific behaviors, however, that can give you the tools to master values-based living. They will provide you with the skills you need to follow your dreams as you journey toward becoming the person God designed you to be.

Behavior Number 1: Attitude

To illustrate the importance of this first behavior, let me tell you about something that happened to me recently. I was in Rochester, New York, preparing for a morning seminar. I had just finished my workout that morning, and I felt tremendous. After showering and dressing, I decided to grab a quick breakfast before giving my morning presentation.

When I arrived at the hotel cafeteria, I said to the hostess, "Great morning."

Her countenance seemed confused as she looked at me. Great morning? What's with this guy? Why's he so excited? It's only breakfast. Just another day at the salt mines.

"Are you here for breakfast?" she asked.

"Yes," I said, "I'm here for breakfast."

She grabbed a menu and asked me if I preferred smoking or nonsmoking. When I said that I preferred nonsmoking, she seated me and asked if I wanted coffee—decaf or regular. After our stimulating dialog, she went to the coffee station where she continued to stare at me, perplexed by her overzealous patron. She returned to my table with a coffeepot, but she stood as far away from me as possible, as if I had a communicable disease. Stretching her arm to the limit of her reach, she poured my coffee. It was the strangest sight. She took two steps back from the table and blurted out, "You have a positive attitude, don't you?"

"Yes, I do," I responded enthusiastically.

She then made a statement that blew me away: "You know, mister, I've always wondered what one of those looked like."

For one of the first times in my life, I didn't know what to say. But it dawned on me that she was probably speaking the truth: This woman did not know what a positive attitude looked like. While still thinking how I could answer her, she asked, "Say, could you tell me how I could have one?"

At that moment, I realized I had a unique opportunity to make a difference in another person's life. During that special

> *"You have a positive attitude, don't you?" "Yes, I do," I responded enthusiastically. She then made a statement that blew me away: "You know, mister, I've always wondered what one of those looked like."*

morning in Rochester, my positive attitude not only made a difference in how I approached my day, but my attitude also made an impression on a person who wanted the same attitude for herself.

Less fearful now, she edged closer to the table. I said, "I'll tell you what, if you keep my coffee cup full, I promise for as long as I'm eating breakfast that I'll give you some of the ideas I use to have a positive attitude. Would that be okay?"

She responded enthusiastically, "Yes, I'd love that."

With that agreement between us, she kept filling my coffee cup and for the next thirty-five minutes I shared with her some of the things we all can do to develop positive attitudes.

Answer These Two Questions

I have two questions for you: (1) Do you know what a positive attitude looks like? (2) What does yours look like? One might also ask, Why is a good attitude important? Isn't success primarily about I.Q., money, power, influence, and a well-bankrolled future? Why the focus on attitude? Those are good questions, and the answer is that attitudes are the only gateways through which we will ever enjoy the fullness of life.

Martin Seligman, professor of psychology at the University of Pennsylvania, has done substantial research in the area of attitudes. He has discovered that people with positive attitudes perform better regardless of their circumstances—the workplace, their family life, their financial investing, their relationships with colleagues, and just about anything else to which they put their minds. In fact, Seligman suggests that such people perform at a level 40 percent higher than those with pessimistic and negative outlooks.

As your coach and mentor, I recommend that you take Seligman's research at face value. With a positive, upbeat, never-say-die attitude alone you'll be 40 percent ahead of those who grouse their way through the day and through life.

One of the questions I continue to ask myself—and one that others keep asking me—is the same one I was asked that morning in Rochester: Just how do you get a positive attitude? With all the troubles of my life, how do I keep a positive attitude once I get one?

Some time ago, a friend handed me a one-page Xerox on attitude written by Chuck Swindoll, best-selling author and president of the Dallas Theological Seminary. I do not know the original source of this powerful quote which reads:

> *The longer I live, the more I realize the impact of attitude on life. Attitude, to me, is more important than facts. It is more important than the past, than education, than money, than circumstances, than failures, than successes, than what other people think or say or do. It is more important than appearance, giftedness or skill. It will make or break a company, a church, and a home. The remarkable thing is we have a choice every day regarding the attitude we will embrace for that day. We cannot change our past. We cannot change the fact that people will act in a certain way. We cannot change the inevitable. The only thing we can do is play on the string we have and that is our attitude. I am convinced that life is 10 percent what happens to me and 90 percent how I react to it. And so it is with you. We are in charge of our attitudes.*

"I am convinced that life is 10 percent what happens to me and 90 percent how I react to it. And so it is with you. We are in charge of our attitudes." **Chuck Swindoll**

It's All about Choices!

Attitudes don't just happen. We choose them. Shad Helmstedter, in his book *Choices,* says:

> *No one else can ever make your choices for you. Your choices are yours alone. They are as much a part of you as every breath you take every moment of your life. You have the ability to choose your strength. You have the ability to choose honesty. You have the ability to believe in yourself. You have the ability to choose your goals and your directions in life. You have the ability to choose to accept others as they are. You have the ability to choose, to make your decisions for yourself. You have the ability to choose to always be responsible for your own actions. You have the ability to choose right from wrong. You have the ability to choose to work for what you believe in. You have the ability to choose to learn from your mistakes. And you have the ability to choose to love and to be loved. And you have the ability to choose every detail of your life, and it all starts with your attitude.[1]*

Grounded in Purpose

Since our choices arise from our attitudes, it's reasonable to assume that we'd be wise to begin each day by making good choices. Fortunately, we don't need to go it alone. Our Creator begins each day with us by granting us the freedom to make these new choices. If a loving God is relaxed enough to give us new choices each day of our lives, then certainly we can follow suit and make new choices of our own.

In the Book of Lamentations, we read, "Through the Lord's mercies we are not consumed, because His compassions fail not. They are new every morning" (3:22–23). What a great way to start the day. What happened yesterday was yesterday, what happens today is today, and what happens tomorrow is something we should not waste our time worrying about. When you live a life based on uncompromising values, when you live a life grounded in purpose, when you live a life tethered to your visions, short-term missions, and daily activities, you can't help but approach each morning with a healthy outlook.

When your attitude is positive, your choices become positive. When your attitude is strong, your choices become strong. When your attitude is weak, your choices become weak. When your attitude is negative, your choices become negative. So how do you improve? The following are three keys to making better choices:

1. Make choices that are values based.
2. Make choices that propel you rather than restrict you.
3. Make choices that are ownership based.

Make Choices That Are Values Based

Starting today, you can begin any day with everything you need to ensure a positive attitude. Let me illustrate that with the following story.

At a recent seminar, I taught the models that I have already shared with you in chapters 1 and 2. After completing the seminar that morning, I agreed to have lunch with several of the executives of the company that had hired me.

We were seated around tables in rounds of ten. Within moments of being seated, I could see that my seminar material would soon be tested. The server was doling out large portions of fettuccine Alfredo to everyone at the table. She started with the people to my left and continued clockwise until she came to me.

I knew I was going to have to make a decision based on my values. Luckily, earlier that morning I had reviewed my clarifying vision statements in relation to God, my body, and my family. So when the server came to my plate, I asked her if she had some steamed vegetables or a plate of rice.

Everyone looked at me, and then one of the gentlemen said, "You know, I was wondering if you were going to walk your talk."

Earlier that morning, I had shared some of my cherished values, one of which is my health. I said that I wanted 25 percent or less of my calories to come from fat and that I wanted to put things into my body that would energize it, not deplete it of its energy. It was gratifying to look across the table and say to that person, "You know, it wasn't that difficult, really. I made a decision based on my values."

To make better choices that lead to a better attitude, you must hold fast in your mind to that which is important to you. You must do the things you must do to fuel their success each day of your life.

Make Choices That Propel You Rather Than Restrict You

When you make choices that propel you rather than restrict you, you find yourself asking the question, If I do this, will it move me closer to or take me farther away from what I value most in life?

Most of us make our choices stuck on autopilot. We choose to eat too much without thinking of our health. We make the choice to drink too much without asking how we'll feel the next day. We make the choice to spend too much money without asking if our decision will protect us financially in the future.

It's all about choices. To make better choices—the kind that will give us the results we want—we must come off autopilot and ask ourselves, Will the choice I'm about to make bring me closer to being my best?

Make Choices That Are Ownership Based

Shad Helmstedter is right when he says that the choices we make by accident are just as important as the choices we make by design. The issue is one of ownership.

When you say to yourself, "This choice is mine," you program yourself not only to recognize how many choices you have available to you in the first place, but you also start working with a new program that tells you, from now on, I will take responsibility for making these choices for myself. There is no more exhilarating freedom than exercising the power to make your own decisions.

> *"The choices we make by accident are just as important as the choices we make by design."* **Shad Helmstedter**

Behavior Number 2: Unleashing Your Power

What happened yesterday is history. What happens today is your foundation for tomorrow. You were born to succeed. God gave you the ability to act, the capacity to think, and the competence to choose. With the combination of those three attributes, you might ask, How can I possibly fail? You fail when you think and act the wrong way.

I discovered this truth while reading Norman Vincent Peale's bestseller, *The Power of Positive Thinking.* One day a man approached Dr. Peale after he'd given a powerful speech on positive thinking. He told the great motivator that he was forty years old and that he'd made absolutely nothing of himself. He wanted to know why inferiority feelings and a lack of self-confidence had tormented him all his life. He begged Dr. Peale to help him develop some faith in himself.

Dr. Peale said, "As you walk down the street tonight I suggest that you repeat certain words which I shall give you. Say them over several times after you get into bed. When you awaken tomorrow, repeat them three times before arising. On the way to your important appointment say them three additional times. Do this with an attitude of faith and you will receive sufficient strength and ability to deal with this problem. Later if you wish, we can go into an analysis of your basic problem, but whatever we come up with following that study, the formula which I am now going to give you can be a large factor in the eventual cure."[2]

The following scripture is the affirmation that Dr. Peale gave to the man: "I can do all things through Christ who strengthens me" (Philippians 4:13).

The man took Dr. Peale's advice and soon began to see his life turn around. Things began to flow to him rather than away from him. He became more self-confident. He accomplished more than he'd ever done before. His personality became so positive that instead of pushing away success, he was now drawing it to him.

Inscribe the following statement in your heart: *God does not want us to fail.* He didn't design us to fail. We were born with everything we need to succeed. To harness the power that God gives us, however, we must allow Him to work in us. When we do that, He gives us everything we need to be everything He wants us to be. In fact the Bible says, "If God is for us, who can be against us?" (Romans 8:31).

The Power of What We Say to Ourselves

Our minds are powerful, but they are also our slaves. They hear without bias and respond without reference to positive or negative input. If our language is negative, no matter how hard we may try to get rich, lose weight, stay off drugs, or thrive in a relationship, we won't succeed. Why? Because our language becomes a coconspirator in the fine art of emotional sabotage. Since our self-image is stored in the subconscious mind, and since it believes the information it stores is true, whether true or not, it is imperative that we send our minds positive images and pictures, even when they do not represent current reality. All new behaviors start in the mind—the imagination—and then work their way outward into reality. What you think is what you get.

Our self-image, that picture we hold of ourselves in our minds, is the platform from which all our actions flow. Each action, feeling, and behavior cannot help but be consistent with this image on our internal mirror. To change our results, we must change the negative blueprint we have created over time. Since repetition created the state of our current image, it will also take repetition to change our state of mind from unhealthy to healthy. This is where most of us break down. We simply don't muster the stamina or the faith to repeat the right behaviors and actions long enough to create a healthy self-image that can lead us to become more than we think we are.

We must build and modify our self-image through encouraging self-talk—those words and pictures that trigger the positive images to give us the power to move in the right direction. Over time, these new directions lead us to feel better about ourselves, enhance our character, and release within us the power to be our best.

Self-talk, Affirmations, and Dreamation

Let's follow through on this important issue of self-talk. If we want different results, we must learn to speak to ourselves differently. This difference is best found in the power of affirmations.

When I was just beginning to understand the life-changing power of affirmations, it was my good fortune to purchase two of Denis Waitley's books, *The Winner's Edge* and *Seeds of Greatness*. Here's the powerful lesson I learned in their pages: Anything we want in life has to be seen before it can be attained. Then, equally important, I learned that we must feed our beliefs until they become reality. I call this process *dreamation*—the art of attaining maximum motivation by living as if our dreams have already come true.

Recently, I had the pleasure of speaking on the same platform with Dr. Waitley, and I told him about this process and what I called it. I also shared with him some of my results. He asked if he could tell our audience how powerful dreamation could be in their own lives.

I have learned that without dreams, we're dead, or at least we're in the process of dying. You and I can be, have, or do anything we want if we will dream it, see it before we have it, and pursue our goal with a never-say-die attitude. The key element that keeps dreamation alive is the power of affirmations. I'm sure affirmations are not new to you, but since it's so easy to forget their power, let's look at them once again:

The Five Keys to Powerful Affirmations

They must be:

> *You and I can be, have, or do anything we want if we will dream it, see it before we have it, and pursue our goal with a never-say-die attitude.*

1. Personal: They must begin with the personal pronoun "I." (For example, "I am earning . . . I am having a relationship with . . . I am enjoying living in a three-thousand-square-foot home at . . .")

2. Positive: They must be articulated as something you have already received, not something you are trying to get rid of. (The latter negative language goes immediately to your subconscious.)

3. Present tense: They must be stated as if they are already achieved.

4. Emotional and benefits driven: They must trigger your emotions.

5. Noncomparative: They must be what you want for you to be your best, not what you feel you must do to be better than someone else.

My Closet Was My Think Tank

Early in my career, I put every goal I had on 8-1/2" x 11" pieces of paper and posted them on the walls of my closet. Each morning when I went in to get dressed, I would spend fifteen minutes reviewing my goals and filling my mind with the end results of my exciting future life. Later, as I accomplished many of those objectives, I took the same concept and made it portable.

As I devoured Dr. Waitley's books and heeded his advice, I began to write affirmations that supported each of my goals. Here's a page of affirmations I wrote in 1984 at the age of twenty-six while working as a loan officer in the mortgage banking business. Each of these goals has come true.

1. I am a professional speaker.
2. I earn in excess of $500,000 per year.
3. I always have $200,000 in cash in the bank.
4. I have ten successful audiocassette albums or videos.
5. I am 100 percent debt-free.
6. I have only healthy habits.
7. I speak over 100 times per year.
8. I own a 5,000-square-foot home at the beach with high ceilings, a large yard, tennis court, pool, and spa. (Well, it doesn't have the tennis court, but I don't play tennis anyway—at least not yet!)

I still carry this list in my wallet to remind me of the power of short, concise affirmations. It is tattered and worn, soft and torn, but it is the most powerful piece of paper I own.

Behavior Number 3: Focus Precedes Success

When your attitude is right, and the power to be your best has been unleashed, it is then time to focus. There is a tremendous difference between having power-energy and having power-focus. I know many people who have a positive attitude and are nowhere close to tapping their potential. In virtually every situation such as this, the common error is a lack of focus. Al Ries, author of *Focus*, says it like this:

> *The sun is a powerful source of energy. Every hour the sun washes the earth with billions of kilowatts of energy. Yet with a hat and some sunscreen you can bathe in the light of the sun for hours at a time with few ill effects. A laser is a weak source of energy. A laser takes a few watts of energy and focuses them in a coherent stream of light. But with a laser, you can drill a hole in a diamond or wipe out a cancer. When we focus, we create the same effect. We create a powerful, laser-like ability to get anything done in our lives that we desire.*[3]

That is what focusing is about; it must precede any action to produce significant results in that area. When we become unfocused, we lose power and the ability to create great results. We become like the sun, releasing our energy everywhere, in any and all areas of our lives, but never producing any significant results.

The key to gaining and maintaining the life you deserve is to focus on those areas you said were most important to you in chapter 2. If you want to lose weight, you must be focused. If you want to create wealth, you must be focused. If you want to have a vital marriage, you must be focused. If you want to enjoy intimacy with God, you must be focused. Focus is everything. Without focus, you will live a life of mediocrity.

Focus is everything. Without focus, you will live a life of mediocrity.

As you concentrate your focus on those things that are important to you, your values, attitudes, choices, and affirmations begin to work together. This process is called *synergism,* proof positive that the whole is always greater and more powerful than the sum of its parts.

Behavior Number 4:
The Best Results Take Time

The date was 1903. The location was Kitty Hawk, North Carolina. The distance was 120 feet. The time in the air was 12 seconds. Nevertheless, Orville Wright had finally achieved a first: He had gotten something heavier than air to stay aloft. That day in Kitty Hawk forever changed the way people traveled. Today, more than five million people worldwide fly daily. Like fine wine, relationships, and a grove of mighty oaks, the best things in life take time to ripen and mature.

Patience—Another Key to Success

Let's look at a few great accomplishments where patience was the deciding factor in success. One man proved to be one of the most patient men in history. When he was seven years old, his family was forced out of their home on a legal technicality, and he had to work to help support them. His mother died when he was nine years old. At twenty-two, he lost his job as a store clerk. He wanted to go to law school, but his education wasn't good enough. At twenty-three, he went into debt to become a partner in a small store. At twenty-six, his business partner died, leaving him a huge debt that took years to repay. At twenty-eight, after courting a girl for four years, he asked her to marry him. She said no. At thirty-seven, on his third try, he was elected to Congress, but two years later he failed to win reelection. When he was forty-one, his four-year-old son died. At forty-five, he ran for the Senate and lost. At forty-seven, he failed as the vice-presidential candidate for his party. At forty-nine, he ran for the Senate again and lost. At fifty-one, he was elected president of the United States. His name was Abraham Lincoln, a man many have considered to have been the greatest leader this country ever had. Like the critic said…some people get all the breaks.

What an incredible story of perseverance, of facing the odds and staring them down, of refusing to allow defeat to beat him. Lincoln regarded his lifetime of unsavory results as building blocks, not stumbling stones. What's the lesson here for you? I hope it's one of encouragement, because you, too, can tunnel through your difficulties, overcome your obstacles, and with God's help, make it to the top. Lincoln is not the only model in a galaxy of stars who exercised patience in overcoming the odds:

1. Thomas Edison estimated that he'd performed more than fourteen thousand experiments in the process of inventing and perfecting the incandescent light bulb.
2. Colonel Sanders tried to sell his chicken recipe to over one thousand different people before someone actually bought it.
3. Michael Jordan didn't make the varsity basketball team until his senior year in high school. As of this writing, he has been awarded ten NBA scoring championships. The next closest man is Wilt Chamberlain with seven. (Wilt does hold the rebounding title with eleven.)
4. Orville Redenbacher conducted more than thirty-five hundred experiments before his lighter, fluffier popcorn was invented. He later sold his patent to Hunt-Wesson Foods for more than $300 million.

One of the keys to your success is never giving up. That's why a life based on purpose is critical to your ultimate achievements.

Everything you want to accomplish will take patience. Ninety-five percent of the people in the world will go 95 percent of the way and settle for only 5 percent of what's available to them. There is another 5 percent who will go 100 percent of the way and demand 95 percent of what's available to them. Which group are you in? One of the keys to your success is never giving up. That's why a life based on purpose is critical to your ultimate achievements.

Speed Kills—Go Slow

It took me fifty years to become an overnight success. That's the way it is in Hollywood sometimes, but not only Hollywood. There is no fast track to real success. Failure happens for many reasons, but one of the most common—and most avoidable—is when we move too fast. Whenever I try to get there faster, write faster, sell faster, or live my life faster, it invariably takes me longer than I had originally planned. The undoing and fixing takes more time and effort than it would have taken to do it right the first time around.

Recently my wife and I were traveling to my family's summer home in Idaho. We flew to Boise and rented a car. After two hours of driving, I realized I had passed the turnoff for the house. Frustrated, I turned the car around and, at about seventy miles per hour, headed back from where we had just come. I was not alone, however. An Idaho state trooper was coming toward me. My first thought was, *Thank goodness. No problem. He's going the other way.* What I forgot was that he had a steering wheel in a car with amazing maneuverability. Faster than you could say "Cop!" I saw all his lights come on. His vehicle went into a four-wheel slide as he turned around and came up behind me. I pulled over to the side of the road.

He collected my license and returned to his patrol car to write me a ticket. I decided to try to talk him out of it. I approached his closed window and gently knocked on it. He rolled it down.

"Officer, are you sure you have to give me this ticket?" I asked.

"No," he said, "but I really want to!"

I got to the family house late. Remember there are no shortcuts. Not to the family place in Idaho or wherever you plan to go today.

Behavior Number 5:
Humility—The Master's Strategy

When I started my company in 1988, I was committed to its uncompromising success. We came out of the gate with a large contract with a national company, and within three years we were doing more than $5 million in sales annually with a staff of only twenty-seven people. It was amazing. We could do nothing wrong. Every day our company grew more and more profitable, and with its seemingly endless success, I became increasingly confident and prideful. I kept thinking, "Hey, look what Todd built. Isn't this incredible—all this money, power, and influence. The sky's the limit."

Things began to unravel over the next six months as we found ourselves up against what appeared to be the inevitable—closing shop. Our cash flow could not meet our obligations.

One day, that limitless, cloudless blue sky began to fall down all around me. The first call came from one of our key clients. Because of what they said were unfavorable market conditions (Have you heard that one before?), they would have to cancel their contract (valued at $150,000). The following month another client called and gave us the same bad news. Within six months, five contracts had canceled, leaving a total of more than $900,000 of receivables on our books—uncollectible.

I called a meeting of all the employees. With their agreement, the executives went on a 50 percent pay reduction while the staff agreed to a 20 percent across-the-board pay cut to help the company try to stay afloat. We had to notify the two hundred vendors to whom we owed money that we would not be able to meet our payment obligations. That's when things got ugly. We fell behind on our rent payments, and the landlord began serving eviction notices. Several vendors filed lawsuits.

Things began to unravel over the next six months as we found ourselves up against what appeared to be the inevitable—closing shop. Our cash flow could not meet our obligations.

I recall one morning when I knew I'd come to the end of my rope. Emotionally overwhelmed and financially unglued, I had no one to turn to, so I fell on my knees in my office and with the door shut I cried out, "God, why me? Why me?" That's when my eyes caught a framed saying that my friend Bob Shank had given me several years earlier.

It read:

TODD
TRUST ME.
I HAVE
EVERYTHING
UNDER
CONTROL.

JESUS

At that moment, I had my first lesson in humility. I had never committed my company or its activities to the Lord (Proverbs 3:5–6). I had not thanked God for any previous success. If anything, I made sure everyone knew that Todd Duncan was the boss, the reason for his company's great progress, and the ultimate master of his own fate! Well, Todd wasn't bragging now. So here's what we (God and I) did. We sold off those businesses we should not have been involved with in the first place. Our primary calling was professional speaking, and if a business we owned didn't include that activity, we got rid of it—or sold it to an employee so they could start a business of their own. We then created a vendor repayment plan that paid back more than $500,000 over twenty-four months. Before long, the lawsuits stopped. My integrity (a core value) would not allow me to file bankruptcy, so we just kept re-engineering our operations until we got ourselves out of hock. The most important aspect of our re-engineering, however, was to commit to a humble spirit and thankful heart.

As I regained my perspective, I started to pay more attention to the life of the greatest man who ever lived—a model for all the world of gentleness and humility. His name is Jesus Christ. In Matthew 11:28–29, Jesus said, "Come to Me, all you who labor and are heavy laden, and I will give you rest. Take My yoke upon you and learn from Me, for I am gentle and lowly in heart, and you will find rest for your souls."

This is the same great man who demonstrated His humility by washing the feet of His disciples. He loved children. He reached out to those members of society no one else cared about. He loved when others expressed only hate. He knew the difference between the urgent and the important. He didn't rush around trying to heal everyone, save everyone, or make sure everyone knew him. His lifestyle was quite the opposite. Now, as I slowly stepped back from my near fatal business experience, I knew I would be wise to spend more time with Jesus than the *Wall Street Journal.*

As you can now tell, I believe the Bible gives us the best road map for positive, effective living, and it provides some of the strongest reasons I've ever found for living life with a humble spirit. Here are but three examples:

By humility and the fear of the LORD are riches and honor and life. **Proverbs 22:4**

Humble yourselves in the sight of the Lord, and He will lift you up. **James 4:10**

God resists the proud, but gives grace to the humble. **James 4:6**

Never lose your spirit of humility. Give thanks to God each day for what He gives to you. Your benefits will be rich beyond measure.

Behavior Number 6:
The Art of Sowing and Reaping

Where you are today is a function of what you did or did not do yesterday. Every result you enjoy or hate is happening because of your choices. It's the same for all of us, no exceptions. Simply put, it's the immutable law of sowing and reaping. You don't have to like it any more than you appreciate the law of gravity, but you would be wise to accept its truth at face value. The behavior of sowing and reaping says, "If you want to enjoy a bountiful harvest tomorrow, you must plant good seeds today." Sounds reasonable, but there's more. The time between these two events—sowing and reaping—must be long enough to allow your seed to germinate and grow. You must water it, fertilize it, weed around it, spray it, and do a host of other things so that when the time to harvest comes, your seed will have matured into an ear of corn, wheat, barley, oats, financial success, or a better relationship with yourself, your loved ones, or with God. Then and only then will you reap the reward of an abundant harvest.

At some point in your life, you probably want to be in a position where you no longer need to trade your time for money. I'm sure most people would like to have the option not to have to work (more on this in chapter 8). Fair enough, but for us to accomplish this worthy goal, we must do certain things now.

Let's say that you want to stop working when you're sixty years old. Let's also figure that for you to enjoy your life at age sixty, you'll need to have $80,000 a year. For that to happen, between now and then you'll need to "plant" $1 million that will earn a minimum of 8 percent so your $80,000 "harvest" can occur. If, for example, you wait until age fifty-nine to plant your seeds, your harvest at age sixty will not come close to meeting your desires. It will be too little too late. To have the power to be your best in your later years, you must plant your seeds early and consistently and then take care of your "field" regularly if your harvest is to be what you want it to be. If you wait until the last minute, the task becomes insurmountable. Look at the following figures:

Age	Monthly Investment @ 8% to reach $1 million by age 60
30	$283
36	$598
42	$1,306
48	$3,103
54	$9,456

Here's the challenging news: Everything you want in life depends on your accumulated actions. Everything counts. Without exception, your abundant harvest will not happen if you fail to plant the right seeds now, which by definition are a consistent execution of the right strategies and a continual feeding of your mind with positive, uplifting thoughts.

When you finally have more free time, when you accumulate more money, when you have gained more knowledge and wisdom, how will you use the excess? The Law of Abundance says that the best way for you to receive more is to commit to giving more; it promises that you can get everything you want out of your life if you just help enough other people get what they want. If we will only heed these words, success beyond measure will be ours. This is the basis for the second element of sowing and reaping—Reciprocity.

When you create reciprocity, you create abundance. The first most important question I want you to ask yourself is this: Are you primarily a giver or a taker? When I say giving, I mean the kind of giving that does not keep score. The investment of time, freedom, and money into the lives and causes that are important to you creates an abundant, positive balance in the emotional and financial accounts of your life. If you fail to invest in

> *The Law of Abundance says that the best way for you to receive more is to commit to giving more. "You can have everything in life you want, if you will just help enough other people get what they want."*
>
> *—Zig Ziglar*

those accounts consistently and only withdraw from them, the day will come when you are emotionally, physically, spiritually, and financially broke. It may take the form of financial troubles, bankruptcy, separation or divorce, shallow relationships with your children and friends, or ultimately a feeling of negative-self worth—the real bottom line. That's why the only way to spell l-o-v-e for your family is t-i-m-e.

To enjoy intimacy with your friends is to be a resource to them. To help create value for your church is to be an active giver of your time, tithe, and talent. To show your spouse how much you love him or her is to be aware that the power of the three words "I love you" goes farther than you will ever imagine. So pour it on. Go 100 percent. Never keep score of your loving deeds, and you will always have a positive surplus in the accounts that are most important to you.

In business, you create reciprocity when you help nurture a prospect's financial health and wealth. As a salesperson, there is no such thing as call reluctance if you know that what you are about to bring to your prospects and clients is worth ten times more than what you are asking them to give to you. When you create massive value for the people and causes you love and serve, you will never have to worry about forward progress in your life. When you are gone, you will leave an enormous legacy.

Importance of a Mortgage Portfolio

One of the most important and most overlooked tools in an individual's financial portfolio is a mortgage. Obtaining a mortgage is typically the single largest financial transaction that anyone makes in his or her lifetime, but it is often dealt with in the same way that we buy electronic components like VCRs. My friend, a highly recognized industry expert, Barry Habib, describes a mortgage as the centerpiece of a solid financial plan. His insight is worth noting:

A mortgage affects a family's tax planning, investments, retirement planning, and can be a vehicle to fund a child's college education. Using a mortgage to tap equity in your home can help in financial planning. A family with a three-year-old child may have concerns about how it will meet future college expenses. A family that draws equity from its home today and invests those dollars with the help of a financial expert should solve the problem. Historically, money invested in mutual funds has yielded an average return of 15 percent per year over timeframes of ten years or longer. This means that your investment should double every five years. An example of $20,000 invested today—when the child is age three—should double in five years to $40,000 when the child is eight. This amount would grow to $80,000 over the next five years when the child has reached thirteen years of age. Finally by the time the child is eighteen and ready for college, the total value of the fund should balloon to about $160,000. This return on investment ensures that the child will be able to afford a solid college education.

Often, this type of cash out can be combined with a lower interest rate or debt consolidation plan that actually reduces the family's overall monthly payments while funding the college education plan. This type of scenario can also have favorable tax consequences since the interest paid on the mortgage is more than likely to be tax deductible. The basic strategy behind this plan can also be applied toward retirement. Retirement is by far the most overlooked part of the average family's financial plan. Many people are dependent upon Social Security for their retirement. If Social Security is solvent by the time an individual retires, the benefits arising from a lifetime of paying into the system will result in an existence that borders on poverty.

Some individuals have contributed to their employers 401(k) plan or have opened up their own IRA accounts. Both plans are steps in the right direction. The problem that still exists, however, is that most people do not start early enough or account properly for the money they will need. Life expectancies are rising and the desired retirement age is decreasing. This demonstrates the need for a better, more sophisticated plan prepared by an expert. Would a computer programmer perform root-canal work on his wife? Obviously not, because he is not a properly trained expert. Why then do most individuals attempt to plan for their financial future and retirement without the help of a financial planner?

Behavior Number 7: The Power of Faith

John Maxwell says, "If you have faith in your future, you will have power in your present. If you have no faith in your future, you are powerless in your present." (I suggest you print this quote on a small card and keep it with you at all times.)

You must have faith in your future to get anywhere in life. You must believe and expect that the visions, goals, aspirations, and objectives you have decided to focus on have already come true. (That's the power of an affirmation.) Without this, you will probably stop short of becoming all God created you to be.

Dr. Norman Vincent Peale observed: "Believe in yourself! Have faith in your ability! Without a humble but reasonable confidence in your own powers you cannot be successful or happy. But with sound self-confidence you can succeed. A sense of inferiority and inadequacy interferes with the attainment of

> *"If you have faith in your future, you will have power in your present. If you have no faith in your future, you are powerless in your present."*

your hopes, but self-confidence leads to self-realization and successful achievement."[4]

Your power of faith and belief will be the final arbiters in your quest for success. Live them with joy. Let them give you the confidence to take action. When your actions fail to create the outcome you hope for, your faith and belief will give you the power to pick yourself up and try, try, try again until you get to where you want to be. With these two elements—faith and belief—fully engaged, you will develop your "never quit" attitude. You will stay focused longer and get the results you want faster. The most powerful book on the planet to teach us how to have great levels of faith is the Bible. Generation after generation has made it the most widely read book of all time. Historically, the human race has put more confidence in its pages than any document ever written. The New Testament alone has hundreds of references to the overwhelming power of faith. Here are a few:

If God is for us, who can be against us?
Romans 8:31

Now faith is the substance of things hoped for, the evidence of things not seen.
Hebrews 11:1

If you can believe, all things are possible to him who believes. **Mark 9:23**

Faith, Belief, and Adversity

The date was April 22, 1987. My brother Jeff was celebrating his twenty-second birthday with my mom in Colorado by skiing at Copper Mountain. The Duncans have always been avid skiers, but on occasion we would throw caution to the wind because, after all, haven't we done this a thousand times before?

Jeff and Mom were coming down a run, when Jeff decided to get some "air" by going off a jump. He picked up enormous speed, but the mogul he hit to get into the air was larger than he realized. He flew sky high. Thrown off balance, he went horizontal. In the blink of an eye, Jeff's life was changed forever. He crashed hard on his back. He finally came to a stop as my mother looked at him from a distance. Jeff wasn't moving. She quickly skied to where he was lying in the snow. When she got there, she heard him muttering, "Mom, I can't feel my legs."

She quickly skied to where he was lying in the snow where she heard him muttering, "Mom, I can't feel my legs."

The ski patrol concluded that Jeff's injury was serious and that he needed to be airlifted to Denver General by helicopter. Since there was no room in the chopper, Mom was forced to make the two-hour drive to Denver not knowing Jeff's condition. When she arrived at the hospital, she learned that Jeff had suffered major back trauma and that immediate surgery was necessary to increase Jeff's chance of walking again. In fact, the doctors did not hold out much hope.

Jeff had shattered his L1 vertebra and had broken his L2 in several places. The surgery took five hours as two twelve-inch rods were laced to his spine to give it the stability it needed to heal.

Eventually, he was transferred to Craig Rehabilitation Center in Colorado where he began an extensive and painful rehab that lasted three and a half months. Sheryl and I were to be married on August 8, 1987. Some months before the accident, I had asked Jeff to be in our wedding. What would happen now? Would he be able to make it? All his life, Jeff had been a championship athlete with a championship attitude; baseball and basketball were his passions. He didn't know the meaning of the word *quit*. With painstaking commitment, he reached deep down with the unalterable belief and faith that one day he would walk again. Would he be able to come to our wedding?

August 8, 1987, arrived. For as long as I live I will never forget watching Jeff at 5:00 P.M. that sunny day as he clutched his cane and slowly but confidently walked the thirty to forty yards to the outdoor gazebo where Sheryl and I were to be married. Tears streamed down my face as inch by inch, foot by foot, Jeff steadied himself, looking down and then up, trying to determine where he was and where his next step would take him, until he finally reached the front of the gazebo.

Later I asked him how he had done it, and he said, "Well, I had faith that I could, and I never stopped believing that I would." As his strong voice uttered those words of confidence, my eyes again welled up with tears. I asked myself then, even as I ask you now: What would your world look like if you had Jeff's attitude? Could you accomplish more? Would you give up a negative outlook as a bad deal? Jeff made it because he was living with purpose. Purpose will cut through the most awful adversity any day of the week because, in the end, it's never a matter of *if* but *when* and *how* we will get through the storm.

The Personal Influence Model

To see how all the elements of this chapter work together, review the diagram on the next page. Everything begins with your faith and your belief. Nothing of value will ever be accomplished without these twin forces working together for your success. Henry Ford once said, "Whether you think you can or think you can't, you're right."

When our beliefs are high, we gain confidence. That confidence leads to the security of taking action, which, when properly directed, will create your desired outcome. Each of the following four quadrants is synergistically related. If one area suffers, so will the other three. If one becomes strong, the others will share in that strength.

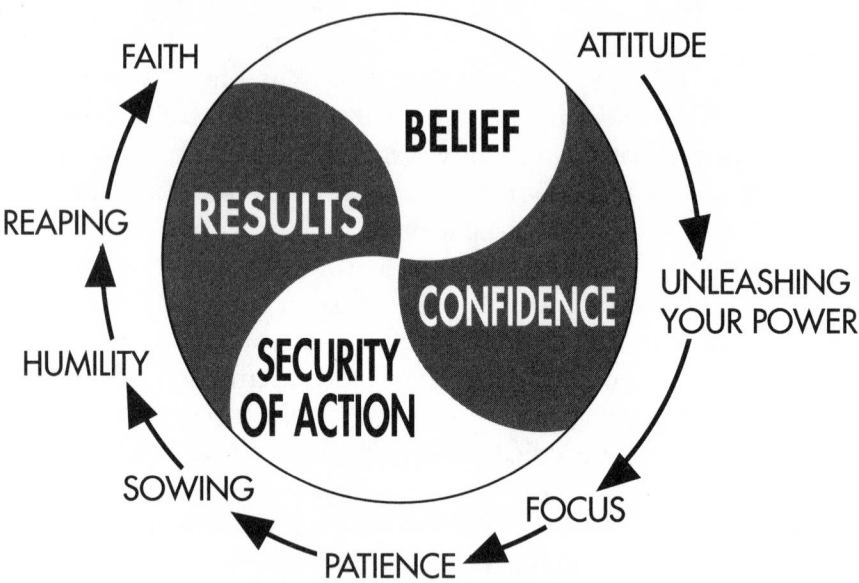

With these seven behaviors now in tow, you have a foundation that will make it easier for you to accomplish everything you laid out in your action plans in chapters 1 and 2. Let's now integrate the first three chapters with the following plan of action.

THE *POWER!* TO BE YOUR BEST!

Plan of Action for More Productive, Effective Living

1. List below three to five positive new choices that you will initiate immediately. Develop a short affirmation statement for each to help keep you on track.

   - _____

   - _____

   - _____

   - _____

   - _____

2. How would you improve your life by providing a concentrated focus to those areas important to you? How will this sustained focus give you a greater edge? How will it get you closer to the results you want? What are those areas? Match them against the clarifying vision statements you created in chapter 2.

   _____

   _____

   _____

3. How are you doing in the area of personal faith? What changes do you feel you should make in this part of your life?

   _____

   _____

   _____

When you have completed these three assignments, go to my website at www.toddduncan.com and register to win a free thirty-minute consultation to discuss any issue of your life in which you would like my assistance. *See you on-line. —TD*

www.toddduncan.com

Action Planner Notes

_____

_____

_____

_____

_____

_____

_____

_____

_____

_____

_____

_____

_____

_____

_____

_____

_____

_____

_____

_____

_____

_____

_____

_____

Part II

Purpose, Passion, Productivity, and Power!

CHAPTER

FOUR

Destination Success: Why Are You Here?

We are here to be excited from youth to old age, to have an insatiable curiosity about the world. . . . We are also here to help others by practicing a friendly attitude. And, every person is born for a purpose. Everyone has a God-given potential, in essence, built into them. And if we are to live life to the fullest, we must realize that potential. ***Norman Vincent Peale***

What is success? I think it is a mixture of having a flair for the thing that you are doing; knowing that it is not enough, that you have got to have hard work and a certain sense of purpose.
Margaret Thatcher

ome 350 years ago, a shipload of travelers landed on the northeast coast of North America. The first year they established a town site. The next year they elected a town government. The third year the town government made the decision to build a small road five miles westward into the wilderness. In the fourth year the people tried to impeach the leaders of the town government because they thought it was a waste of public funds to build a five-mile stretch of road into the western wilderness. Who needed to go there?

What's wrong with this picture? Here was a group of battered and bruised pioneers who had a compelling vision that drove them three thousand miles across an ocean, overcoming great hardships to get there. In five years' time, however, they could not see the need to venture five miles out of town. They had lost their pioneering vision. They had lost their purpose.

I've discovered that it's not just the pioneers in this story who have lost their vision. Millions of people across this land once had goals, hopes, and dreams for a better future for themselves and their families. Eventually they chose to settle for less. Compromise took its toll. That's why in this chapter, I want to help you move beyond where you are and to see you recapture your vision and your compelling purpose for living.

What Is Your Compelling Purpose?

Let's look at the derivations of some of these words. *Compelling* is the adjective form of the verb *compel*, which comes from the Latin words *com* (meaning "together") and *pellere* (meaning "to get or bring about by force—power"). *Purpose* is when you make an uncompromising commitment to get or do something. When you put these two Latin words together, you outfit yourself with the energy that can give you what you want in your life. But you need more than two words from a "dead" language to propel you in your new direction. You need a proven, effective plan that you can make work for you. That's what I am going to give you in the next few pages.

The Art of Virtue

Benjamin Franklin was born in Boston on January 17, 1706, and died in Philadelphia on April 17, 1790. During his eighty-four years, he created one of the most effective plans for living most of us will ever see. At the heart of his many literary works was *The Art of Virtue.* In 1760, referring to this manuscript, Franklin wrote to his close friend, Lord Kames:

> *I propose...a little work for the benefit of youth, to be called the Art of Virtue...Many people lead bad lives that would gladly live good ones but do not know how to make the change. They have frequently resolved and endeavored it; but in vain, because their endeavors have not been properly conducted. To expect people to be good, to be just, to be temperate, etc., without showing them how they should become so, seems like the ineffectual charity mentioned by the Apostle, which consists in saying to the hungry, the cold, and the naked, "Be ye fed, be ye warmed, be ye clothed," without showing them how they should get food, fire, and clothing.*
>
> *Most people have naturally some virtues, but none have naturally, all the virtues...If a man would become a painter, navigator, or architect it is not enough that he is advised to be one, that he is convinced by the arguments of his adviser that it would be for his advantage to be one, and that he resolves to be one, but he must also be taught the principles of the art, be shown all the methods of working, and how to acquire the habits of using properly all the instruments; and thus regularly and gradually, he arrives, by practice, at some perfection of the art...*

95

My Art of Virtue has also its instruments and teaches the manner of using them...Such as are naturally well disposed, and have been so carefully educated as that good habits have been early established and bad ones prevented, have less need for this art; but all may be more or less benefited by it. It is in short, to be adapted for universal use.[1]

Aren't you glad some principles are so powerful that they stand the test of time? Let's look particularly at Franklin's concern that "Many people lead bad lives that would gladly live good ones but do not know how to make the change." It was a concern for him in the eighteenth century, and it should be a concern for you and me today. Perhaps he was talking about you. You may be dissatisfied with the results you are seeing in your life. You want to get out of your rut, but feel you don't have the tools to do so—until now.

Franklin's approach to teaching others how to change led him to create what he called his Ladder of Success. This twelve-runged ladder can still lead those who desire it toward a purposeful and fulfilling life. Even with his enormous scientific, social, and political accomplishments, Franklin admitted he had not finished all he had set out to do. By living his life according to almost sacred principles, however, he noted, "On the whole, though I never arrived at the perfection I had been so ambitious of obtaining, but fell far short of it, yet I was, by the endeavor, a better and happier man than I otherwise should have been if I had not attempted it."[2] Franklin recognized that life, if anything, is a journey.

"On the whole, though I never arrived at the perfection I had been so ambitious of obtaining, but fell far short of it, yet I was, by the endeavor, a better and happier man than I otherwise should have been if I had not attempted it."
—Ben Franklin

Life's Both a Journey and a Ladder

When we prepare for a road trip, one of the first things we do is get out a map. We study it intensely to learn the best routes, determine the number of miles we'll have to travel, pick out interesting places to visit, decide how far we can get in a day, and estimate expenses. On the journey, the map is our constant companion, and we consult it frequently throughout each day. We couldn't get along without it. And, without consulting it regularly, making sure we are on course, we're likely to end up off course or lost.

It's the same with life, the greatest journey of all. Without a map, you will never arrive at being all you are designed to be. You'll never have it all wired or completely figured out. If your goal is perfection, you're doomed to fail. The journey, however, that's something else! On your journey you can always correct your course, choose another road, stop and ask for directions, read books, listen to tapes. The journey is where the dynamic of life happens, not at some imagined destination. With this premise in mind—that the greatest joy of life is in the journey and not the end result—let's change our metaphor to that of a ladder and the vital steps we must take to grasp the power to be our best.

Look at Ben Franklin's Ladder of Success. Read the words on the twelve rungs quickly, starting at the bottom, and then read them again. As you read them a second time, think seriously about your own life as you ask yourself two questions: Do you believe what Ben Franklin says is true? If what he proposes is true, are you making these principles work for you in your life? Write notes to yourself in the margin.

Ben Franklin's Ladder of Success

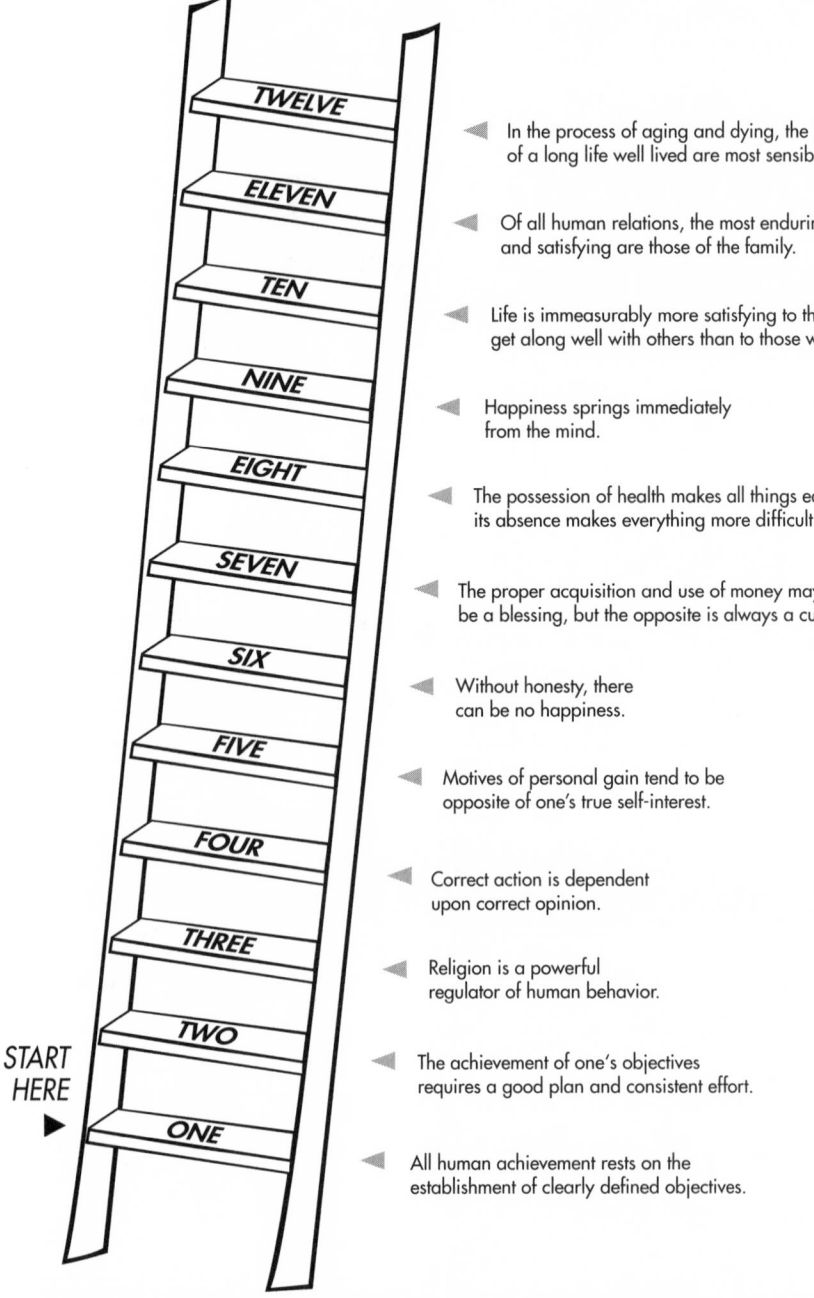

TWELVE — In the process of aging and dying, the fruits of a long life well lived are most sensibly felt.

ELEVEN — Of all human relations, the most enduring and satisfying are those of the family.

TEN — Life is immeasurably more satisfying to those who get along well with others than to those who do not.

NINE — Happiness springs immediately from the mind.

EIGHT — The possession of health makes all things easier, its absence makes everything more difficult.

SEVEN — The proper acquisition and use of money may be a blessing, but the opposite is always a curse.

SIX — Without honesty, there can be no happiness.

FIVE — Motives of personal gain tend to be opposite of one's true self-interest.

FOUR — Correct action is dependent upon correct opinion.

THREE — Religion is a powerful regulator of human behavior.

TWO — The achievement of one's objectives requires a good plan and consistent effort.

START HERE ▶ **ONE** — All human achievement rests on the establishment of clearly defined objectives.

From Benjamin Franklin, *Benjamin Franklin's The Art of Virtue: His Formula for Successful Living,* ed. George L. Rogers (Eden Prairie, Minn.: Acorn, 1990), 12–13.

What thoughts went through your mind as you moved from the first rung to the last? Do you agree with Franklin's premises? What would your life be like if you worked harder at implementing these principles in your daily living?

Getting Off Autopilot

One of the goals of this book is to cause a transformation within you—to help you tap the power (already at your disposal) and move the tectonic plates of your mind so dramatically that you'll never be the same person again. For that to happen, you must read each page of this book with an active mind. As you do this, you will begin to see changes. Some of these transformations will be subtle, almost imperceptible. Others may border on the miraculous. You may even ask, How did I make that happen? It won't be just you either. As others see changes occurring in you, you may hear the "miracle" word coming from their lips as well: It's a miracle that he lost all that weight...It's a miracle how much she has accomplished...It's a miracle that's he's become such an outstanding public speaker.

When you begin to see change in yourself—and when others volunteer that they see it too—you are, by definition, in the midst of a major transformation. How does it happen? It happens when you get off autopilot and consciously decide to live intentionally. It happens when you no longer simply careen from wall to wall praying for good luck or hoping against hope that things will somehow work out. You change because you have the determination, discipline, and drive to unleash the power to be your best. You change because you now live with a compelling purpose.

Expand Your Power Reservoir. Your purpose, something you determined for yourself in chapter 2, has now become the focus of everything you do. Your purpose governs your plans, establishes your goals, directs your activities, and pushes you toward positive, corresponding actions and results. It is the trigger that prompts you to act.

> *As others see changes happening in you, you may hear the "miracle" word coming from their lips as well: It's a miracle that he lost all that weight. . . . It's a miracle how much she has accomplished...*

When your purpose is linked to your values, you begin to live your life on purpose. The longer you live your life on purpose, the more you will accomplish, because you create a power reservoir that keeps expanding. The larger your capacity for this power, the more power becomes available to you. Conversely, if your reservoir is half-full or going on empty, you will not even come close to becoming the person God designed you to be.

Renew Your Mind. In an interview with my colleague and friend, Glenna Salsbury, I was reminded that "a transformed mind is the source of wise decisions." When Glenna made that statement, my mind began to whirl. Where had I just read about the transformed mind... the newly shaped mind...the renewed mind? I then recalled I'd been studying the Book of Romans in the Bible where the apostle Paul wrote, "And do not be conformed to this world, but be transformed by the renewing of your mind" (12:2). Paul knew that change is always an inside job.

Change starts with a housecleaning, a cobweb removal of our minds. Change happens when we make decisions based on what matters most to us. When we do this, we begin the critical turnaround from wrong to right behavior and move from autopilot living to living our lives on-purpose.

New Thinking, New Choices. Glenna gave me another gift. She introduced me to *The Fifth Discipline,* written by Peter Senge. In this amazing book, Senge demonstrates how a typical organization can become a learning organization: "Great organizations are never built by trying to emulate another, any more than individual greatness is achieved by trying to copy another great person. Individual greatness only comes through being

THE *POWER!* TO BE YOUR BEST!

transformed by the reinventing of how you think, and how you associate with the physicalities of choice. New thinking creates new choices. New choices create new outcomes. New outcomes raise your level of thinking."[3]

The general theme of Senge's work asserts that people need to take a critical look at old ways of thinking, attempt to be more open with others, come to grips with how their company functions, and develop a plan of action on which all can agree. Simply stated: New thinking creates new choices that create new outcomes that leads to transformation.

Let's Hear It from a Dolphin

There's a Sea World entertainment park about ten minutes from my home in La Jolla. Often, I'll take my two-year-old son, Jonathan, to this lively place because he loves the nonstop excitement and action. When I pull into the parking lot, he can hardly wait to get out of his car seat so he can run over to the kids' play area. So we always hang out there first. Here's what I've observed. Each time he plays on the swings, goes down the slide, or builds his castles in the warm noonday sand, Jonathan seems to develop a higher level of thinking. Yes, parents, it is possible for a "terrible two" to develop a higher level of thinking. What was difficult the last time for Jonathan is always easier the next time. What was easy during our last outing is a snap this time around.

The Greeks, as we might expect, have a word for this phenomenon. It's called *metanoia*, which means a shift of mind. The word has a rich history. For the Greeks, *metanoia* meant fundamental change, or more literally, transcendence (*meta* meaning "above or beyond," as in metaphysics) of mind (*noia* from the root *nous*, meaning "of the mind"). To grasp the meaning of *metanoia* is to understand the deeper significance of "learning," for true learning demands a fundamental shift in thinking.

Metanoia is alive and well in young Jonathan's heart, but it also thrives in the huge dolphin and whale tanks at Sea World. If you've been to one of these attractions, you've seen some amazing things as trainers and dolphins and whales work together. In the early stages of their interaction with dolphins, the trainers do nothing. They simply wait for the dolphin to jump on its own and then reward the desired behavior by giving the dolphin a nice fat fish. So far, so good. Each time a dolphin jumps of its own accord, the trainer is patterning behavior, something that's further reinforced through the growing emotional connection with the trainer, the dolphin's positive anchor. The two now start working together as a team. They begin to trust each other. The dolphin thinks, *When I do, apparently, what you want me to do, I get a fish. Thank you.*

Once this pattern is stabilized, the dolphin continues to do the trick. Then suddenly there's a change in the pattern. The trainer withholds the reward, and this causes immediate discomfort for the dolphin. *Hey, what's going on. Where's the fish?* So what does the dolphin do? It gets out a Greek dictionary and fins the pages until it comes to the "m's," where it quickly locates the word *metanoia*. Being highly intelligent (but mostly wanting another fish), the dolphin dives to the bottom of the pool and thinks of a way to outdo his previous performance so it can avoid the pain of "no fish" and attain the usual reward. It is certain that the dolphin will now execute the old trick in a new way. It may jump higher, swim faster, engage in more theatrics, or do whatever its new thinking may create, but it will do something different just to get the reward.

> *Hey, what's going on. Where's the fish? So what does the dolphin do? It gets out a Greek dictionary and fins the pages until it comes to the "m's" where it quickly locates the word metanoia.*

> *The greatest rewards in life are always in direct proportion to our capacity to think beyond what we once believed were our limits.*

Now two things happen: The dolphin never knows which trick will be rewarded, and the trainers know they cannot continue to reward the dolphin 100 percent of the time for fear it will become too comfortable and stop thinking of ways to achieve new goals and meet the increasingly higher demands. The message: The greatest rewards in life are always in direct proportion to our capacity to think beyond what we once believed were our limits.

Becoming an On-Purpose Person

During my interview with Glenna, she told me she had met Kevin McCarthy, a wonderful person and creative thinker and author of the book *The On-Purpose Person*. Shortly after that, he and I got together in Orlando, Florida. Here are some notes I took during that interview:

- People are happiest and most productive when what they do is purposeful.
- When we live on-purpose, our lives will be filled with meaning and significance.
- There is no such thing as a dimmer switch in life; we are either on-purpose or we are off-purpose.
- The more on-purpose we are, the more frequently we will enjoy peak experiences.
- If our purpose is clear, we can affect tremendous change in those areas important to us: spiritual, family, financial, physical, professional, intellectual, and social.
- Purpose is the why behind your existence. Kevin made this point: "One's world-view affects one's self-perspective. Here's how: If you believe the world is here by accident, a quirk of fate emanating from some primordial slime, then the natural extension of my perspective is that I'm here by accident with no design, no plan, no designer, and no purpose. On the other hand, if my perspective allows for the world being created by design, then there's a design, a plan, a designer (call the designer God), and a reason why it all exists. It follows, therefore, that I am part of the design, there

is a plan for my life, and I have a purpose. So the key to a life of hope begins with seeing the design and our fit within it. From there, we articulate our fit in the world by way of our purpose statement. When we align our lives to our purpose, then we're being on-purpose!"

I was thinking of Kevin in chapter 2 when I walked you through how to determine purpose for your life. I taught you how to drive that purpose through each of your value areas so it would propel you toward your vision, mission, and daily objectives. Now I want to show you in more detail how living on-purpose can empower you to move even more quickly toward the life you desire.

Green Grass Requires Water

Bob Gundaker was one of my best clients. He was head of sales production for Meridian Mortgage Corporation in Trevos, Pennsylvania. Every year he would invite me to teach his people how to be more productive. It was fascinating. Each year we saw how new thinking and new behaviors always led to powerful new results.

One afternoon I was with Bob and ten people from his sales team when Joe, a team member said, "But Citibank doesn't do it that way."

I loved Bob's response. "Then why don't you go to work for Citibank?" he asked.

The salesperson was stunned. Then Bob said, "Look, Joe, the grass is only greener where you water it."

There is always creative tension between relying for your success on yourself or someone else or on some other company's special way of doing things. In the end, though, you must make the decision to water your own. That's where *metanoia* comes in again, that internal shift that alerts you to do something to change. Until this "inside" job is accomplished, all external appearances of finding "something better" elsewhere will be a mirage. To make your own way in life is a process. There are no shortcuts to success. You can't make it to the land of your dreams in one great leap forward. Your success in life simply demands that you make measurable progress in reasonable time.

What's John Doing Anyway?

John is my good friend. He and I grew up in the business world together when we were in our twenties. After a time, we even worked for the same company. When I decided to start our seminar business, John continued to work in the industry we grew up in, real-estate finance.

He and I have stayed in touch throughout the years. In fact, every fourteen to eighteen months or so, I still get a call from John. "Hey, Todd, I'm with a new company now, and it's going great. Fantastic opportunities here. Just wanted you to know." Then, sure as clockwork, I'll hear from him again about a year and half later. "Hey, Todd, I'm with a new company now, and it's going great. Fantastic opportunities here. Just wanted you to know." Same John. Same message. Always a new company.

During the past decade, John has probably been employed by six different sales organizations. By now I'm wondering if my friend will ever make the time to check inside for the seeds of his success, or will he forever search out greener pastures on the other side of the fence. Lush green grass elsewhere can be seductive for us all. It's our job to water the grass under our own feet.

Acres of Diamonds

There is no better tale to illustrate this point than the story of Russell Conwell. In my career I have heard this story told by Earl Nightingale, Robert Schuller, W. Clement Stone, and most recently, Denis Waitley. If you have heard it before, please hear it again. If it's new to you, read it, believe its message, and pass it on to others.

After years of sacrifice and effort, Russell Conwell turned a night school in his church basement into Temple University.

There are no shortcuts to success. You can't make it to the land of your dreams in one great leap forward. Your success in life simply demands that you make measurable progress in reasonable time.

To raise money for books, facilities, and faculty, Conwell became a prominent lecturer and wrote sixteen books. He gave his most famous lecture some six thousand times over two decades. It was entitled "Acres of Diamonds," and it was spellbinding. Its message is as relevant today as it was when Conwell traveled the nation sharing it with students, business leaders, politicians, and anyone else who would listen.

The story begins with Conwell's finding himself on the Tigris River with a party of English travelers. The year was 1870. Their guide was an elderly Arab who had been hired to show the visiting group the ancient cities of Assyria. Much more than a guide, however, the old Arab was a consummate storyteller who felt compelled to weave a tale of intrigue and romance at each bend of the trail.

"And now I will tell you a story I reserve for my particular friends," he said one evening, as he introduced the acres of diamonds story that Conwell later shared with hundreds of thousands of listeners.

"Not far from the River Indus, there once lived a Persian farmer by the name of Ali Hafed, who owned a large farm with orchards, grain fields, and gardens. He was a wealthy and contented man—contented because he was wealthy and wealthy because he was contented. One day he was visited by an ancient priest, a wise man from the east. The priest sat by the fire and told Ali Hafed how the world was made.

"He said the Almighty thrust a finger into the fog and slowly tuned it round and round, increasing the speed until it gradually became a ball of fire. Then he said the ball of fire rolled throughout the universe, burning its way through other cosmic fogbanks and condensing the moisture until it fell in floods of rain upon its surface, which cooled the outer crust.

"When the melted mass burst out and very quickly cooled, it became granite. That which cooled less quickly became silver, and even less quickly, gold.

"'And diamonds,' said the ancient priest, 'diamonds are congealed drops of sunlight.' Declaring diamonds the highest of God's mineral creations; the priest said that one stone the size of Ali Hafed's thumb could purchase the whole country. If Ali Hafed had a mine of diamonds, he could place his children on

THE *POWER!* TO BE YOUR BEST!

the thrones of the countries throughout the world.

"Ali Hafed went to bed that night a poor man—poor because he was discontented and discontented because he thought he was poor. 'I want a diamond mine,' he repeated to himself throughout his sleepless night.

"He woke the priest early the next morning. 'Will you tell me where I can find diamonds?' he asked.

"'Diamonds,' said the priest. 'What do you want with diamonds?'

"'I want to be immensely rich,' replied Ali Hafed candidly.

"'Then go along and find them, that's all you must do,' advised the priest.

"'But I don't know where to go,' Ali Hafed pleaded.

"'Well,' said the priest, 'if you look for a river that runs over white sands between high mountains, you will always find diamonds in those sands.'

"'I don't believe any such river exists,' Ali Hafed challenged.

"'Of course it does, there are many of them,' said the priest. 'All you have to do is find them.'

"Ali Hafed went to the window and looked out; his gaze fixed on the mountains that bordered his farm. 'I believe you. I will go!' he resolved.

"He sold his farm and collected his money. Leaving his family in a neighbor's care, he went off in search of diamonds, starting with the nearest mountains. Next, he searched in Palestine. Finally, he wandered Europe. When the last of his money had been spent, he stood in rags at Spain's Bay of Barcelona, watching the waves roll in. Soon the penniless, hopelessly wretched man cast himself into the oncoming tide and sank beneath the water, never to rise again.

"Declaring diamonds the highest of God's mineral creations; the priest said that one stone the size of Ali Hafed's thumb could purchase the whole country."

"One day the man who had purchased Ali Hafed's farm led his camel into the garden to drink. As the beast lapped the brook's clear water, Ali Hafed's successor noticed a curious flash in the shallow stream's white sands. Reaching into the water, he withdrew a black pebble with an eye of light that reflected all the colors of the rainbow. He took the curious stone into the house, put it on the mantel, and returned to his chores.

"Some days later, the ancient priest visited him. The moment the priest saw the gleam from the mantel, he rushed to it. 'There's a diamond here!' he shouted. 'A diamond! Has Ali Hafed returned?'

"'No, he hasn't returned and that's no diamond,' the new owner answered. 'It's nothing but a stone from out there in the garden.'

"'But I know a diamond when I see one,' the priest insisted, 'and I tell you that's what this is, a beautiful diamond.'

"Together they rushed to the garden stream. They stirred the white sands with their fingers, and they discovered more stones, even more beautiful and valuable than the first. Thus was the diamond mine of Golcanda discovered—the most magnificent in history, exceeding even the Kimberly diamond mine. For decades, every shovel from near that stream revealed gems that would decorate the crowns of monarchs. Had Ali Hafed remained at home and dug in his own garden instead of wandering aimlessly into a life of frustration, poverty, and suicide in a strange land, he would have had acres of diamonds."

No story in the literature of mankind better illustrates that your greatest riches are within your own reach, in your own backyard. You can stop looking on the outside for wealth and happiness. Water yourself. Immerse yourself with the awareness that your acres of diamonds are within you. Mine them and you will be rich.

From a Life of Coal to a Life of Diamonds

Texas oil billionaire Bunker Hunt was once asked what it takes to be a success. He said, "First, you must decide what you want specifically; second, you must make the decision that you are willing to pay the price to make it happen and then pay the price."

> *What's happening in your life is not nearly as important as how you interpret what's happening.*

To get the life you want, you need to decide ahead of time what it will look like, determine how you'll need to think to get there, figure out how to manage the challenges that will creep in during the journey to discourage you, and never back away from the price you promised to pay for your success.

Power Problem-Solving

Problems are a matter of interpretation. Steady rain for a farmer may be a welcome sight, but it can make an evening at the ballpark miserable. The rain is not the problem. It's how the rain is interpreted. What's happening in your life is not nearly as important as how you interpret what's happening. Something is always happening. We can't go through a day without something happening. We have to learn, and it is a lifelong learning process, to use our x-ray vision to see through the challenges of our immediate experiences so we can discover the positive potential outcomes that ultimately will emerge. The faster we learn this drill, the sooner we will make our dreams come true.

The question then is not whether or not we will have problems, but rather how we choose to think about them. When we harness the power of our problems with an equally powerful strategy to deal with them, we will neutralize their effect and minimize the consequences they might have had in our lives.

Here are four questions I've asked myself over the years that have helped me manage my problems. They have empowered me to become my best in the midst of conflict, disappointment, and even despair:

1. If this is the first time I have encountered this problem, what can I do now so that I don't encounter it again? If I have faced this problem more than once, why does it continue, and what must happen now to avoid its recurrence?

2. What good is there in this problem that will create growth and advancement for me as I deal with it?

3. How can I build up my resistance during the time it takes to fix the problem?

4. How can I change my perspective so my problem impacts me more positively?

You'll recall how my company got into serious trouble several years ago. I had every right to see this impending financial collapse as a problem. That would have solved nothing, however, and I would have most certainly failed. Instead, I chose to engage in *metanoia* and made a major shift in my thinking. Here's what I wrote in my journal about that situation several years ago.

How can my purpose be manifested in or by this problem? In the midst of financial collapse, I am realizing that my purpose—making a difference—is not happening like it should because I am so caught up in the problem. I think the reason for this is that the company had grown too big and is not being managed correctly. So, if I am to use this problem to be able to live my purpose more intentionally, the company has to become more manageable more quickly.

THE *POWER!* TO BE YOUR BEST!

Every decision from that point forward was easy because my purpose was driving it. I could have done many things, but my diamonds were right there. I just had to find them.

1. **If this is the first time I have encountered this problem, what can I do now so that I don't encounter it again? If I have faced this problem more than once, why does it continue and what must happen now to avoid its recurrence?**

My business problem was a first-time experience. I had not yet repeated enough wrong behaviors for my problem to recur; however, I needed to do something immediately so this problem would not return to haunt me in the future. *Solution:* I did twenty-six things within four months to assure me that this problem would not return. After working through those decisions, I was finally able to say I was happy the problem had occurred in the first place.

2. **What good is there in this problem that will create growth and advancement for me as I deal with it?**

You'll recall how my company got into serious trouble several years ago. I had every right to see this impending financial collapse as a problem. That would have solved nothing, however.

My problem was the best thing that ever happened to me. At the time, my company owned a software system that we had created. We had two thousand users. When the independent contractor filed a copyright infringement suit against me for continuing to sell the product when we were behind in commissions to him, I became angry. Hey, it was my idea. I brought this guy on board. We had an agreement that I owned the "code" of the software and he had simply been hired to design it. My mistake? I continued to use him as an independent contractor rather than make him an employee, an error in judgment that landed us both in front of two lawyers.

Remember that I was trying to make sense of this mess, dig out the good in the midst of turmoil, and find it. With my shift in thinking, I did just that. Here's what *metanoia* thinking produced for me. Without the software division, I would have five fewer employees (all of whom could now work for the independent contractor), I would lower my overhead by as much as $30,000 per month, I would no longer need to keep upgrading the programs to feed the voracious appetites of a user group, and I would have no more customer complaints because I would no longer be involved with the product. My positive list of reasons grew so long that my attitude soon became *I can't wait to get rid of this part of my company.*

3. How can I build up my resistance during the time it takes to fix the problem?

This question drove me to reach out to two mentors who called me every week to support and coach me during the crisis. My friends were straight shooters. They would not let me sit on the pity pot. They loved me and helped me keep my focus. They also reminded me that the greatest resource in the world, prayer, was my vehicle for unlimited power and strength. That was something I was allowing to lie dormant. The light was there to provide illumination for my troubled path, but I was so worried about my problem that I didn't bother to throw the switch. My mentors reminded me that I did not have to stumble in the dark. I took their advice.

4. How can I change my perspective during the time it takes to fix the problem?

I engaged in end-result thinking. I kept my affirmations alive. I remained present-tense positive. I could see the end of the road, even though it often seemed like light-years ahead. I continued to think how my character would ultimately be molded for the better because of my problem. I learned that we all have a choice when it comes to how we "interpret" the stones that litter our path: We can either regard them as stumbling blocks that keep us off course, or as steppingstones that provide the footing to guide us to greater success.

How to Make Every Day Worth Living

Charles Garfield in his book *Peak Performance* says, "Alignment is when what you do fulfills your greater purpose and goals." He's right. Think for a moment how it would feel to know at the end of every day for the rest of your life that each day had been truly worth living. Wouldn't that be an incredible feeling? Every day would be better than the day before. How close are you to getting there? If you're even one step closer today than you were yesterday, then you're on your way, because success is simply the progressive realization of worthwhile goals. To live a guilt-free, anxiety-free life is to live your life on purpose. Problems? Yes, you'll have your share, perhaps more than your share at times, but you can now live with the confidence that everything you attempt, whether you get the immediate results you want or not, is part of your LifeQuest Pyramid in chapter 2. Wow! What a way to live. What power to be your best!

If you want new directions, you must make new decisions. When your decisions are purpose-based, you are more likely to see your destiny tomorrow reflect the plans you make today.

Everything you experience in life, the power you receive and the power you lose, is a result of the decisions you make. If you want new directions, you must make new decisions. When your decisions are purpose based, you are more likely to see your destiny tomorrow reflect the plans you make today. Here are five keys to help you maintain an on-purpose attitude:

Key Number 1: Let your purpose guide your every decision. As you do this, do you believe it will allow you to live a life of greater abundance (relationships, finances, business, etc.)? What is your answer?

Key Number 2: Make every decision subject to your most cherished values. Ask yourself: If I do this, will it help me make positive strides toward the things in which I believe most? (God, health, family, money, friends, etc.)

Key Number 3: Make every decision without wavering. Stay committed. Studies indicate that the most successful people are clear on their purpose and values. This is why they are able to make decisions quickly (#1 and #2 above) and change them slowly, if at all.

Key Number 4: Journal every poor decision. Insanity has been defined as doing the same thing over and over while expecting a different result. I have been keeping a journal for years where I note each decision I make that has produced an undesirable outcome. I review this journal whenever I have an important decision to make because I do not want to make the same wrong decision twice. I encourage you to create such a journal for your miscues as well.

Key Number 5: Pray before every decision. God is a good God. He wants the best for you. It is we who mess things up, not God. This is especially true in the area of decision making. Here is some clear biblical instruction on the importance of relying on the Almighty for strength and wisdom in making decisions:

Be anxious for nothing, but in everything by prayer and supplication, with thanksgiving, let your requests be made known to God; and the peace of God, which surpasses all understanding, will guard your hearts and minds through Christ Jesus.
Philippians 4:6–7

---

*But you shall receive power when the Holy
Spirit has come upon you.* **Acts 1:8**

*Your kingdom come. Your will be done...
Give us this day our daily bread.*
Matthew 6:10–11

God created you, and He created me. He created our
world and the vast multitude of known and unknown universes
that lie beyond. He wants to put a song in our heart and plant
words of joy on our lips. We need not pour our energies into
pain and suffering. Life is too good. Even better when lived on-
purpose. The good news for us who struggle to become our
best is that we do not need to struggle alone. Since we live
under God's sovereign law, we can ask Him to be our faithful
friend and guide. Through prayer and meditation, we can ask
Him to make clear our decisions before we dare make them
ourselves. He will keep us honest, and He will keep us pure.

This is what right living and living right are all about. As
I review Benjamin Franklin's commentary on virtue, these five
mandates on the purpose of living come to mind:

Thought Number 1: Work on the improvement of your
character. Of all the ambitions to which your heart must aspire,
none are nobler or will have greater permanent value than the
improvement of your character. The richness of your life will be
your reward for being a person of honor.

Thought Number 2: Pursue moral perfection. Only in
the pursuit of moral rectitude will you obtain a full measure of
happiness and achievement in your life.

Thought Number 3: Be on guard always. Weeds will
enter the garden of your mind uninvited and unnamed. You
must know what you want from your life, or someone will surely

sell you a bill of goods. Put down the forces that would destroy you by living your life on-purpose.

Thought Number 4: Replace bad habits with right habits. Bad habits must be eliminated and good ones acquired before you can expect to become the person you were created to be.

Thought Number 5: Your life is all about progress, not perfection. You'll never be perfect, but you can and will make progress. There are no shortcuts. To the end of our days, life will remain a lesson imperfectly learned. So what do you have to lose? Live your life on-purpose. Throw yourself over the bar and your heart will follow.

We began this chapter with a quote from Norman Vincent Peale who wrote "We are here to be excited from youth to old age, to have an insatiable curiosity about the world." We are also here to help others by practicing a friendly attitude. And, every person is born for a purpose. Everyone has a God-given potential, in essence, built into them. And if we are to live life to the fullest, we must realize that potential.

I hope you will use Dr. Peale's words of inspiration and the message of this chapter to help you throw yourself over that bar of on-purpose living, and push you even closer to becoming an on-purpose person as you take further action to become the individual you were designed to be.

Plan of Action for Becoming an On-Purpose Person

1. On a scale of 1 to 10, 10 being the best, rate how you are doing for each of the rungs on Benjamin Franklin's Ladder of Success. Go back to the ladder on page 98 and enter your score beside each rung.

2. List three things you need to be doing immediately to help you to live a more on-purpose life.

    * _____

    _____

    * _____

    _____

    * _____

    _____

3. Are you looking for "acres of diamonds" in your own backyard? If not, what actions are you prepared to take to become more of an "internal" person rather than one who keeps looking for success "where the grass is greener?"

    * _____

    * _____

    * _____

4. To help you start winning more, what areas of your life could use some new decisions? Be specific.

    * _____

    * _____

    * _____

When you've completed
these four assignments,
go to my website at
www.toddduncan.com
and listen to my Audio Success
Snapshot: The Winner Within.
See you on-line. —*TD*

www.toddduncan.com

Action Planner Notes

_____

_____

_____

_____

_____

_____

_____

_____

_____

_____

_____

_____

_____

_____

_____

_____

_____

_____

_____

_____

_____

_____

_____

Visions, Values, and the Art of Flying

Courage is the price that life exacts for granting peace. The soul that knows it not, knows no release from little things.
Amelia Earhart

We [my plane and I] took off rather suddenly. We had a report somewhere around 4 o'clock in the afternoon before that the weather would be fine, so we thought we would try it.
Charles A. Lindbergh

I had been seated for less than half an hour when the plane's captain came on the intercom and announced that we would be departing Sydney for Brisbane in about ten minutes. After two weeks of enjoying nothing but Aussie accents, the captain's American voice came first as a surprise, then as a pleasant reminder that before long I would be back in the States with my family and friends.

I asked the purser, "Would you mind telling the captain that there's an American on board who'd like to say hello?" She nodded, walked to the cockpit, and returned within minutes. "Captain McDonald has invited you to visit him in the cockpit," she said. "Would you like to follow me?"

Trying to hide my boyish delight at receiving this gracious invitation, I quickly got up and began moving from my seat to the aisle when she stopped me and said, "Bring your bags. I think you're in for a treat."

A treat! Now I was really getting excited, not letting anyone know, of course. Without questioning the purser, I grabbed my computer bag and walked with her to the nerve center of our Boeing 767 jetliner. She introduced me to Captain McDonald, and he introduced me to the first officer and flight engineer. I was like a kid in a candy store. The captain then said something that any passenger ready to speed along in a giant tube at thirty thousand feet loves to hear. They are also the words that, when implemented, promised to offer you and me one of our best options to enjoy the ride of our life here on the ground.

Captain McDonald said, "Todd, why don't you have a seat behind me, get buckled in, and put the headset on. We are just now going through our preflight checklist, and we will be on our way to Brisbane as soon as everything checks out."

A preflight checklist. What a concept. What a clever way to travel in safety from here to there. What a marvelous tool for maneuvering several tons of expensive airplane and precious human cargo effectively . . . and what a wise means to ensure the safest journey possible through something as challenging and complicated called life.

As I listened to the three pilots talk back and forth on my headset, I was overwhelmed as they engaged in what seemed like an effortless, thorough checklist of more than forty-five different items to ensure our plane not only took off properly, but that it would reach its destination safely. After they had finished their routine checks, the tower gave us clearance; we taxied down the runway and took off for Brisbane.

Once in the air, I enjoyed a stimulating conversation with Captain McDonald about flying, Australia, America, and mortgages, probably in that order. I had traveled to Australia to work with Aussie Home Loans, the biggest nonbank lender in the country. Every few minutes, the captain would interrupt our conversation while he and the other pilots changed settings and corrected headings so we would remain on course. As soon as they made their adjustments, the captain and I would drift back into conversation.

As we approached Brisbane, we stopped talking as the three pilots made their preparations for landing. Now here's the truly amazing part of this scenario. In the last thirty minutes of flight, I witnessed more than two hundred separate commands, computer adjustments, conversations with the tower, and instrument evaluations by three pilots who brought our 767 in for one of the smoothest landings I have ever felt in or outside the cockpit.

What a thrilling experience. As I sat there in the cockpit, I was impressed with the idea that the key to our safe, noneventful, smooth flight had happened on the ground in Sydney before we took off and then in the short time prior to our landing in Brisbane. The preflight check made all the difference, and unless some of the passengers were pilots themselves, it's likely that few had ever given it a moment's thought. If I had not been in the cockpit with the captain and his crew, I'm sure I would not have given a preflight checklist a minute's thought.

You see where I'm heading, don't you? What if you and I worked through a daily preflight checklist? I doubt if we would have to go through two hundred items to give ourselves a leg up on the day, but what if we even checked ourselves out on ten things, even five? Do you think that would make a difference in how effectively we lived our day? I think it would.

Without a preflight checklist, we are admitting we do not know where we are going. If we don't know where we are going, how do we dare assume we will not crash en route to our destination? Perhaps you are not yet even at the checklist stage. You may still be wondering if it's really *possible* to fly. If that's where you are in your journey, fine; however, to help push your thinking to greater heights, I want to tell you a story.

While a local bishop was visiting the president of a small denominational college in 1870, he expressed his firm biblical conviction that nothing new could be invented. Everything that was worth anything had already arrived on the scene, he insisted. The bishop could not be persuaded otherwise.

The educator, of course, disagreed. "Why, in fifty years I believe it may be possible for men to soar through the air like birds!" said the college president.

The bishop was shocked at this reckless talk that bordered on sacrilege. "Flight is strictly reserved for the angels," he insisted, "and I beg you not to repeat your suggestion lest you be guilty of blasphemy!"

Ironically, that mistaken bishop was Milton Wright, father of Orville and Wilbur, two young men who thirty-three years later would make their first flight in a heavier-than-air machine—the forerunner of the legions of planes that now dot our skies and the craft that had carried me from Sydney to Brisbane. Yes, it is possible to fly, but you must make the decision to get aboard, engage your preflight check, and take off.

> *"Flight is strictly reserved for the angels," he insisted, "and I beg you not to repeat your suggestion lest you be guilty of blasphemy!"*

Here's another observation I made on that flight. Captain McDonald did not engage the autopilot on our 767 until he was confident that all systems were functioning. He was patient. He was in no hurry to sit back, relax, and leave the driving to advanced technology. He made sure everything was working before he relinquished control, and even then he did not remain on autopilot throughout the flight.

Another lesson: You and I will make greater progress in reasonable time when our lives are in relative control before we engage our autopilot, which too often is little more than mindless thinking, an assumption that life never changes and that all we need to do is hang on to past behaviors as we float in comfort to a life of success. That is not the recipe for becoming our best. We must monitor our instruments constantly, "talk to the tower" always, and continually seek the counsel of others in our "cockpit" if we are to stay on course and make a favorable landing in this business called life.

Takeoff and Landing: Your Keys to a Smooth Flight

Your model for getting the life you desire is now in place if you have completed the assignments in chapter 2. You have begun to modify certain significant behaviors if you have implemented the information in chapter 3. Your purpose is now clearer, and you are thinking at a higher level because of what you learned in chapter 4. Now, it is time to fly! How high do you want to go? As your value areas drive your purpose, your life will assume greater significance, but you still must know where you want to go.

Too many people I know are like the cowboy who jumped on his horse and rode off in all directions. Perhaps it was his brother who ran to the counter at the airport and demanded a ticket. "To where?" asked the agent. "I don't know, and I don't care. I've got business everywhere." I guess that's possible. Any of us can jump in a car, hop a plane, or board a train and go *somewhere*. That's the easy part. The challenge is to be sure you are in the right car, on the right plane, or on the right track. Perhaps you remember the beloved conversation between Alice and the Cheshire cat on this subject.

> *The Cat only grinned when it saw Alice. It looked good-natured, she thought: still it had very long claws and a great many teeth, so she felt that it ought to be treated with respect.*
>
> *"Cheshire Puss," she began, rather timidly, as she did not at all know whether it would like the name: however, it only grinned a little wider. "Come, it's pleased so far," thought Alice, and she went on.*
>
> *"Would you tell me, please, which way I ought to go from here?"*

"That depends a good deal on where you want to get to," said the Cat.

"I don't much care where," said Alice.

"Then it doesn't matter which way you go," said the Cat.

"—so long as I get somewhere," Alice added as an explanation.

"Oh, you're sure to do that," said the Cat, "if you only walk long enough."[1]

The crew had done this hundreds of times before, but with all their experience, they did not take their history of error-free flying for granted. They, thank goodness, regarded this journey from Sydney to Brisbane as the most important flight of their lives. Because it was!

The issue, however, is not "walking long enough." Just about anyone can do that. The key is to know where you are going and how long is a "reasonable time" to get there.

I made another observation while watching the three pilots in action from my front-row seat. They were supremely confident in their work. They made decisions quickly, knowing in advance that their decisions were correct. The crew had done this hundreds of times before, but with all their experience, they did not take their history of error-free flying for granted. They, thank goodness, regarded this journey from Sydney to Brisbane as the most important flight of their lives. Because it was!

To get where you want to go in life, you simply cannot afford to slide along, go with the flow, or hope that "things will somehow turn out." Of course there's room for fun (in fact, a loose muscle will always respond more quickly and effectively than a tense one), but to get to where you want to go, you must be focused and stay focused on the same purpose, all the time maintaining the same intensity and certainty of those pilots who were responsible for a few tons of airplane over eastern Australia. It's all about the *art of flying,* whether flying a high-performance airplane or living a high-performance life. Now if you suspect that I spend a lot of time in airplanes, you are right . . . hence, another story.

I had just completed a talk in Owensboro, Kentucky, and was on a commuter flight to Alabama. As he approached the beginning of the runway, the pilot revved the engines of our twin turboprop and we were on our way. A few seconds later, the right engine sputtered, then white smoke poured out of it. We were thrust forward as the pilot reversed the props to slow us down to avoid what would have been a disastrous takeoff.

As we pulled from the active taxiway, the pilot came on the intercom and said, "Folks, we seem to have a little problem with the right engine. We are going to go back to the gate area and check it out."

You can imagine the thoughts going through our minds. *Check it out? What are you, crazy or something? Let me off this death trap!*

> It's all about the art of flying, whether flying a high-performance airplane or living a high-performance life.

The pilot then asked everyone to stay on board for a few minutes while they determined what the problem was. That was *real* reassuring. Ten minutes later he returned to the plane, entered the cockpit, revved the engines four or five times and let them run for several minutes. I can assure you that even all this activity was less than reassuring.

What about all that white smoke and sputtering earlier. What if it happens again when we're airborne? Then what do we do?

As he let up on the throttle, the engine slowed to an idle. With serenity in his southern-accented voice, he said, "Well, folks, everything seems to check out. We're going to give it one more try."

What? You can't be serious. Let me off this thing! Before we could mount a sizable protest, we were rolling once again. A confident pilot revved the engines, and we were off. As the plane ascended, you could cut the tension in the air of the cabin with a knife. As we climbed, holding our collective breath, we slowly fell in step with the confidence of the people in the cockpit, knowing that we were safely on our way.

There is not a pilot alive who would have done what our pilot did unless he or she was absolutely confident the plane would fly and arrive at its destination. How could our pilot be so confident? He reviewed his checklist, consulted with people on the ground, checked and rechecked their gauges (remember this from chapter 1?), and when finally confirming everything was okay, he took action.

There was something else, though, while the pilot went through all this checking and rechecking—he never stopped thinking of his destination. He knew where he was going; he had filed a detailed flight plan (course of action), and once we were in the air, he and his crew made hundreds of in-flight corrections en route. The lesson: You and I must attend to our lives as conscientiously as a pilot of an airplane tends his craft if we are soar in the value areas of our lives.

Where Is Your Cadaver?

I was thirteen years old at the time. We had returned to my birthplace for a family vacation. My mom and dad had moved to Ohio in 1953 so my dad could attend medical school at the University of Cincinnati. It was great living in the shadow of a great university, because it allowed me to get a jump-start on some things I may not have learned until adulthood, if then, like the day my dad took me to a room near his lab I'd never seen before.

The corridors were sterile. It was quiet. Suddenly, we turned a corner that led us to the physiology and anatomy lab. I thought this would be another room filled with test tubes, wires, lotions, and potions. Suddenly the most terrible smell assaulted my nose. *What in the world was that?* I asked myself, as Dad gently opened the door to the lab.

That's when I saw them for the first time in my life, lots of dead bodies, cadavers covered with white sheets, lying on tables throughout the lab. Now the smell was really getting to me. I asked Dad what it was.

"That's the formaldehyde we use to preserve the bodies," he said. "Would you like to see one?"

As he pulled back one of the sheets, exposing the face, Dad looked at me and said, "Todd, doctors work on these dead bodies in the lab so when they work on a live body, they will know what to do."

See one? You mean . . . really see . . . one? With my heart racing and my eyes big as saucers, I mumbled a reluctant yes. As he pulled back one of the sheets, exposing the face, Dad looked at me and said, "Todd, doctors work on these dead bodies in the lab so when they work on a live body, they will know what to do."

In situations like this, doctors and pilots are much the same. Both train themselves in "pretend" situations before the actual event: Pilots fly long hours in simulators and doctors work on cadavers. Pilots work through scores of items on their preflight checklists; doctors review data collected from the dead before they attempt to administer life and health to the living. Imagine having a doctor operating on you without the benefit of working on cadavers.

Imagine being on an airplane, knowing the pilot is hoping against hope that she can land the plane because she's never done this kind of thing before. A responsible pilot would never put herself or others in harm's way. She is certain she can land the plane. She has taken off and landed hundreds of times. Yet, every time, she follows a checklist. She has negotiated disaster after disaster, problem after problem, and has learned the art of flying. I'm pushing this analogy hard because only after you and I simulate what doctors and pilots do to perform their best will we achieve the results we want in our lives. If you are to capture the visions outlined in chapter 2, then you must have a checklist every day to help you fly through your day with confidence, knowing that you can navigate the most difficult situations because you've been there before.

Always Practice More Than You Play

We must practice before we play. Every great performance requires practice, practice, practice, whether by a pilot, a doctor, a salesperson, an athlete, a musician, or you and I endeavoring to live the life we have imagined.

I had just entered the lounge in San Diego to await the departure of my flight. After a few minutes, I noticed that Joe Montana, the retired football legend, was seated quietly in the corner. I had always admired Montana as a quarterback throughout the years, and I wanted to thank him for the great performances he gave us while at Notre Dame and with the 49ers and the Chiefs. Primarily, I wanted to get his autograph for my brother Jeff. (Really, it was for *Jeff*, not for me. Honest!)

A bad golf swing practiced regularly produces a bad golf swing. A perfect golf swing practiced regularly gets you closer to par. Not to engage in perfect practice sets you up to lose to the competition and afflicts you with mediocrity, complacency, adversity, and setbacks.

I approached him, introduced myself, and paid him the compliment I had intended. Then, after a brief conversation, which led to getting his autograph, I asked, "Joe, as a quarterback, how many hours would you spend weekly preparing for game day?"

"Between, viewing films, reviewing the play book, and actual on-field practice," he said, "I'd say forty to fifty hours per week."

Forty to fifty hours a week . . . for sixty minutes of game time? No wonder he was so good. What a ratio: 40–50 to 1. Here's my question: What would happen if you increased your ratio of practice to performance? What if it were 10 to 1? 5 to 1? Even 3 to 1? Are you practicing (simulating the actual game) enough? Are you practicing *more* than you actually play? Most of us don't do that.

We figure, hey, we show up, do

our thing, kibitz a little with our friends, abhor Mondays, live for Fridays, hope for the best, and we'll be successful. Actually, that's the language of the poor, not the prosperous. This attitude will not propel you to the top; instead, it will be an anchor on your soul and drag you to the depths.

To live the life you have imagined, you must practice every day, and only when you have mastered your craft, will you be ready for the game. One other thing—and I learned this from Denis Waitley—it's not practice that makes perfect: *Only perfect practice makes perfect.* A bad golf swing practiced regularly produces a bad golf swing. A perfect golf swing practiced regularly gets you closer to par. Not to engage in perfect practice sets you up to lose to the competition and afflicts you with mediocrity, complacency, adversity, and setbacks. To practice more than you play promises you at least three major benefits:

1. *Constant forward progress.* Simply put: The best way to go forward is not to retreat. You cannot afford to be stagnant. Constantly flowing water gathers no moss. It has no time to do so.
2. *Constant sharpening of skills.* To play at a higher level requires better execution than you are currently delivering. You cannot afford to enter the game just "hoping" to win. You must enter the game prepared to win.
3. *Increased confidence while playing.* The more you win, the greater your opportunity to develop a winning mindset, which sets you up to win again and again and again. Any salesman will tell you the best time to make the next sales call is on the heels of a successful sales call.

It's Time to Take Off

Let's fly! The space shuttle uses most of its fuel in a time-distance ratio during the first minutes of flight. Once off the ground, it uses its remaining fuel to stay its course. The same is true for you and me. We will always use most of our energy to combat the inertia of getting off the launching pad.

For this initial blast we need to be physically, financially, socially, spiritually, and relationally fit. We need all we've got going for us to get us where we need to go. When we approach our blastoff in this manner, we discover we will need less fuel and energy to maintain our desired course. It's a law of physics, and it's a law of life. Chapter 2 introduced you to the LifeQuest Pyramid of Success. You'll recall that after you discovered your purpose and determined your value areas, I had you ask yourself one important question: *In this value area, where do I want to go?* I will assume you have answered that question for the five to eight value areas you have discovered. I also assume that you have taken that vision and created a *clarifying vision statement* that embodies it.

As we approached the end of that chapter, I showed you the next two levels of the pyramid: mission (short-term actions leading to the fulfillment of your vision) and daily fulfillment activities (daily and weekly actions that fulfill your mission). Since most of your results will come from the last two levels of the pyramid, I would like to dig deeper to help you determine your mission and the importance of specific daily activities. Let's explore these so you will be prepared to harness the power that the rest of this book can give you. Then at the end of this chapter, I will give you a "Life by Design" checklist. I want you to use this checklist as a navigation tool for the rest of your life as your journey leads to a place called peace—the feeling you get when you are living the life you desire.

Don't Sabotage Your Success

Before we talk about setting goals, let me ask you some questions:

Have you ever set goals only to see your drive to accomplish them dissipate over time?

Have you ever written down your goals at New Year's and then wondered why you broke your promises before month's end? (More on this in chapter 10.)

Have you ever set a goal, accomplished it, and then wondered why you didn't experience the happy feelings you were expecting?

Have you ever shared a goal with someone, only to hear them say, "Hey, that's too big a goal for you. You're crazy. You'll never make it happen!"

Have you ever tried to set goals for your life but gave up because you felt they just didn't work?

There are more questions I'd like to ask you, but if you answered yes to any of these, pay close attention to the next several paragraphs. First, and this may seem like motivational heresy, I believe traditional goal setting simply doesn't work. Perhaps it's because I have witnessed the profound impact that nontraditional goal setting has had in my life and in the lives of thousands of others who have attended my seminars. In the next few pages you will learn to change the way you think about goals, so that from now on goals will become friends to help you capture the power that emerges from pursuing them with passion.

God's Goals and Yours

It estimated that about 96 percent of the American people believe in God and own at least one Bible, and 90% of Americans say they pray. In one survey the data showed that 80 percent of those polled named the Bible as the most influential book in human history. An amazing 58 percent said that they believe the Bible to be accurate in every detail. Still, for years, some polling groups and sociologists who specialize in tracking the religious behavior of Americans have been at odds trying to get a handle on how many of us go to worship services on a regular basis. Two of the best-known names in religious polling—the Gallup Organization and Barna Research Group—say about four in ten Americans go to church weekly, a figure that has remained fairly consistent since 1939, when Gallup first began collecting such data. These men, women, and children attend a variety of

> *These men, women, and children attend a variety of churches, hear a variety of messages, and each week come away with a variety of convictions on what they hear. I wonder how many are taught anything about goal setting from God's point of view.*

churches, hear a variety of messages, and each week come away with a variety of convictions on what they hear. I wonder how many are taught anything about goal setting from God's point of view.

Is it possible that God's plan for your life might be better than your plan for your life? It's true that the Book of Proverbs tells us to determine our plans. We are not to wait for a message from heaven that tells us to turn right or left or go straight ahead. It's up to *us* to look at our options and make an intelligent decision; however—and this is an important *however*—one verse goes on to say that we are to let God direct our steps (Proverbs 16:9). Simply stated, God has a plan for your life, and He wants you to experience it in all its fullness.

If you set your goals without trying to understand what His goals are for you, you are more than likely going to wind up being off purpose. How will you know this? When you fail to accomplish your major goals, or upon completing them, you have a vague feeling that you've somehow missed the boat just when you thought your ship had finally come in.

To be effective in your goal setting is to be close to God and to know His will for your life. There are some people, however, who try to fool themselves and others in "pretend" goal setting. It reminds me of the man who was driving along a narrow, winding road in rural New England when he saw a barn with five bull's-eyes painted on the side of it, and right in the middle of each one was an arrow—a perfect bull's-eye. The man's curiosity got the best of him. He pulled over, got out of the car, and went to the house near the barn, hoping to meet the person who was such an incredible marksman.

The farmer was surprised that anyone would take such interest in his marksmanship and invited the stranger outside for an exhibition of his shooting skill with the bow and arrow. He carefully loaded the bow and swiftly shot the arrow into the side of the barn. Then he went inside the barn, came out with a paintbrush and a bucket of paint and carefully and meticulously painted a target around the arrow, making sure that the arrow was right in the middle of the bull's-eye. Goal setting . . . after the fact. Cheating would be another word for it, and millions cheat themselves every day, knowing they live a life that's a fraud, but continuing to do it anyway.

That's why we have God's Spirit as our helper. The Bible tells us He will provide for our emotional, physical, spiritual, and psychological needs. If we trust in Him, He will make our paths straight (clear). Furthermore, we are not to lean on our own ways or our own methods exclusively. Instead, we are to acknowledge Him in our plans, and He will help us (Proverbs 3:5–6).

You bought this book to gain the power to be your best. I hope you now understand that the greatest power you will ever know comes when you tap in to the incredible plans that God has waiting for you. Once you come to grips with this eternal truth and believe it with all your heart, you will have all the confidence you'll ever need to know He will never leave you or let you down.

Becoming a Person of Prayer

One of the things I enjoy most is teaching Sunday school about thirty times each year. It forces me to spend more time in God's Word, and it encourages me to see so many others come to faith as they embrace the eternal truths found in the Scriptures. One of my most popular classes is when I teach students how to use the Lord's Prayer to gain clarity and guidance for their lives.

Whether you go to church regularly or not, I'm sure you have heard the prayer that Jesus taught his disciples to "pray this way." I offer it to you now to illustrate the strategy this prayer provides for us to be everything we can be.

In this manner, therefore, pray:
Our Father in heaven,
Hallowed be Your name.
Your kingdom come.
Your will be done
On earth as it is in heaven.
Give us this day our daily bread.
And forgive us our debts,
As we forgive our debtors.
And do not lead us into temptation,
But deliver us from the evil one.
For Yours is the kingdom and the power
and the glory forever. Amen.
Matthew 6:9–13

Here is how author Bob Beltz interprets the Lord's Prayer in his book, *Becoming a Man of Prayer.*

1. **"Father."** Prayer begins with a conscious act of seeking to enter into the presence of God. I call this component "Getting Started."
2. **"Hallowed be Your name."** Having entered into the presence of God in prayer, Jesus instructs us to direct our attention to God Himself. This component becomes what I call "Getting Focused."
3. **"Your kingdom come."** This is the goal section of prayer. As a third component of prayer, Christ extends an invitation to appropriate His intervention in our lives and the needs we and the world have. In light of this, our third area will be called "Experiencing Divine Intervention."

4. **"Give us this day."** It is not until this fourth component is reached that our focus shifts from God's agenda to our agenda. "Praying for Provision" becomes the time we pray about our own needs.

5. **"Forgive us our debts."** Under the category of Experiencing Forgiveness we learn to utilize the resources made available by the finished work of Christ to keep our lives in line with God's moral imperatives.

6. **"Deliver us."** The sixth component is labeled "Developing Spiritual Protection." This area of prayer will become a time to build a spiritual defense system around our lives and families.

7. **"Yours is the kingdom and the power and the glory forever."** The seventh and final component of the pattern is a closing time of affirmation. Having moved through all the dimensions of the pattern, it is appropriate to bring our time of prayer to a close with the declaration that God is the King and His is the kingdom. These will be our final issues.[1]

The key element for goal setting is #3, "Your kingdom come. Your will be done on earth [our life] as it is in heaven [His plan for us]." Wow! There it is. The essential element to effective goal setting is to align ourselves with God so that our plans are in concert with His. That is what He wants for you and me. The secret to knowing His will for your life is to realize you are living in it every day. Whether you are doing what He wants you to do or not, it is still His will. He is omniscient. He knows everything that is best for you. Therefore, you are wise indeed when you listen to what He wants to teach you.

To listen to God is to know the formula for peace. To be silent in His presence is to hear the answer you seek to your most profound question. When you listen to the Father, truly listen, you discover a dimension to your life you did not know existed. You suddenly begin to live with the peace of knowing that your plans (mission) and how you live them (daily fulfillment activities) are what your gracious heavenly Father wants for you. The greatest benefit to you in the process is that you will be backed forever by His power.

Read these words of Scripture carefully:

Therefore I say to you, do not worry about your life, what you will eat or what you will drink; nor about your body, what you will put on. Is not life more than food and the body more than clothing? Look at the birds of the air, for they neither sow nor reap nor gather into barns; yet your heavenly Father feeds them. Are you not of more value than they? Which of you by worrying can add one cubit to his stature?

Matthew 6:25–27

Christ said that because the birds fail to set goals, they receive no harvest, still the Father takes care of them. You and I are not birds, though. Imagine if we were to align our plans with God's and got some sowing going. We would receive a bumper crop of rewards—financial, spiritual, physical, and emotional. In the process, we would start to get the feeling that we were now getting the very best.

Are You Listening?

For me, prayer and meditation are the most effective methods to learn and understand God's plans for my life. When I pray, I outline my purpose and the key value areas of my life. My visions, missions, and activities become a reflection of what God puts on my heart during my time alone with Him. I want you also to give this a try.

Here's what I want you to do. Bring the great, important, difficult issues of your life to God and say, "Father, speak to me.

Tell me what you want for my life in these areas." Then, listen. Listen. Listen for a few minutes, perhaps even as long as five or ten minutes, though that may seem like an eternity. Eventually, you will hear your answer. This is God's way of nudging you into knowing that you are on the right track.

You suddenly begin to live with the peace of knowing that your plans (mission) and how you live them (daily fulfillment activities) are what your gracious heavenly Father wants for you. The greatest benefit to you in the process is that you will be backed forever by His power.

From that moment forward, as you continue to pray and meditate, you will know the direction you should go in every area of your life. You will have an inner peace that money, real estate, stocks and bonds, and big cars will never provide. Most important, you will have at your disposal the peace and the power to live life to the fullest. The prophet Isaiah once wrote, "You will keep him in perfect peace, whose mind is stayed on You, because he trusts in You" (Isaiah 26:3).

Life by Design: Are Your Wheels Balanced?

One of the most memorable business meetings of my life was with my colleague and friend Jim Cathcart. We were having lunch in La Jolla, where we both live, when I told him I needed counsel on some decisions I needed to make in my life. During our lunch, Jim introduced me to a model for living that has made a huge impact on my life and in the lives of others as I've shared it with them over the years.

In the circle on the next page, you will notice there are eight spokes. Think of the outer ring as the wheel; think of the inner circle as the hub. You are the hub, and the outer wheel is your life. Depending on how you are doing on each of the spokes, your life either rolls smoothly, or because your spokes are not "trued," your wheel wobbles.

Worst-case scenario, your wheel has a flat spot that makes it impossible for it to roll at all. I have put my value areas on the spokes as an example.

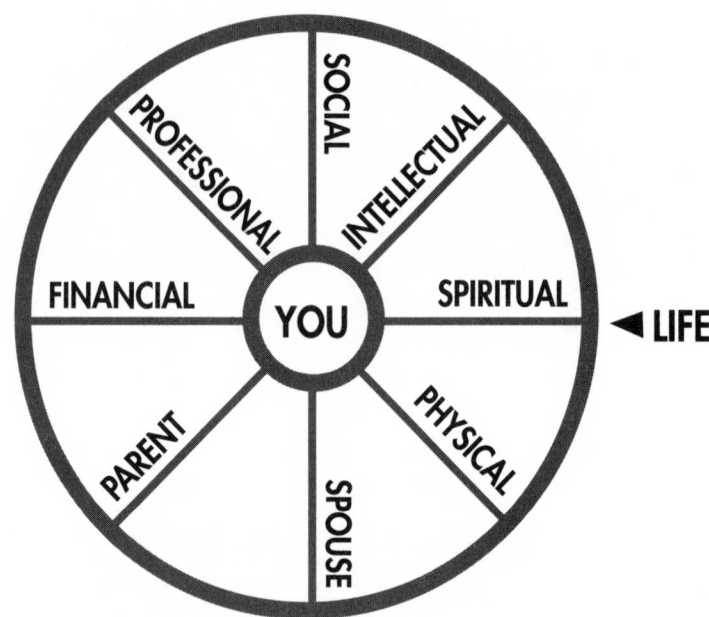

On each of the spokes below, I want you to write one of your value areas from chapter 2. Proceed clockwise and write down your eight value areas, rotating every other spoke with four value areas until you have gone around once. Then continue to add four more value areas on the spokes that remain. Second, rate yourself honestly on how you are doing in each of these areas. Put a dot on each line where you think you are at this moment. A rating of 1 is next to the hub, 10 is at the end of the spoke. A rating of 1 indicates this area of your life isn't working as well as you would like; a rating of 10 suggests this area is working extremely well. Complete the rating for each of the spokes. Don't sabotage yourself! Be honest. It's your life.

Here's the last step. Choose any one of the dots on any spoke, and with your pen or pencil connect that dot moving clockwise to the next dot. Continue clockwise to the next dot until you have gone all the way around, ending with the first

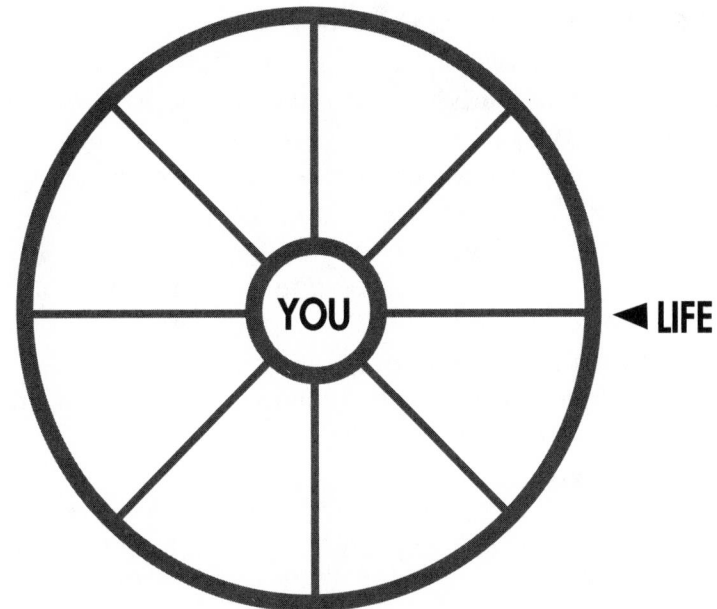

dot. This is your life, your current wheel. How does your real life now compare with the round one that encircles it? Do you have any flat spots? Are there any dents? If yours is like mine, I'm sure your answer will have to be yes. This is where your goal setting begins. The areas where you need improvement begin when you are clear on where you and God want you to go.

Questions to Get You Thinking

I want you to take inventory of where you are right now by asking yourself a series of important questions. I've designed them to help you become more intentional about what you feel you must become to sense your true significance. Just as pilots go through routine checklists, this is your checklist—something to be read every day to ensure that you enjoy safe takeoffs and smooth landings. After you review these questions, I will provide you with a detailed plan to help you integrate your answers into a formidable plan of action. Then, in chapter 6, I will show you how to take your plan and accomplish it with the highest degree of certainty possible.

The Life by Design Checklist

1.   Am I missing anything in my life right now that is important to me?
2.   What am I passionate about? What gives meaning to my life?
3.   Who am I? Why am I here today?
4.   What do I value that gives me true happiness?
5.   Where do I want to be? What do I want to be doing in the next five, ten, twenty years?
6.   What gifts has God given me that I am now in the process of perfecting? Which ones am I not using as effectively as I might?
7.   What am I willing to die for?
8.   What is it, if anything, about my job that makes me feel trapped?
9.   What realistic changes can I make in my employment that will give me more freedom?
10. What steps should I take today that will ensure my meaningful future?
11. With regard to money, how much is enough for me? If I have more than I need, what purpose does my excess money serve?
12. Am I living a balanced life? What areas of my life need more focus?
13. Where do I seek inspiration, mentors, and working models for my greater success?
14. How do I want to be remembered?
15. What legacy do I want to leave for my children?
16. Where will I go when this life is over?

Let's Take Massive Action

In chapter 2, I told you after completing the pyramid and "finding your rock," that you should spend fifteen minutes a day:

- reviewing all that is important to you in life. (These are your value areas.)

- reviewing the vision you have for your value areas.

- reviewing the mission you have for your short-term goals.

- reviewing your activities that, when completed, fulfill your vision and allow you to live your life with purpose.

With all the information you now have—and now that you have had some time for chapters 1–4 to sink in—spend as much time as it takes to complete the following forms. These are the practical tools you will use during your fifteen minutes each day to stay on course. When you need to make a decision, review your answers immediately. When you have to make a choice, consult them. When you become discouraged and lose your nerve, tap in to them. If the results of your life are not what you want, reflect on them. If you want to raise the bar, upgrade them. These are the "tracks" on which your life now runs.

There are ten forms, five of which contain the most frequent value areas. The other five are for other value areas you will discover as you play with this process. It is important that you use all the information you have received so far. Review all previous action plans.

Now go to a quiet place and reflect on the importance of your life. It is the only life you will ever have to enjoy on this earth. As your coach, I want to help you make it the best you can. Go through the checklist above. Get serious about your direction. The purpose of this exercise is to help you clarify where you are and where you want to go.

As we come to Part 3: The Art of Creating Wealth, the focus will shift to help empower you in the major areas of importance in your life. Then, by the time you complete chapter 12, you will have a 360-degree plan of action for every area of your life, giving you the power to be your best today, tomorrow, and for the rest of eternity.

By now you should be crystal clear on your purpose and your five to eight value areas. It is not necessary to repeat steps one and two of the LifeQuest Pyramid here. These ten forms address the creation of your vision (Step 3), the development of a mission statement to embody your goals in each value area (Step 4), and ask what actions you must take consistently to attain your goals and fulfill your vision (Step 5). Refer back to chapter 2 if you need to reacquaint yourself with this process. When you do this, your response to these questions will take on added significance. When you have completed your answers, go immediately to the next chapter, and I will show you how to use them to the highest degree of efficiency possible.

Life by Design Planner

Step Number 3: Develop a Clarifying Vision Statement. What do I want to be, have, or do long term in this area? This vision statement clarifies my long-term vision in the **spiritual** area of my life:

_____

_____

_____

Step Number 4: Develop a Mission Statement. What do I want to be, have, or do short term in this area? This mission statement embraces my short-term goals in the **spiritual** area of my life:

_____

_____

_____

Step Number 5: Daily Activities. What do I need to do today? What activities need to be scheduled today to move me closer to my goals **spiritually?**

1. _____

2. _____

3. _____

4. _____

5. _____

Life by Design Planner

Step Number 3: Develop a Clarifying Vision Statement. What do I want to be, have, or do long term in this area? This vision statement clarifies my long-term vision in the **health** area of my life:

_____

_____

_____

Step Number 4: Develop a Mission Statement. What do I want to be, have, or do short term in this area? This mission statement embraces my short-term goals in the **health** area of my life:

_____

_____

_____

Step Number 5: Daily Activities. What do I need to do today? What activities need to be scheduled today to move me closer to my goals **physically?**

1. _____

2. _____

3. _____

4. _____

5. _____

THE *POWER!* TO BE YOUR BEST!

Life by Design Planner

Step Number 3: Develop a Clarifying Vision Statement. What do I want to be, have, or do long term in this area? This vision statement clarifies my long-term vision in the **family** area of my life:

_____

_____

_____

Step Number 4: Develop a Mission Statement. What do I want to be, have, or do short term in this area? This mission statement embraces my short-term goals in the **family** area of my life:

_____

_____

_____

Step Number 5: Daily Activities. What do I need to do today? What activities need to be scheduled today to move me closer to my goals **relationally?**

1. _____

2. _____

3. _____

4. _____

5. _____

Life by Design Planner

Step Number 3: Develop a Clarifying Vision Statement.
What do I want to be, have, or do long term in this area? This
vision statement clarifies my long-term vision in the **professional**
area of my life:

_____

_____

_____

Step Number 4: Develop a Mission Statement. What do I
want to be, have, or do short term in this area? This mission
statement embraces my short-term goals in the **professional**
area of my life:

_____

_____

_____

Step Number 5: Daily Activities. What do I need to do
today? What activities need to be scheduled today to move me
closer to my goals **professionally?**

1. _____

2. _____

3. _____

4. _____

5. _____

Life by Design Planner

Step Number 3: Develop a Clarifying Vision Statement. What do I want to be, have, or do long term in this area? This vision statement clarifies my long-term vision in the **financial** area of my life:

_____

_____

_____

Step Number 4: Develop a Mission Statement. What do I want to be, have, or do short term in this area? This mission statement embraces my short-term goals in the **financial** area of my life:

_____

_____

_____

Step Number 5: Daily Activities. What do I need to do today? What activities need to be scheduled today to move me closer to my goals **financially?**

1. _____

2. _____

3. _____

4. _____

5. _____

Life by Design Planner

Step Number 3: Develop a Clarifying Vision Statement.
What do I want to be, have, or do long term in this area? This
vision statement clarifies my long-term vision in the _____
area of my life:

_____

_____

_____

Step Number 4: Develop a Mission Statement. What do I
want to be, have, or do short term in this area? This mission
statement embraces my short-term goals in the _____
area of my life:

_____

_____

_____

Step Number 5: Daily Activities. What do I need to do
today? What activities need to be scheduled today to move me
closer to my goals _____?

1. _____

2. _____

3. _____

4. _____

5. _____

Life by Design Planner

Step Number 3: Develop a Clarifying Vision Statement. What do I want to be, have, or do long term in this area? This vision statement clarifies my long-term vision in the _____ area of my life:

_____

_____

_____

Step Number 4: Develop a Mission Statement. What do I want to be, have, or do short term in this area? This mission statement embraces my short-term goals in the _____ area of my life:

_____

_____

_____

Step Number 5: Daily Activities. What do I need to do today? What activities need to be scheduled today to move me closer to my goals _____?

1. _____

2. _____

3. _____

4. _____

5. _____

Life by Design Planner

Step Number 3: Develop a Clarifying Vision Statement.
What do I want to be, have, or do long term in this area? This
vision statement clarifies my long-term vision in the _____
area of my life:

_____

_____

_____

Step Number 4: Develop a Mission Statement. What do I
want to be, have, or do short term in this area? This mission
statement embraces my short-term goals in the _____
area of my life:

_____

_____

_____

Step Number 5: Daily Activities. What do I need to do
today? What activities need to be scheduled today to move me
closer to my goals _____?

1. _____

2. _____

3. _____

4. _____

5. _____

Life by Design Planner

Step Number 3: Develop a Clarifying Vision Statement. What do I want to be, have, or do long term in this area? This vision statement clarifies my long-term vision in the _____ area of my life:

_____

_____

_____

Step Number 4: Develop a Mission Statement. What do I want to be, have, or do short term in this area? This mission statement embraces my short-term goals in the _____ area of my life:

_____

_____

_____

Step Number 5: Daily Activities. What do I need to do today? What activities need to be scheduled today to move me closer to my goals _____?

1. _____

2. _____

3. _____

4. _____

5. _____

When you have completed at least five worksheets for your five top value areas, please visit my website at www.toddduncan.com and listen to my Audio Success Snapshot—Born to Win. *See you on-line. —TD*

www.toddduncan.com

Action Planner Notes

_____

_____

_____

_____

_____

_____

_____

_____

_____

_____

_____

_____

_____

_____

_____

_____

_____

_____

_____

_____

_____

_____

Values-Based Living: The Art of Time Efficiency

You must learn to be still in the midst of activity, and to be vibrantly alive in repose.
Indira Gandhi

For fast-acting relief, try slowing down.
Lilly Tomlin

---

ne morning as I looked out over Darling Harbor in Sydney, Australia, from my hotel room, I again reminded myself how most people seemed to live their lives: it's go, go, go—pause, deep breath, throw the shoulders back, exhale—go, go, go some more. Everywhere I looked I saw taxis hurrying, cars racing, and people scurrying. Pedestrians were looking at their watches, tapping their feet impatiently as they waited for the traffic lights to change. They smoked too much, drank too much, worried too much. Everything was just another rush hour for them, and that lifestyle continued nonstop, not only here in Sydney, but in cities and towns around the globe.

The string is tightly wound around the heads and hearts of millions. Bigger is better. Faster is better. More is better. Few, it seems, have made the effort to read E. F. Schumacher's great book *Small Is Beautiful* or understood its message that we do not need to be the biggest, the brashest, the fastest, or the noisiest to win in the game of life.

How about you? Do external forces drive your life or are your days ordered by simplicity? Have you found that the game of managing your time eludes you, or are you the master of your time? Have you ever crafted what you knew was a foolproof plan of action only to see it messed up by midmorning? Once in a state of disarray, can you recall how difficult it was to get yourself back on track? If you are not living your life on-purpose, which includes managing your time on-purpose, chances are you will never harness your full power nor order your days as efficiently as you must to become the person you were designed to be.

> *If you are not living your life on-purpose, which includes managing your time on-purpose, chances are you will never harness your full power nor order your days as efficiently as you must to become the person you were designed to be.*

Values-Based Living

Emily Dickinson once said, "To live is so startling, it leaves little time for anything else." Once you commit to a values-based lifestyle, your life will reflect such magnificent form that you will have little time to live the lesser life of mediocrity, complacency, laziness, or excusitis. You will move forward, not backward. Life will pose challenges, not problems. Objects obstructing your path will no longer be stumbling blocks, but rather steppingstones to your brighter future. When you live your life to the maximum, all the rules change because your values clarify your thinking. Still, you will always face the question, Am I just being busy or am I being productive? Welcome to the club!

Life Productive Behavior is the conduct that sets the stage for you to live your life with control, organization, fulfillment, and rewards, allowing you to get what you want because you are focused on the right things. In the first five chapters of this book, you built your model. You should now be clear on your purpose (your five to eight value areas) along with your vision and mission in those areas (your long- and short-term goals and your daily activities). In this chapter I want to help you create a workable strategy so you can incorporate your daily activities into a manageable course of action.

Here's Where It All Started

"In the beginning . . ." is the opening line of the most famous book in all history, which is still being read today in hundreds of languages and by millions of people. Still, with all the Bible buying and recitation of its thousands of verses, the power of those first three words remains overlooked. Their significance is either glossed over or reckoned unimportant. Yet those first words from the book of beginnings must be considered seriously, because they contain infinite truth that demands at least partial comprehension by our finite minds. Those words tell us that we live in a world that has a beginning and, by extension, an end—that we live in a world of time.

Lynn Grant Robbins reminded me of a startling truth. She said that there is only so much time. If you were to look at your calendar, you will find it to be the same as everyone else's with respect to the number of days in the week, the number of hours in the day, and the number of days in the year. The chief difference in the calendars of those who lead rich and fulfilling lives

When you live your life to the maximum, all the rules change because your values clarify your thinking. Still, you will always face the question, Am I just being busy or am I being productive? Welcome to the club!

159

and those who do not is simply a difference of understanding time value. How each activity done in that time either leads you to a greater level of values congruency or creates a barrier for you getting to a stage where you feel good about how you are spending your time.

We only have so much time, twenty-four hours to be exact. We have no more, no less than anyone else. Time is the great equalizer. Therefore, it is not good enough for us to say we do not have time. We do have time, and it's all the time we will ever need. Whatever we accomplish, we will do in the span of time allotted to us. We cannot buy, beg, or steal one extra hour, one more minute. Benjamin Franklin once observed, "To love life is to love time." Time is the stuff life is made of. If this is true (and it is), than why do we waste so much of it?

Your Power Comes from Your Choices

Albert Einstein once remarked, "Time has no independent existence apart from the order of events by which we measure it." Gottfried Leibniz, a brilliant German mathematician and philosopher of the early 1700s, after doing much research on the subject, observed, "Time is merely the order of events, not an entity itself."

If we are not in control of the events in our lives, we will never be able to live the full lives we have imagined.

Time waits for no one. We cannot blockade it. We cannot stall it. It is like a rushing torrent that demands we deal with it, work with it, and use it. It is an ongoing continuum of events that have happened, are happening, or will happen in the future.

Our success in the game of life comes from how we merge the activities and events that we say are important into a planned time to execute them. That is why executives are called executives, but we do not need a corner window with a view of the city to be an executive. When we learn to merge our activities into a planned time for execution, we become executives. We receive immediate feedback—like stepping on a rake—because we know immediately whether we are living on purpose or by accident. It is always our choice.

We not only choose our events, we also choose when we will do them. The operative word here is choose. This is the platform for our success.

In the game of time, our power to live the life we have designed is in direct proportion to our effectiveness in getting things done. If we are ineffective or inefficient in controlling our life events, we will fall short of achieving the power to be our best. If, however, we focus on moving our events into a plan of action, then our power grows and so does our performance. If we are not in control of the events in our lives, we will never be able to live the full lives we have imagined. This is one of the central themes that runs throughout the remainder of this book.

Control Is the Key

How do events and controlling those events work together? Peter Drucker in his book *The Effective Executive* says that the task of a time manager is to control time whenever possible. When I interviewed Hyrum Smith, he told me that *control* is the key to making sure our events are not only scheduled but also completed. Since time is essentially the accumulation of events and control is the key to making sense of those events, then the secret to taming time is, logically, the fine art of *event control*. This means that we not only choose our events, we also choose when we will do them. The operative word here is *choose*. This is the platform for our success.

Productivity Follows

Here are eight truths about most people and their productivity behaviors:

1. **People spend 75 percent of their time on things that are urgent and important or urgent and not important.** We wrongly believe that, generally speaking, we are doing the best we can. We can all do a better job to lower this percentage.

2. **If people are not preventing, they will always be reacting.** Whenever things get messed up in our lives, it is usually our own fault. Of course, there are those circumstances over which we have limited control. Some events will happen regardless of planning, but while we may not be able to control all events in life, we can and must control our responses to these events. In most cases, everything that happens to us is fixable.

3. **People need to spend 75 percent of their time in those areas that are not urgent but important.** Too many of us believe we will never accomplish all that we want to do. This is a myth. To accomplish future goals, we must first be patently clear on what is important to us today.

4. **Until people clean up the messes in their lives, productivity will not happen.** If we are not preventing, we are reacting. The question we must ask ourselves is Are we in control or are we on

If we use our new values platform to move away from making a mess, toward living with mastery, then every positive step in that direction secures a new direction. Remember: Success is simply the incremental achievement of worthwhile goals. It is the journey, not the destination.

THE *POWER!* TO BE YOUR BEST!

autopilot? Have we accepted, wrongly, that idea that this is poor me and my miserable life and I guess I can't do much about where it's heading? If so, progress is impossible. If, however, we use our new values platform to move away from making a mess, toward living with mastery, then every positive step in that direction secures a new direction. Remember: Success is simply the incremental achievement of worthwhile goals. It is the journey, not the destination.

Most of us do not know how to plan an effective day. If we do not define our day and put demands on it, the day will define us, rule us, and squeeze us into its own mold.

5. **Most people live a life that is in conflict with their values.** We live this way because, not knowing our values, we have no frame of reference on how to use our time. Additionally, most of us do not know how to schedule blocks of time that allow us to get the right things done. The "first things first" mentality is the key to making this work.

6. **While we cannot control everything, we can control more things.** The Law of Responsibility comes into play here. When we take ownership of our lives, we move beyond mediocrity toward new visions of what is truly possible.

7. **People will never be able to manage their time effectively 100 percent of the time; however, we can all do a better job than we are now doing**. Most of us do not know how to plan an effective day. If we do not define our day and put demands on it, the day will define us, rule us, and squeeze us into its own mold.

8. **The number-one way to be better at using our time is to be proactive, to begin the process with the end in mind.** We have two choices: control or be controlled. There are no other options. We either control our time, or we do not.

Recently, a friend gave me the following piece on the importance of time for seven people with different perspectives. Which of these statements do you relate to most?

The Importance of Time

To realize the value of one year:
Ask a student who has failed a final exam.
To realize the value of one month:
Ask a mother who has given birth to a premature baby.
To realize the value of one week:
Ask an editor of a weekly newspaper.
To realize the value of one hour:
Ask the lovers who are waiting to meet.
To realize the value of one minute:
Ask a person who has just missed the bus, train, or plane.
To realize the value of one second:
Ask a person who has survived an accident.
To realize the value of one millisecond:
Ask a person who has won a silver medal in the Olympics.

Time waits for no one. Treasure every moment you have. When you do, you will find, not only is time important, but there is a time for all things. As the Old Testament preacher said long ago:

To everything there is a season,
A time for every purpose under heaven:
A time to be born, And a time to die; A time to
plant, And a time to pluck what is planted;
A time to kill, And a time to heal; A time to break
down, And a time to build up;
A time to weep, And a time to laugh; A time to
mourn, And a time to dance;
A time to cast away stones, And a time to gather
stones; A time to embrace, And a time to refrain
from embracing;

THE *POWER!* TO BE YOUR BEST!

*A time to gain, And a time to lose; A time to keep,
And a time to throw away;
A time to tear, And a time to sew; A time to keep
silence, And a time to speak;
A time to love, And a time to hate; A time of war,
And a time of peace.*

Ecclesiastes 3:1–8

There is also a need to spend time:

- with God
- with our mate
- with our children
- with our health
- with our finances
- with our profession
- with our mind

There is time for everything that is important. Our task is to get rid of the unimportant and schedule the important by using our values as the tools and motivation to make this happen.

The following concept can change your life forever: When you combine "the value of time" with the truth that "there is a time for everything," you will possess the most powerful, effective, life-changing tool for powerful living. Determine what is most important to you; then schedule to get it done in a timely manner.

Time Management Is Values Management

When you manage your time, you manage your values. When you manage your values, you begin to enjoy inner peace because everything about you and your life is becoming consistent. When your values are clear to you, the decisions on how to use your time no longer appear challenging. Your job is to continue aligning your values with your activities. Consider this excerpt from *Time Management* by Richard Winwood:

> *Ken Blanchard and Spencer Johnson in* The One-Minute Manager *have stated, "People who feel good about themselves produce good results." The direct relationship between our sense of self-worth and our personal productivity is a relatively new concept in management. In time management, because its basis is personal productivity, the relationship is vital. A person may possess many practical skills and be able to apply them well and yet have a very low self-esteem. This person may feel a great discomfort at the thought of having to learn a new skill or having to change his environment in any meaningful way. Another person with a high self-esteem may be lacking in practical skills but having no fear of learning or of confronting a new environment can quickly and enjoyably learn and adapt to different situations. In the latter example, the person had confidence in his or her ability—based on a healthy self-esteem.[1]*

To live life on-purpose, you must get far enough ahead of the curve to bolster your confidence and take more control. Your esteem is enhanced when you do; it suffers when you do not. If you fail to control the events in your life, then events will put a choke hold on you. You will feel like a victim and not know why. Your productivity goes up when you are in control; it goes down when you are not. In that weakened state, you will make weak decisions, and every weak decision will affect your productivity, seducing you

To live life on-purpose, you must get far enough ahead of the curve to bolster your confidence and take more control. Your esteem is enhanced when you do; it suffers when you do not.

to accept less of what you truly want. To enjoy the healthiest life possible, you need to:

1. Know your key value areas.
2. Determine specifically what you want in those areas.
3. Learn new skills, if necessary, to be more effective in those areas.
4. Schedule activities that give you a sense of accomplishment in those areas.
5. Repeat your behaviors consistently. This is vital, because it brings about an alignment between what you are doing, and what you know is value-based.

Once you have done this, this alignment should look like the diagram below.

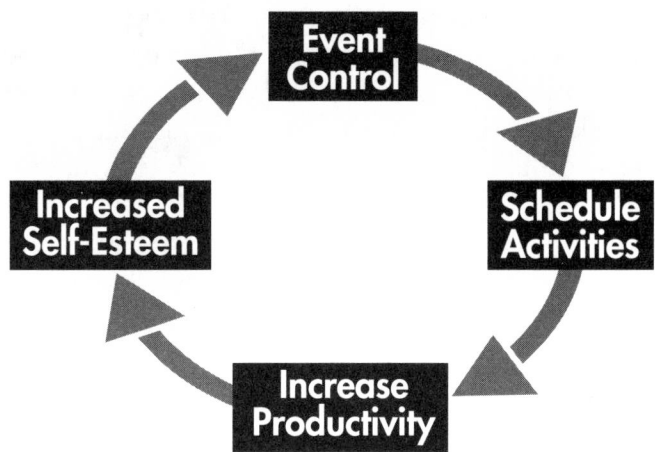

As each of the elements in this diagram improves in quality, the other elements also improve. Gaining control of events that strengthen you and help you achieve your highest priorities is the foundation you must have to live the life you want to live. Once you start along this path, you will find that everything begins to come together. Within weeks, even days, you can make more progress than you have in years past. The key is to plan.

A $25,000 Thank You

One of the earliest success stories on the importance of planning as a discipline concerns Charles Schwab, the president of Bethlehem Steel. In a discussion with a management consultant one day, Schwab threw out this challenge: "Show me a way to get more things done with my time, and I'll pay you any fee within reason."

Ivy Lee, the consultant, handed Schwab a blank sheet of paper and said, "Write down the most important things you have to do tomorrow and number them in order of their importance. When you arrive in the morning, begin at once on number one and stay on it until it's completed. Once you've completed the first task, recheck your priorities and begin number two. Stick with your task all day if necessary, as long as it's the most important one. If you don't finish all your tasks, don't worry. You probably couldn't have done so with any other method, and without some system you'd probably not even decide which one was most important. Now, make this a habit every day. When it works for you, give the idea to your management. Try it as long as you like. Then send me a check for what you think it's worth."

Several weeks later, after the idea had been tried and found worthy, Schwab sent Lee a check for twenty-five thousand dollars, an enormous sum for the 1930s, along with a note saying that the idea was the most profitable one he had ever learned.

How much would such a suggestion be worth to you? What would happen to your business, family, and social life if you prioritized the activities you knew would make the greatest difference? What if you carried out this disciplined planning every day without fail? What would your life look like three months, six months, one year from now, especially if you took Ivy Lee's advice to heart every day? I think you know the answer. You would revolutionize your thinking, which would in turn revolutionize your bank account, your relationships, your social life, and your view of a brighter future.

The Art of Delegation

Greg and Devon are enjoying their lives in Albuquerque, New Mexico, in an exquisite seven-thousand-square-foot home on two lush acres of beautifully manicured lawn. During a recent trip to visit them, I was impressed with the many things Greg and Devon delegate so they can enjoy the life they have designed. For example, they have a pool person, a rose gardener, a full-time housekeeper and handyman, and a cook. I think they have it figured out. The money they have chosen to spend on this kind of help frees them up to do what is important to them: spend time with each other and with their children.

Washing the car and mowing the lawn may appear to be noble manifestations of an ingrained work ethic, but if you would use that time to focus on what is truly important—and if you did this consistently, week after week and year after year—before long, you would see incredible results.

You may not have the income Greg and Devon enjoy; your income is not crucial. If delegation is a fundamental principle, then as a principle, it must work for everyone. A ten-year-old child can hire other kids to shine shoes "representing his firm," take a 25 percent cut, and be profitable. Why? Because the ten-year-old knows how to delegate. She learned the basic principle that if you want to be wealthy, you have to make money while you are sleeping, or at least when you are not working. It is called delegation. It's also called being smart!

You too have the ability to delegate numerous things that would give you many extra hours to focus on the important things of your life—your values. Washing the car and mowing the lawn may appear to be noble manifestations of an ingrained work ethic, but if you would use that time to focus on what is truly important—and if you did this consistently, week after week and year after year—before long, you would see incredible results.

Efficient Time Management

Here's another truth, and it is a simple one: You can accomplish more simply by managing your time more efficiently. Let me give you an example. I now get up an hour earlier because I am a father of two. (I was a father of one when I began writing chapter 1!) Having two children, however, does not alter my need to nurture two of the values that are important to me: spiritual intimacy and the maintenance of my health. If anything, that fact only increases their importance.

Before I had children, I would work out at 6 A.M., after which I would have my devotions and prayer time. Now, with two children, I have to get up at 5 A.M. to fulfill those two value areas in my life. This was not a difficult choice because values-based living is neither grievous nor painful. All I had to do was adjust my timing. Now if these had not been my core values, do you think I would get up in what seems like the middle of the night to sweat and pray? Not on your life. I would have thought of every reason in the world to stay between the lily whites. I didn't.

Here's the point: You don't have to spend money or debate long and hard before making decisions when they are grounded in your values. You simply need to do what Nike keeps telling us to do, Just do it! Decision making is not a matter of time or money; it is a matter of values.

Do the math on this. If you truly want to get things done in your life that until now you have not been able to do, then, as your coach, I want you to get up an hour earlier or stay up an hour later each day. This will give you an extra 365 hours each year to do what is important to you. It will not cost you a dime, but it will require an investment in a life of discipline. Why is it important for you to make this part of your hard wiring? For these reasons:

1. If you want to be in a different place than where you are, you must follow a different course of action than you have been following.
2. Your new course of action requires that you know which activities, when repeated, will form habits to lead you to

the great accomplishments you already see and feel. (Remember the importance of present tense, "Believe it before you see it" affirmations?)

3. These activities must be scheduled and carried out consistently for them to be integrated into your new life.

4. For this new way of thinking to work for you, you must cut out the clutter and develop a focus on those things you value. When "stuff" gets in your way and you allow it to remain an obstacle, you will veer off course. There is no way around it. That is why any activity that is not values-based should be either eliminated or delegated immediately.

5. If your life remains disorderly and confused because of too much urgency and not enough priorities, you will never get to where you want to be. You will fail to develop the power to be your best. No matter how positive you are, no matter how much faith you have in yourself, no matter how great your beliefs, if your life remains a clutter of undifferentiated stuff that keeps you in a perpetual state of fear and anxiety, you will never make reasonable progress in measurable time.

To get the life you want demands that you master the art of planning, delegating, and scheduling. Then you must use your values as your sole motivator for living and do the most important things before you do the urgent and less important things. Your ultimate goal is to distance yourself from the tyranny of the urgent and move yourself closer to the wisdom of doing only what is important.

The Art of Making Things Simple

God made us plain and simple, but we have made ourselves very complicated.
Ecclesiastes 7:29, TEV

Here it is, straight and honest. The person we face in the mirror each morning is the one who has created most of the confusion in our lives. It is not the economy, not the government, not a mean father, or the fact that mother loved someone else more. Those are excuses, not reasons. Why have we made such a muddle of things? The uncomplicated answer is that we have taken something simple and made it incredibly complex. Until you simplify your life, you will be forever challenged in your efforts to gain and maintain the life you have imagined, desired, and deserve. You need a garage sale of the mind where you clean up the mess, get rid of old thinking that no longer works, slow down, reevaluate, and begin to live your life intentionally. Prizes are handed out at the end of the race, never at the beginning. It will be the same with you. Your new life demands a different kind of action now; your results will come later. Don't be like good ol' Charlie Brown who was convinced he couldn't do new math. After all, he whimpered, I have an old-math brain. No more excuses!

> *The advertisements, however, never admit that the happiness and fulfillment you so fervently desire will never arrive. If you succumb to the pitch, the wizards of words win again at the game of Gotcha!*

I did not say this would be easy. Everything around you is going to work against you. Everything! Madison Avenue does not preach simplicity. Our world has become a kind of compulsive, "got to have it today," "upgrade now," "toss out the old and give me the new" joke. Advertising has one objective: to make you so unhappy with what you have that you feel compelled to buy more of what you do not need with money you do not have. The advertisements, however, never admit that the happiness and fulfillment you so fervently desire will never arrive. If you succumb to the pitch, the wizards of words win again at the game of Gotcha!

It is time to reorder our private world. To do so, simplification is our mandate. In the words of Chuck Swindoll:

To reorder one's own private world, the need to simplify is imperative. Otherwise, we will find ourselves unable to be at rest within, unable to enter the deep, silent resources of our hearts, where God's best messages are communicated. And, if we live very long in that condition, our hearts grow cold toward Christ and we become objects of seduction in a wayward world. What perils await us in that condition! . . . Busyness is an enemy wherever it raises its ugly head! . . . Envy is another enemy of simplifying life. Locked into a horizontal syndrome of judging, comparing, and regretting, our focus turns from the things of God and becomes riveted on others as well as ourselves. Instead of being contented (one of the wonderful by-products of simplicity), we are consumed by envy. Our standard of contentment is raised so high; we can never measure up.²

Not to choose a life of simplicity is to live at a frantic pace. Then, as we try to do even more, we feel drained, strained, fretful, and out of physical and emotional gas. Is this were you are? Doing too much with too little reserve? If the pace, the push, the clutter, and the crowds are getting to you, it is time to stop the nonsense and find a place of solace to refresh your spirit.

If the pace, the push, the clutter, and the crowds are getting to you, it is time to stop the nonsense and find a place of solace to refresh your spirit.

This Might Be the Last Moment of Your Life

I will never forget the call for as long as I live. I can still hear the sirens in the background. As if it were yesterday, I can hear the paramedics as they worked on my screaming twelve-month-old son. I can hear Sheryl saying, "Honey, we've been in a very serious accident. We're alive, but Jonathan may be seriously injured. The paramedics said we were hit at around sixty miles an hour while our car was standing still. They are going to take Jonathan to the trauma center at children's hospital. You need to meet us there. The car is a total loss." To this day I do not know how Sheryl had the composure to speak so lucidly. She was so concise. After all, she had been injured too.

Every moment I had ever enjoyed with Jonathan flashed before my eyes. In the fifteen minutes it took to drive to the hospital, I recounted every memory. Oh, they were so great. I did not want to lose my son. Our life together had just begun.

The minutes seemed to become hours as I waited for the ambulance to arrive at the hospital. Then I heard the sirens. An eleven-doctor trauma team was waiting. Then I saw the paramedics wheel Jonathan from the back of the vehicle. He was covered with blood. He clutched his blanket. His screams were deafening. Four hours later, we learned that he was going to make it. There were no internal injuries. Most of the blood was from flying glass. His eyes were not damaged (the doctors originally thought the glass had cut his cornea). All the bones in his tiny body seemed to be okay.

Wow! Talk about a life-changing moment. Let me tell you this: I'm so glad I had learned to live my life based on my values and simplicity. What would it have been like to feel guilty for the rest of my life for not having spent quality time with Sheryl and Jonathan had they been taken from me?

Are You Doing What Counts?

You are now at a crossroads in this book and, hopefully, in your thinking. From this point forward, your complete, uncompromising focus must be to create a master plan that takes each principle you have discovered so far—including the Life-by-Design plans you completed in the previous chapter—and put them to use. I now want to share with you the basis of the philosophy taught here after which I will show you a practical plan to schedule your most important activities.

To quote Ben Franklin: "It was about this time I conceived the bold and arduous project of arriving at moral perfection. I wished to live without committing any fault at any time; I would conquer all that either natural inclination, custom, or company might lead me into. As I knew, or thought I knew, what was right and wrong, I did not see why I might not always do the one and avoid the other."[3]

Franklin first developed a list that stated his most important values (he called them virtues and prioritized them). In these areas he sought perfection. You declared your values in chapter 2, and now it's time for you to strive toward perfection in fulfilling them. Yes, perfection! Then Franklin, to define the action to be associated with each of his virtues "annex'd to each a short precept, which fully express'd the extent I gave to its meaning." Simply, he predetermined the behavior that would be ideal within the framework of the value. Here are his virtues—these differ from the Ladder of Success rungs you studied earlier.

- **Temperance**. Eat not to dullness; drink not to elevation.
- **Silence**. Speak not but what may benefit others or you; avoid trifling conversation.
- **Order**. Let all things have their places; let each part of your business have its time.
- **Resolution**. Resolve to perform what you ought; perform without fail what you resolve.
- **Frugality**. Make no expense but to do good to others or yourself; that is, waste nothing.
- **Industry**. Lose no time; be always employed in something useful; cut off all unnecessary actions.
- **Sincerity**. Use no hurtful deceit; think innocently and justly; speak accordingly.
- **Cleanliness**. Tolerate no uncleanliness in body, clothes, or habitation.
- **Tranquillity**. Be not disturbed at trifles or at accidents common or unavoidable.

- **Chastity**. Rarely use venery [sexual intercourse] but for health or offspring, never to dullness, weakness, or the injury of your own or another's peace or reputation.
- **Humility**. Imitate Jesus and Socrates.[4]

As Franklin went on to discover, it is not enough simply to state objectives. There is also a need to establish some means of keeping our goals in mind. Here is how Franklin measured his progress:

> *I made a little book, in which I allotted a page for each of the virtues. I ruled each page with red ink, so as to have seven columns, one for each day of the week, marking each column with a letter for that day. I crossed these columns with thirteen red lines, marking the beginning of each line with the first letter of one of the virtues, on which line, and in its proper column, I might mark, by a little black spot, every fault I found upon examination to been committed respecting that virtue upon that day.*
>
> *I determined to give a week's strict attention to each of the virtues successively. Thus, in the first week, my great guard was to avoid every least offense against Temperance, leaving the other virtues to their ordinary chance, only marking every evening, the faults of the day. Thus in the first week, if I could keep my first line marked T, clear of spots, I supposed the habit of that virtue so much strengthened, and its opposite weakened, that I might venture extending my attention to include the next, and for the following week, keep both lines clear.[5]*

Every week Franklin would cycle through his list. It was his goal, each quarter, to perfect his habit in that "Virtue Area."

TEMPERANCE							
Eat not to dullness; Drink not to elevation.							
	S	M	T	W	Th	F	S
T							
S	*	*		*		*	
O	**	*	*		*	*	*
R			*			*	
F		*			*		
I			*				
S							
J							
M							
C							
T							
C							
H							

Your Platform to Make It Work

Whether it is people like Ben Franklin, Charles Schwab, Chuck Swindoll, or Ivy Lee, there is a thread to success of these individuals: focus. Every day each of these individuals did what mattered most to achieve fulfillment in those areas most important to them. They simplified their lives. They lived with a sense of "first things first." They knew if the first things did not get done, then nothing else would matter. I have shared their stories with you to set the stage for a final thought: activity management.

In your value areas, there are activities you have determined or will determine to be of critical importance to living the life you have imagined. To help you format your value areas, I'm going to give you some examples from my own experience. My values demand that I:

- Read the Scriptures at least three days each week.
- Have one quality date with my wife every week.
- Spend a minimum of one hour every day with each of my children in uninterrupted, quality time.
- Arrange one major event per month that involves my entire family.
- Spend two hours a week on self-development (books, tapes, videos).
- Review my financial investments for at least thirty minutes twice each week.
- Spend three quality days with my extended family each year.
- Maintain a low-fat food intake daily.
- Workout four days each week for a minimum of one hour.
- Attend worship services every Sunday and attend one study class per week.

The following diagram represents one week.

TIME-BLOCKING SCHEDULE

	MONDAY	TUESDAY	WEDNESDAY	THURSDAY	FRIDAY	SATURDAY	SUNDAY
5 am							
6							
7							
8							
9							
10							
11							
12 pm							
1							
2							
3							
4							
5							
6							
7							
8							
9							
10 pm							

VALUES-BASED LIVING: THE ART OF TIME EFFICIENCY

You will also note this week has not been defined. Enter the powerful tool of a time-blocking schedule, something you will develop over the next several days, weeks, and months. This is not a traditional time-management system. Instead, it is a means to reorder your life and your world so you can accomplish your important activities. To recap: You began in chapter 2 by discovering your purpose, value areas, vision, and mission. In chapter 5, you revisited your vision and mission and then determined what activities needed to happen for you to reach your goals, subsequently fulfilling your vision for that value area. Now, time blocking gives you a visual tool to help you fulfill your activities. The more frequently you accomplish your goals and allow them to become synergistic with your other values, the more likely you will develop a habit in that value area. While time-blocking may seem regimented at first, ultimately it will become so valuable to you and those you love that it will become your personal vehicle for freedom. Here then are the essentials of time-blocking:

There is nothing more important than doing what is most important.

1. For each of your value areas, capture a sense of how frequently you want to do or will need to do certain things. For example, I know I need to work out at least four days each week
2. Determine how much time you will need to carry out your activity. Each of my workouts needs to last one hour.
3. Determine when you will do that activity. I am going to workout on Tuesday, Wednesday, Thursday, and Saturday.
4. Decide at what time during the day you will do this activity. On Tuesday, Wednesday, and Thursday, I will work out from 5 to 6 A.M.; on Saturdays from 1 to 2 P.M.
5. "Block" the time necessary to make this an important part of your schedule. I have included an example of my time-blocking schedule.

	MONDAY	TUESDAY	WEDNESDAY	THURSDAY	FRIDAY	SATURDAY	SUNDAY
5 am	Devotion	—Workout / Devotion—			Devotion	Free Time	Personal Time
6	Kids / Breakfast	Kids / Breakfast	Kids / Breakfast	Kids / Breakfast	Kids / Breakfast		
7						Mens Group Study	Teach Sunday School
8							
9	Work	Work	Work	Work	Family Day	Family Outing	Attend Church Service
10							
11							
12 pm						Workout	
1							
2						Free Time	
3							Dad/Sons Time
4							
5	Family	Family	Family	Family	Social Outing Friends		
6							
7						Sheryl Date Night	
8							
9	Reading	Portfolio Review	Reading	Portfolio Review			Weekly Planning
10 pm							

6. Note the activities that do not need to be block scheduled but which are still key intentional behaviors you want to "live" that day. Things like being smoke free, alcohol free, fat free, frugal, serene, etc., along the lines of Franklin's virtues. These are activities you plant in your brain in the morning and review throughout the day as your affirmations. Affirmations are your self-contained, inner dynamos to help you maintain a positive mental attitude as you take your daily steps toward developing the power to be your best.

7. By now, you should be spending fifteen to thirty minutes each day reviewing your LifeQuest Pyramid and the Life-by-Design planning sheets you completed in the previous chapter. With that said, your time blocks can take on two identities:

    • First, there will be activities that once scheduled become routine and therefore a habit. For example, I no longer need to schedule my workouts because they are part of my habitual routine.

    • Second, if, in my quiet time with God, I sense there are important activities to which I have not paid serious attention recently, I can schedule them for that day or at some later time in the week. For example, suppose I realize I have not shown Sheryl enough appreciation recently. Solution: I may schedule a surprise picnic lunch with her. Or perhaps I haven't had what I feel is quality time with my children, then I would block off an hour to spend time only with them.

Your values are your motivation. Your vision and mission are your guidelines and boundaries. Time-blocking guarantees that you schedule activities that, over time, help you form new habits, break bad ones, enhance your self-image, engage in more positive self-talk, and live your life on-purpose. As your coach, I promise you that time blocking is the most exciting thing you will ever experience. Once you get into it, your life will never be the same. There is nothing more important than doing what is most important.

THE *POWER!* TO BE YOUR BEST!

Plan of Action for Implementing Values-Based Living

1. In what areas of your life do you feel you are less than effective in planning and scheduling?

    *   _____
    *   _____
    *   _____

2. What clutter in your life can you begin to get rid of (or delegate) to help you focus more intensely on those values that are truly important to you?

    *   _____
    *   _____
    *   _____

3. What are five things you can do to simplify your life now? Be specific.

    *   _____
    *   _____
    *   _____
    *   _____
    *   _____

When you have completed
these three assignments,
go to my website at
www.toddduncan.com
and download a *time blocking
master* to help you complete
your new schedule.
See you on-line. —*TD*

www.toddduncan.com

Action Planner Notes

_____

_____

_____

_____

_____

_____

_____

_____

_____

_____

_____

_____

_____

_____

_____

_____

_____

_____

_____

_____

_____

_____

_____

_____

Part III

The Art of
Wealth

CHAPTER SEVEN

For Men Only

We can do no great things—only small things with great love. **Mother Teresa**

Remember, your family spells love: T-I-M-E **Zig Ziglar**

When I was a child, I used to speak as a child, think as a child, reason as a child; when I became a man, I did away with childish things. **1 Corinthians 13:11,** NASB

---

he women I have asked to preview what you are about to read have told me that this may be the most relevant chapter in this book. That's because it underlines the short-comings most men manifest in the areas of relationships, parenting, and overall decision making. I should warn all men who read beyond this point that you should deposit your ego at the beginning of this paragraph and leave it there. What follows is nothing but straight talk. I want to help you be all you can be in these areas. I am not there yet (Sheryl will tell you), but regardless of my imperfections, I have some workable solutions to help you get everything you want in your relationships whether you are dating, married, separated, or divorced and whether you have children or not.

I want to start by recalling a beautiful June day in Los Angeles, California, when I was with my dad and seventy-five thousand other men who were learning how to be better men, dads, and fathers. It was one of the most exciting days of my life. Dr. Tony Evans was part of that special day as he spoke about meeting the challenge of being the best man one can be. Evans is a passionate African-American pastor from Texas, and when he wants to make a point, he does so emphatically.

On this day Evans said that one of our major responsibilities is to help give meaning to the lives of our wives and children. If they are to be secure in this world, then in addition to their relationship with God, they must have a fully functioning relationship with a husband and a father. He reminded us that if we are not fully functioning, then we cannot play this vital role in the family relationship. Here is what he said:

> *If the man is messed up and he is in a relationship, then the relationship is messed up.*
>
> *And, if a messed-up man is in a messed-up relationship that happens to be a marriage, then the marriage is messed up.*
>
> *And, if a messed-up man is in a messed-up relationship that is a messed-up marriage and that marriage happens to have children, then the family is messed up.*
>
> *And if a messed-up man is in a messed-up marriage that happens to be a family and the family is messed up and that family lives in a community, then that community is messed up.*
>
> *And if a messed-up man is in a messed-up marriage that is a messed-up family in a messed-up*

community and that community is in a city, then the city is messed up.

And if a messed-up man is in a messed-up marriage that is a messed-up family in a messed-up community in a messed-up city and that city is in a state, then the state is messed up.

And if a messed-up man is in a messed-up marriage that is a messed-up family in a messed-up community in a messed-up city in a messed-up state and that state is in a country, then the country is messed up.

And if a messed-up man is in a messed-up marriage that is a messed-up family in a messed-up community in a messed-up city in a messed-up state in a messed-up country and that country is in the world, then you have a messed up world.

So if we don't want a messed-up world, it starts with not having messed-up countries, which comes from not having messed-up states, which results from not having messed-up cities which means there are no messed-up communities, which requires families that aren't messed up which only happens if marriages aren't messed up. And the best way to make sure of that is to not have messed-up men.

Guys! It starts with you and me. It's not just Tony Evans's mandate, it's God's command that we be the best we can be. This is the first requirement for any successful relationship. No matter what your background, how dysfunctional your family (remember, no one has an exclusive claim to a dysfunctional relationship), or how bad your life has been to this point, there are steps you can take to turn it around. It comes down to a choice, the choice to be or not to be the man God designed you to be. In this and the next chapter I want to give you some powerful ammunition to help you be that man.

Drop the E and Go

It may be tough medicine to swallow, men, but about 95 percent of our problems occur because we cannot get out of the way of our egos. How you deal with this single important issue determines the quality of your relationships with your wife and your children, the atmosphere in your home, and ultimately whether you make the right kind of impact. I am learning this lesson in my own life in more ways than I can count. When I think I have it under control, my ego erupts, bigger than life, and I blow it, becoming powerless and useless to the ones I love. We have to learn that the best way for our relationships to mature is for us to drop the *e* from our ego so we can *go* forward. Imagine this headline on the front page of your local newspaper one morning:

At a Promise Keepers' conference in 1996, Bishop George McKinney Jr. said, "When you don't listen to your wife, you miss at least 50 percent of what God is trying to tell you." I found this out for myself the hard way, naturally.

Sheryl and I had left our home in Newport Beach to go sailing with John and Jan Parker in San Diego. This would be Sheryl's first encounter with the Parkers. We arrived at the dock, and before long we were sailing in the bay. John and I started talking business, and I learned that John had a profitable speaking practice and Jan owned a successful speaker's bureau. These were definitely my kind of people.

For most of the afternoon, we discussed the possibilities of joining forces to create a new training-and-development business. It would be a fantastic opportunity for all of us. While I spoke with John, Sheryl spent time with Jan. It was a great, glorious southern California day.

When the sun began to set, we said our thanks and good-byes and headed home. Before we left, I assured John and Jan that we would be talking again the following week about the exciting possibility of working together.

As we drove home, I turned to Sheryl and asked, "Well, what do you think, Honey?"

She said, "I'm not sure. I didn't get a good feeling about Jan at all. I'm not sure I trust her."

"How's that?" I asked. "What did she do or say to give you that feeling?"

Sheryl said, "I'm not sure, it's just this feeling I have."

It may be tough medicine to swallow, men, but about 95 percent of our problems occur because we cannot get out of the way of our egos.

Well, I needed something a little more concrete than that. As much as I love my wife, this was *my* business and I would make the final decision, thank you very much! (How's that for an open mind!) Within a month, John and I agreed to form a new corporation which would be headquartered in Jan's offices. She had plenty of room, and we would grow from there. We were on our way to fame and fortune.

John was about thirty years my senior, and so my goal was to learn from him and build the business so that when he eventually slowed down, he could retire with the sure-to-be-successful enterprise falling into my capable hands. All was going well in our new partnership until the day I landed a huge contract. Based on our financial relationship, John would receive 25 percent of the revenue I earned, and he would cover all expenses.

Within a month, however, after I had paid him the agreed-upon percentage of my income, John's attitude changed. As I began to make more money than he did, instead of supporting my economic growth, he suddenly wanted all the money to go into a pot to be distributed evenly between the two partners. Not a bad idea, I suppose; however, it was not our agreement, and so it was a bad idea. John was slowing down, and I was accelerating my pace in the business. I did some quick math and knew his idea would not work for me.

Within eighteen months, our partnership was in trouble. Jan was throwing roadblocks in my path, speaking unkindly about me, and made it a point to spread the chasm even wider between John and me. Within twenty-four months we were history. It cost me twenty thousand dollars to dissolve the partnership, another two hundred thousand dollars in lost income, and thousands of dollars more to create a new company—everything from legal counsel, computers, office equipment, letterhead and supplies, right down to the postage stamps.

After that tempestuous relationship with John and Jan with all its relational and economic twists and turns, I ended up where Sheryl wanted me to be in the first place: in my own business. No partners. I should have listened to her!

As Sheryl predicted, our new company took off, and in the middle of our growth spurt, we ended up leasing seventy-five hundred square feet of office space in one of the town's high-rent districts. Sheryl warned me not to go so far, but I countered her with the usual keen insights: *Come on Sheryl, not again. Please! This time I know what I'm doing. The thing with John and Jan was a fluke!* I explained that the high-class, high-rent, high-visibility environment would be good for the employees we were hiring. Here, again, I had hired twenty-eight people, and Sheryl told me not to do it. I explained that their salaries would be financed by our expected growth.

You will remember this story from chapter 3. The results of my brilliant decision? We grew too fast, spent too much, got too cocky, and came crashing down at a total cost of $750,000.

You have stories of your own, don't you? You too have made decisions against the advice of your mate only to wish you had taken her wise counsel. For once in our lives, men, let us learn this truth: The women in our lives have an instinct we will never have. That's why it is imperative that we listen to their intuition and take it into consideration whenever we have major decisions to make.

It makes no difference what the decision is: The women in our lives have the answers to our questions. So put your ego aside and pay attention to your wife! To listen to her, really listen, and to realize her counsel is right most of the time, is to (a) be smart and (b) create an atmosphere that the best outside consultant could never provide. The impact of our response will fill voids we never knew existed; our loving and listening will strengthen the cement that keeps our relationships alive forever.

Guys, Serve Your Wife

For all our good intentions, however, our egos cannot play dead forever. The least nudge or threat to our testosterone-saturated egos resurrects its desire to take over, do the caveman thing, and show the world how a real man rises to the occasion. Granted, part of this is the way we men are wired. When a couple is looking to buy a home, the man invariably is ready to buy long before the woman decides which is the right one. The man usually buys the car he wants, not the one his wife desires. The man usually thinks about his own sexual satisfaction, oblivious to the sexual needs of his wife. The man rarely admits he is wrong, even when what the woman says makes sense.

For once in our lives, men, let us learn this truth: The women in our lives have an instinct we will never have.

What is it about our ego that leads us into this divisive behavior? The central issue is our self-centeredness, a negative expression of unmet needs that pushes intimacy and rapport out of reach. This is the opposite of the command we men receive from the Bible on how we are to care for our wives. We are told to "love your wives, just as Christ also loved the church." If this is our model, then we must see ourselves as "servants" to our wives while still being the "leaders" in our homes. The two roles are not contradictory, although our egos will fight us all the way. God has outlined a plan to make marriages thrive, outlined in Ephesians 5.

Today, when we mention concepts such as "authority" or "submission" in polite conversation, the dialog often suddenly becomes impolite: You've got to be kidding. That's the language of the dinosaurs. Get with it. Who believes that stuff anymore! We need to hear the whole message and not get hung up on a couple of words.

This is one of the most gentle, fair, loving passages in all Scripture. The man is not to become a "dictator" in the marriage, nor is his wife to assume the role of "slave." To the contrary, the message says the man is to "lead" by demonstrating his "love." The wife should "submit" only when there is manly leadership in the home, not overlordship. A woman is invariably drawn to the man who provides loving leadership and resists making self-centered demands. A wife submits gladly when her husband makes good decisions for himself and for the family. She takes over only when his leadership wanes.

There is no such thing as dictatorial marriage. This adjective and noun do not belong together. Only a marriage formed of love, compassion, trust, service, caring, and mutual respect will thrive and stay alive. If you do not serve your family, you are not qualified to lead your family.

> *A woman is invariably drawn to the man who provides loving leadership and resists making self-centered demands. . . . Only a marriage formed of love, compassion, trust, service, caring, and mutual respect will thrive and stay alive.*

The Power Platform

Authors Gary Smalley and John Trent offer these insights in their book *The Hidden Value of a Man*, a great treatise on marriage and the husband-wife relationship:

> *When God speaks of authority and submission, in no way is He endorsing "Lording it over" the other. To the world, headship in the home has come to mean the dictatorial, demeaning authority of a*

man. But from God's Word, it's clear that a man is to lead in one thing: love.

"Husbands, love your wives, just as Christ loved the church and gave himself up for her to make her holy, cleansing her by the washing with water through the word." Again we read, "In this same way, husbands ought to love their wives as their own bodies." (Ephesians 5:28)

Submission has come to stand for knuckling under, swallowing your real feelings, backing yourself into a corner, turning off your brain, and being dysfunctional and codependent. [This is where the women's movement does not get it. If it did, they would be the happiest women on earth. —TD] *But that's exactly the opposite of what the Bible means when it tells women to submit to their husbands. In Ephesians 5, before wives are called to submit, we read, "Submit to one another out of reverence for Christ" (vs. 22). In Greek, the original language of the New Testament, being "subject to" another person was actually a military term. It's a word that speaks of support, voluntary allegiance, and cooperation. It leaves room for creativity and even questioning while maintaining a high commitment. It carries with it none of the damaging misconceptions of high control or manipulation but instead connotes teamwork and mutual respect."[1]*

If we only withdraw from our accounts without making regular deposits, we will fast be overdrawn if we are not already.

The goals of a successful relationship must be mutual respect and teamwork, not unilateral submission from one party. If these two defining characteristics are missing, any relationship is headed for failure. Guess what, men? It is up to you and me to initiate the process. The most direct way you can do this is to add value to your wife's life.

The Art of Adding Value

I wonder if you own the kind of bank account that keeps replenishing itself. The kind that requires no deposits but spits out great sums of money every time you need to make a withdrawal. Every month your statement shows a growing balance. There is never a question about there always being enough in your account. In fact, the bank calls you and asks if it can give you even more. In your sweet dreams! The truth is that neither banks nor life work that way. Nor do marriages. If we only withdraw from our accounts without making regular deposits, we will fast be overdrawn if we are not already.

Men, our wives are telling us that they need more regular deposits into their accounts.

Men, our wives are telling us that they need more regular deposits into their accounts. They need to know that we love them more than anyone or anything else in our world. They need to know we are unequivocally committed to their success and happiness and to our children's well being. They also need to know that we will never ever leave them. This is the first step in the fine art of adding value.

Dr. John C. Maxwell, founder of Injoy Ministries, says that to add value to those relationships most meaningful to us is the single greatest way to protect our relationships. It is the uncompromising effort to make an ongoing difference in the lives of those people who are important to you: your wife and your kids.

Go 100 percent of the way. If you want to add value to the most important earthly relationship you have, then learn how to not keep score. When you stop at 50 percent because you feel you have done enough and it's "her move," you are violating the most important key to a thriving relationship—reciprocity. The greatest way to "get" in the relationship with your wife is to "give" unconditionally.

Remember, you can choose to subordinate the *e* in your ego so you can really *go*. If your marriage lacks vitality and closeness, you need to give more. If you have been giving and you do not feel it is working, assess your motivation. Have you been giving to get or have you been giving to give? In any event, from this day forward, pour it on. Go all out in loving your wife with the suggestions and ideas that follow and you will be amazed at your results. Let me share six ideas with you on how to add value to your wife.

1. Honor her accomplishments: Praise her out loud where she and other people can hear you. Has your wife ever done something that made you especially proud? Do you regularly look for positive things you can acknowledge? I would suggest that you might ask yourself every day, How can I praise or acknowledge my wife today?

Go 100 percent of the way. If you want to add value to the most important earthly relationship you have, then learn how to not keep score.

I am not suggesting a canned speech that sounds hollow and false. Say it from your heart, not your head; say what you mean and mean what you say. If you do not tell your wife you love her, how will she know you appreciate her? If you do not recognize her accomplishments verbally, how will she have the confidence to feel good about herself when she is with you?

You do not need this attention as much as she does. As men, we recognize ourselves, praise ourselves, and emphasize our "good side" more often than we realize and to the extent of being prideful. Our wives do not do this. They wait for us to tell them how wonderful they are. Here's something to remember: 45 percent of communication comes from our words and how we say them. There's a lot of difference between, "Dear, when I look at you, time stands still," and, "Honey, you have a face that could stop a clock." Isn't it amazing how similar the words are in those two sentences? Yet one will elicit a hug and the other has much harsher repercussions.

Some of the best compliments you give your wife are brief statements that mean you still care for her: "Honey, you look fantastic!" "Sweetheart, you worked so hard on that delicious dinner, let me clean up the kitchen tonight." "You know, I love you more now than I did when I married you." Of course, the nicest thing you can say when you have a newborn is, "Don't get up. I can change-feed-rock him. You go back to sleep." You know what you can say and what she'll appreciate. Practice in front of a mirror if you have to. The gist of the matter is that you should get accustomed to saying words of appreciation to your wife. She may faint in disbelief the first time she hears you say something like this, but it's worth the risk!

2. Set goals together. Setting goals together as a couple is a powerful way to show how much you care. It is a cliché, but a good one: Your wife will never care how much you know until she knows how much you care. Goal setting is a great way to demonstrate that you are not going to do this alone. Goal setting fosters unity. It's a bond and shows a singleness of purpose.

Smalley and Trent have some great insights to offer here, too. "Without first determining your direction as a couple and as parents, you'll never reach the level of fulfillment you could. In fact, the absence of clear goals is one of the biggest problems we see in families around the world. Husbands and wives simply do not know where they are going, and without clear, overall goals of headship and submission guiding a relationship can be impossible."[2]

What does your family stand for? Where do you want to go together? What does your family value? Are you living those values? What is your vision for these areas? What should your family unit be doing regularly to fulfill its goals? When your family does things together, it grows together; when it grows together, individual family members feel good about who they are and the contribution they make. Your wife is the most important member on your team. Take her out to dinner and set some goals with her. Using the insights in chapter 2, work with her to complete the exercise of building her pyramid. If you are a woman, have your husband complete chapter 2. A boat will never reach its destination unless everyone rows in the same direction.

3. *Invest in her goals.* One of the most meaningful things I think Sheryl and I ever did was to invest in her schooling. For many reasons she was unable to attend college after high school. Shortly after we were married, however, she expressed an interest in pursuing her education. Since we had no children at the time, this made sense. We made the decision and put out the money that allowed her to study for her bachelor's degree in nursing. Six years later, she completed her goal. One of the proudest days of my life was when I sat in the amphitheater at Point Loma College and watched Sheryl receive her diploma. To top it off, she graduated *cum laude*. I cannot tell you what those six years did for her self-worth, but I can summarize some of the benefits we gained as a family because her education empowered her as a person, a wife, and later as a mother. The results have been amazing and far outweigh the financial and other sacrifices we made during those six years. All men should want to make a major investment in the women with whom they share their lives.

Sheryl wants to be the best mother she can be. I recognize that. I also was determined that she should be the best mother she could be. Therefore, we made a decision to eliminate some of the things that traditionally hinder her achieving this goal. Think for a moment about some of the things you might do to make such an investment in your wife's life. Perhaps you can have someone come in once a week or once a month to tidy up the house and maybe help with the laundry. If it's your wife's desire to be the full-time mother she wants to be and you're financially able, have someone come in every day to clean the house, do the laundry, and cook the meals. This does not require you to be financially independent, nor does it assume that your wife doesn't work. What it suggests is that when you realign your priorities, you can and will find the money to allow you and your wife to realize your mutually agreed-upon worthy goals.

When you make this kind of investment, you create an environment that brings you together, rather than keeping you away from each other because of umpteen chores. I emphasize that you do not need to be financially independent. You just figure it out!

4. Touch her meaningfully. Lee Shapiro, one of my colleagues, is a retired judge. In San Diego he is known as the "hugging judge." Every time he sees you, he gives you a big bear hug and then, after anointing your lapel with an adhesive red heart, he instructs you to find someone you can hug and "transplant" the little red heart to his or her lapel.

What a great act of repetitive love! I can think of no better way to add value to your wife than to demonstrate this love for her through meaningful touch. Do not forget the Mars-Venus thing. You can tell your wife you love her until the cows come home, but words will never carry the weight of a hug, a kiss, or a tender caress. While words and tonality are 45 percent of the communication process, body language communicates 55 percent of our message. Our women need to *feel* our presence as well as *hear* it.

> While words and tonality are 45 percent of the communication process, body language communicates 55 percent of our message. Our women need to feel *our presence as well as* hear *it.*

When I come home from the office each day, I tune my radar in for Sheryl. Although the first people I may see are my two little boys—and I sweep them off their feet and hug them—the one I am really hunting for is Sheryl. I want my two sons to know that she is my priority. I once read of a brother and sister who, when older, told their friends, "We always felt secure growing up, because we knew that Daddy loved our mom even more than he loved us." That is a powerful truth and one of the prescriptions for the lifelong self-esteem sadly lacking in so many of our grown children.

5. Celebrate the milestones. Sheryl's favorite calendar date is February 5. It is more important than any other day of the year. Why? It's her birthday, and she loves to celebrate it. In fact, in our family, she has the reputation of turning this one day of joy into a virtual two-week festival. I cannot make it any more clear when I say to clients, wherever they are in the world, "Folks, I just don't miss this one." Because February 5 is so special to Sheryl, I always know I will do something magnificent for her on that day. Two years ago I wrote a poem and gave it to her in an envelope on the morning of her birthday. I am sharing this with her permission.

Your birthday is near!
It's time to toast.
We're on our way,
up the California coast

This is the year
to give you the best.
Because after September,
you'll need your rest. [Our first child]

So pack your bags—
our flight's at eleven.
With three stops to go,
we're in seventh heaven.

An awesome view,
such a wonderful treat.
A weekend for you,
complete with a suite.

Alone and in love
in this beautiful place.
Dinner, romance,
and a fireplace

I love you, Sheryl,
with all of my soul.
Your happiness and peace
is my wish and my goal.

Happy Birthday

Also in the envelope were two airline tickets and some spending money. Since the plane was leaving in just three hours, we had to hustle. We quickly packed and within hours, we were at one of our great hideaways in Santa Barbara.

If you want to be a hero to your wife, give something like *that* a try!

Aside from your wife's birthday, one of the most important days of your life together was the day you two said, "I do." Most of us wait until the last minute to figure out how to honor this date and do something meaningful for our wives. We probably spend more time arranging our golf games than we do celebrating the most important day in our married life. Why not get into the habit of honoring this special day every day, or at least one day each month? Let her know that your marriage is the most important event of your life. Do it with flowers, a note, cooking dinner that night (even if you have to get some help), taking her out, giving her breakfast in bed, cleaning the house, or giving her the day off. You name it. You are a genius at the office, guys, now be a genius at home! The important thing is to honor and cherish her. Make being married exciting!

6. *Date her regularly.* When was the last time you opened the car door for your wife? When was the last time you pulled her chair out for her at a restaurant and then rose to seat her again after she returned from the ladies room? Men, nobody does this. So why not set the trend? When was the last time you brought her a single red rose before you went out? When was the last time you wrote her a letter or sent her a card? What did you do to win her before you married her, and why aren't you still doing it?

One of the best ways to add value to your wife's account is to be as passionate today as when you dated her. Why did you move heaven and earth to get her, and now you won't even move a chair to help seat her? The answer is simple: We do not have to.

Oh, really? As I write this, I am in Australia, but Sheryl will receive three cards from me during the two weeks that I am away. I wrote these cards to Sheryl and my sons before I left the country, and they are being sent at prescheduled times. When speaking with her today on the phone, she had just received the first one and was overwhelmed at my thoughtfulness. I'm not bragging. I have to work at this sort of thing because it does not come naturally to me, and it may not come naturally to you. So what! The proper golf swing is not natural either. We have to work at it, practice it, and keep doing it until we get it right. It's the same for a marriage. Good communication is hard work.

Here's something to keep you accountable: On your dates, for good measure, have your wife rate your performance as a husband, a dad, a friend, a lover, and as the spiritual head of the home.

One of the most effective ways to deplete the account with your wife is to take her for granted. In marriage, it is not how you start that counts but how you finish. Most of the men I know are losing this battle. Marriage is not a matter of convenience; it is a mission of commitment. We need to suck it up and finish big. It is one thing to get our marriage going, but another to keep it flowing. There is no better way to keep the fire burning than to keep the dates churning. That's right, one date right after another.

Now that you understand the power of time blocking, you should have your dates time-blocked as nonnegotiable. Here's something to keep you accountable: On your dates, for good measure, have your wife rate your performance as a husband, a dad, a friend, a lover, and as the spiritual head of the home. If you want to add value to her life, ask her where she thinks you need to add it. You cannot lose with this approach! If you are always getting better, and you communicate that you want to be the best you can be, what woman would not get excited by that approach? Try it today. You will see results within a week. If not, give me a call and I will refund the money you paid for this book.

In summary, here are your keys to a successful marriage:

- Honor your wife.
- Be a meaningful communicator.
- Appreciate each other's strengths and weaknesses.
- Touch her like you love her.
- Bond together by being together.

Make your marriage the most amazing relationship in your life.

Plan of Action for Being the Husband God Designed You to Be

1. What is keeping you from developing complete intimacy with your wife? What will you do to get rid of these distractions?

    _____

    _____

    _____

2. What are your thoughts on how you might be a better leader in the home? How might your new approach to leadership affect your wife?

    _____

    _____

    _____

3. List up to five behaviors you can begin to do to add value for your wife:

    • _____

    • _____

    • _____

    • _____

    • _____

4. What are the two most important things you have committed to start doing today with your wife?

    • _____

    • _____

When you have completed
these four assignments,
go to my website at
www.toddduncan.com
for ten inspirational quotes
to help you be the husband
God created you to be.
See you on-line. —*TD*

www.toddduncan.com

Action Planner Notes

EIGHT Date Your Daughters and Knight Your Sons

Train up a child in the way he should go, even when he is old, he will not depart from it. **Proverbs 22:6,** NASB

hild rearing is a tough topic, but if you are to develop the power to be your best, then your children must also have the power to be their best, and that, my friend, is up to you. The simple rule: Get to your kids before their peers and society does. Our kids are in trouble, and it is up to you and me to do something about it. There is a war raging in the streets of America for the lives of our children. We simply must win that war because, frankly, the statistics are against us.

Steve Farrar, in his book *Point Man,* compiled the following statistics. Some of them, we've heard before. The rest are shocking:

- One out of two marriages end in divorce.
- The median age for divorce is thirty-four for men and thirty for women.
- In 1960 a woman maintained one out of every ten households with no husband present; in 1986 a woman maintained one out of every six households with no husband present.

- Tonight enough teenagers to fill the Rose Bowl, the Cotton Bowl, the Sugar Bowl, the Orange Bowl, the Fiesta Bowl, and the Super Bowl will prostitute themselves to support a drug habit.
- One million teenage girls will get pregnant out of wedlock this year.
- Five hundred thousand of those pregnancies will be aborted.
- Of all fourteen-year-old girls alive today, 40 percent will become pregnant by their nineteenth birthday.
- 60 percent of all church-involved teenagers are sexually active.
- 60 percent of American high school seniors have used illegal drugs.
- Every seventy-eight seconds, a teenager in America attempts suicide.[1]

When our marriages are right, we add to our accounts rather than withdraw from them. That kind of addition generates emotional energy that we can use on growing our kids to be people of principle and character, where personal integrity, pride, moral absolutes, purity, and spiritual intimacy are more important than peer acceptance.

If you are to develop the power to be your best, then your children must also have the power to be their best, and that, my friend, is up to you. The simple rule: Get to your kids before their peers and society does.

When the family unit functions properly, a new list of statistics emerges—positive ones. Joe White surveyed one thousand kids from his summer camps, which draw over five thousand youngsters, mostly from God-centered homes where mom and dad are committed to each other. Here is the encouraging news:

- 95 percent of the boys say their fathers regularly tell them, "I love you."

- 98 percent of the girls say their mothers tell them regularly, "I'm proud of you" or "You're doing a great job."
- 91 percent of the kids say their parents play games with them.
- 94 percent say their fathers attend their athletic events.
- 97 percent of the boys say they get hugs from their dads regularly.
- 100 percent of the girls say they get hugs from their mom and dads.
- 100 percent of the girls remember having stories read to them by their mothers; 85 percent of the boys recall having stories read to them by their fathers.
- 89 percent of the boys say their fathers have taken them fishing.
- 100 percent of the girls say their parents have taken them to Sunday school.
- 80 percent of the kids say they are against premarital sex.
- 92 percent have never touched an illegal drug.[2]

One of the most important things I hope you will glean from this book is this: If you are not spending time in meaningful activities with your family, then you will create less of the right results with your spouse and kids.

How would your kids answer the survey? One of the most important things I hope you will glean from this book is this: If you are not spending time in meaningful activities with your family, then you will create less of the right results with your spouse and kids.

Everything we need to know about raising our daughters to be women and our sons to be men can be found in one great verse from the Bible: "Fathers, do not provoke your children to wrath, but bring them up in the training and admonition of the Lord" (Ephesians 6:4). We must do the things that help our kids become the women and men God designed them to be.

Sex and Drugs

The single greatest contribution parents can make to help their children move into authentic adulthood is to teach them what God has to say about the key issues of life. Let's look again at the words from Ephesians 6:4, "Fathers, do not provoke your children to wrath, but bring them up in the training and admonition of the Lord." Men, we know that our wives play a major role in the raising of our children, but it is our responsibility to lead that effort. What our kids need most are full-time dads.

The two most negative forces in our kids' lives today are sex outside of marriage and drugs and alcohol. You know the statistics, and whether you believe in God or not, I submit that it would be impossible to argue against the Bible's approach in addressing these issues. I am sure you would also rather have your kids respond to survey number two above, rather than the first one. Here are a few thoughts to help prime you for some tough words that will appear in the next several pages:

You shall not lie with a male as with a woman. It is an abomination.
Leviticus 18:22

Do not be deceived. Neither fornicators, nor idolaters, nor adulterers, nor homosexuals, nor sodomites, nor thieves, nor covetous, nor drunkards, nor revilers, nor extortioners will inherit the kingdom of God. ***1 Corinthians 6:9–10***

It is good for a man not to touch a woman. Nevertheless, because of sexual immorality, let each man have his own wife, and let each woman have her own husband. Let the husband render to his wife the affection due her, and likewise also the wife to her husband.   **1 Corinthians 7:1–3**

Now the works of the flesh are evident, which are: adultery, fornication, uncleanness, lewdness, idolatry, sorcery, hatred, contentions, jealousies, outbursts of wrath, selfish ambitions, dissensions, heresies, envy, murders, drunkenness, revelries, and the like; of which I tell you beforehand, just as I also told you in time past, that those who practice such things will not inherit the kingdom of God.
Galatians 5:19–21

Marriage is honorable among all, and the bed undefiled; but fornicators and adulterers God will judge.   **Hebrews 13:4**

Dads who are effective at parenting don't let their daughters or sons grow up to practice homosexuality, engage in sex outside of marriage, or be drunkards and do drugs. Instead, dads bring them up in the discipline of the Lord. Each of these unacceptable behaviors comes from ineffective parenting, media influence, and peer pressure, not from genes or heredity. Please understand, if you said you would rather have your kids be the ones who responded to the second survey, then these are the moral absolutes you must represent and strive to help shape your kids future. Let me share with you some eye-opening thoughts on these issues.

Homosexuals are not born; they are made through ineffective parenting and role identification. In a book endorsed by the National Institute of Health, *Growing Up Straight*, Peter Wyden explained:

> *Research findings overwhelmingly indicate that homosexuals are not born but bred...there is increasing agreement that homosexuals rarely (if ever) occur without some important (or controlling) contribution from parents. Many parents underestimate their own importance as models for the behavior of their children especially while the children are still young...they should appreciate that a mother's acceptance of her role as a truly feminine woman will communicate itself to a daughter at a remarkably early age; and that a mother's respect for the father's role as head of the family will help a small boy to grow up to be masculine. On the other hand, if parents themselves are unsure about what constitutes appropriate male and female behavior today—or, especially if they are competitive with each other—their children are bound to become confused about their own place in the scheme of things.[3]*

A father recently asked his son, "Is rock star Michael Jackson a man or a woman?" The young boy, not knowing any better, answered, "Both." I agree with George Gilder who said,

"I do not want my son to be told that he does not have to be masculine to succeed as a man. I don't want my daughters to grow up to be like feminist leaders now reportedly longing to have children as they approach their fifties."[4]

Sueann Robinson Ambrom offers this thought in her book, *Child Development*: "In gender role development, the evidence points to fathers as having the more important influence, not only in fostering a male self-concept in boys, but femininity in girls. Mothers do contribute to their daughters' adoption of the feminine role, but have little influence on the masculinity of their sons."[5]

As dads, we need to establish a role model that defines authentic manhood. We must teach our boys what God says about their role as a boy, a man, a husband, and a father. This is the "instruction" to which Ephesians 6 refers. More on this later in the chapter.

A father recently asked his son, "Is rock star Michael Jackson a man or a woman?" The young boy, not knowing any better, answered, "Both."

What Is Safe Sex?

When it comes to educating your kids about sex it is up to you, dad. Dr. Howard Hendricks says, "We should not be ashamed to discuss that which God was not ashamed to create." When it comes to teaching, answering questions, how it works, and why it is important, you are it. It is imperative that your kids get the straight talk on sex from you. If they do not, guess where they will hear about it? I do not think that is the result you want.

It is important to recognize that there is no such thing as safe sex outside of marriage. Ask Magic Johnson, the former basketball superstar with the Los Angeles Lakers, if sex is safe outside of marriage. The apostle Paul said that the reason you are to take a wife is to make sure that you do not fall prey to the temptations of immorality. That is why you and I must teach our children—by what we say and do—to understand why the marriage bed is to remain undefiled and pure.

Dr. Ed Cole spoke to this when he shared the following with more than fifty-five thousand other dads: "The purity of marriage and the loss of virginity is the actual completion of the marriage bond. It signifies the complete and pure commitment that two people are making to one another. And, if one or the other has had sexual relations, then this bond cannot happen, for it has happened before. If they have not had sexual intercourse previously, then when the penis penetrates the hymen and the blood of the woman covers the male part, the covenant of marriage has been completed. Marriage and sex were created by God. Isn't it fascinating to see the correlation between this and His son's death on the cross, and the shedding of his blood which covers our sins. This is God's covenant to us."

When it comes to educating your kids about sex it is up to you, dad. Dr. Howard Hendricks says, "We should not be ashamed to discuss that which God was not ashamed to create."

According to Cole, there are seven principles of fatherhood:

1. The father must establish the atmosphere in the home.
2. The father must love his family redemptively.
3. The father must let the children see his decisions.
4. You're either a fabulous father or a deadly dad.
5. The father must walk his talk.
6. The father must teach absolute truth.
7. The father must give his family four things: (1) intimacy, (2) discipline, (3) love, and (4) values.

In the stadium in which Cole spoke to thousands of fathers and sons, he asked every unmarried boy and man in that audience who were virgins to stand and make a pledge in front of God and their dads, if they were with them, to remain pure until the day of their marriage. If they had already had sex outside of marriage, he asked them to recommit to a life of purity until they were married. Unfortunately, the alternative today to that kind of experience is "sex education" being taught in "health" classes throughout America's schools.

Of course, my first question is, Why is the school teaching my kids about sex? That is my job as a dad. I cannot speak for you, but I do not want my daughter or son seeing a movie at school that shows two unwed people preparing for sexual intercourse. I certainly do not want the instructor to give my kids the impression that this is normal behavior. I definitely do not want the instructor to pass out condoms to my thirteen-year-old daughter and then, as part of a class exercise, teach her to roll it over a boy's extended finger as "practice" for the real thing.

Why is the school teaching my kids about sex? That is my job as a dad.

Add to this amazing reality that teachers promote condom use to make sure our kids do not get AIDS when they are having unwed sexual relations. There is no safe sex outside of marriage. Condoms are porous; they have holes in them. The holes are measured to 50 microns, and they do not allow sperm to pass through because sperm is measured at approximately 400 microns. The biological structure for HIV, however, is only 4 microns. How many of those can fit through one 50-micron hole in a condom? No thanks! I do not want my son or daughter to take that risk and see their lives altered forever.

Dating Our Daughters and Knighting Our Sons

The best way for our kids to grow up to be sexually pure, reserving for their marriage the awesome gift of sex that God created for them to enjoy, is for us as dads to be an early resource to them. This means that we would be well advised to "Date Our Daughters" and "Knight Our Sons." Dr. Peter Blitchington explains: "Fathers play a strong role in their daughter's future sexual adjustment. Women who have a strong, stable relationship with a loving father usually find the adjustment to mature femininity much easier. They are usually more secure in their sexual nature and they find it easier to love their husbands."[6]

Recently my friend Bob Shank, president of Priority Living and father of two married daughters, shared the following story with me. "I decided when Erin and Shannon were about six that I was going to start dating them," Bob said. "I wanted my girls to understand what it would be like to date the right guy." He wanted to demonstrate the characteristics that he wanted them to look for in the men his daughters would later be dating and specifically in the men they would ultimately marry. So, on every date, he did things like open the car door for them, pull their chairs out for them, order for them, show interest in them, and talk about God in front of them. Bob created a frame of reference for them so that they would have high standards.

Women who have a strong, stable relationship with a loving father usually find the adjustment to mature femininity much easier. They are usually more secure in their sexual nature and they find it easier to love their husbands.

When his daughters approached their teen years, their discussions began to center on sex. Bob told them what was appropriate and what wasn't appropriate while dating. He explained that the greatest gift they could give their husbands would be purity on their wedding night. He also emphasized that purity should also be the criteria for the man they married. For each of the girls, when the time was right, he gave them a "promise ring." It was a ring that symbolized that they would remain pure until the day they were to be married. The two girls wore the rings every day as a reminder to themselves and to the guy they were dating of what the rules were.

Bob told me, "I will never forget when I was standing at the back of the church on Shannon's wedding day. As we were having a private time prior to walking down the aisle together, she looked at me, raising her left hand and removing her promise ring, and said, "Dad, I kept my promise." What an incredible moment that would be for any dad. This is what Ephesians 6 means when it says, "Bring them up in the training and admonition of the Lord."

Now, what about our boys? How do we communicate the importance of sexual purity to these bodies with raging hormones? One of the best illustrations on how to teach your son about the perils of sex outside of marriage is found in the "wisdom book," the Old Testament Book of Proverbs. The context of Proverbs 5 is that Solomon wants his son to know how to handle his sexuality. Solomon talks with his son about how to deal with sexual situations, the penalty of not dealing with temptation, and the reward to be received if handled appropriately.

In this amazing chapter, there are more than fifty salutations to his son as the king gives his boy firm instruction on godly living. Pick up a Bible and read these powerful truths. You will never be the same dad again.

- In verses 1–6, Solomon tells his son about the kind of woman who can destroy him.
- In verses 7–14, he tells his son to avoid this kind of woman, suggesting that the best way not to be tempted is not to get too close to the flame.
- In verses 15–23, he shares with his son the joy of the victory if he saves himself for a pure, fulfilling sexual relationship within the bond of marriage.

One of the books on my must-read list is Robert Lewis's book, *Raising a Modern Day Knight*. I agree with Lewis when he says:

In my estimation, fathers today are coming up short with their sons at three critical points. First, we have failed to deliver to our sons a clear, inspiring, biblically grounded definition of manhood. How critical is that? It's comparable to a hunter without a gun...or a soccer game without a ball...or a cross-country trip without a map. Telling a boy to "be a man" without defining manhood is like saying, "Be a success." It sounds good. But practically, it takes you nowhere.

Second, most fathers lack a directional process that calls their sons to embrace the manhood they should be able to define. Typically, what passes for masculine training in most homes is vague and hit-or-miss. We assume our sons will somehow "get it." This hit-or-miss pattern sends conflicting signals and suffers under the weight of its own inconsistency.

A third shortcoming involves the loss of ceremony. A pioneer of the secular manhood movement, Robert Bly, makes this penetrating observation: "There is no place in our culture where boys are initiated consciously into manhood." Manhood ceremonies have, in fact, become a lost art form. And sons have lost these powerful, life-changing moments where, in the presence of Dad and other men, they can mark either their progress toward or passage into manhood. In the absence of these special ceremonies, sons are left to wonder, Am I a man?[7]

Lewis illustrates his key points by using the medieval paradigm of how a boy first became a page at the age of seven. At this young age he began his formal instruction into manhood. He learned about armor, weapons, jousting, and falconry. He also learned to perform household tasks for the queen of the castle. At fourteen, he became a squire. At this age he was attached to a knight and for seven years he studied everything necessary to be eligible for knighthood. At the age of twenty-one, he became a knight. The system defined three significant moments that marked the boy's ascent into manhood. Perhaps our model should be the same. Here's how it might look:

- At age seven, begin the process of sexual, gender, and character-based training, including the connecting of puberty to manhood.
- At age fourteen, begin the process of preparing for the disciplines of being a man, including parenting, vocation, and financial issues. (As an example, a rich tradition for Jewish people everywhere is to honor their sons' and daughters' coming of age at 13 with either a Bar Mitzvah or a Bat Mitzvah.)
- At age eighteen to twenty-one, plan a formal ceremony to honor his entry into manhood.

To have our sons grow up and mature within the right boundaries and parameters so that they can make a solid transition from adolescence to manhood, Lewis says we need to teach our sons four things:

1. *Reject passivity.* Real manhood begins with the decision to reject social and spiritual passivity when it is the more comfortable, natural option.
2. *Accept responsibility.* Authentic manhood revolves around three primary responsibilities: a will to obey, a work to do, and a woman to love. He must be schooled in these arts and trained from an early age by the mentor in his life, his dad.
3. *Lead courageously.* Men must not relinquish their leadership role. Earth's first man, Adam, relinquished his, and his wife, Eve, paid the price by yielding passively to the feelings and emotion of the moment, seduced by the serpent instead of embracing the counsel of God. Leadership demands that men muster the courage to master their passions and bridle themselves with the principles of truth.
4. *Expect the greater reward—God's reward.* The writer of the Book of Hebrews describes what we should teach our sons to do: "Let us run with endurance the race that is set before us, looking unto Jesus, the author and finisher of our faith, who for the joy that was set before Him endured the cross, despising the shame, and has sat down at the right hand of the throne of God."[8]

I have tried to paint a compelling picture of the importance of raising children with a proper understanding of their strong sexual orientation. I am passionate about this subject. I refuse to hold back God's truth. It is the only truth that will save our children and civilization as we know it. In that context, it is vital that we help our children preserve their virginity until they marry—surely the greatest of all character builders. In pursuing excellence in your relationship with your kids, here are some additional thoughts on being a dad of value.

1. Be a dad of tenderness. You cannot hug your daughters or sons enough. I am forty years old and my dad is seventy. We still hug every time we see each other. Every survey I read indicates that our daughters and sons will grow a healthier self-esteem if we demonstrate affection. As your daughters and sons mature into young women and men, do not stop hugging them. They long for your affection, and they will use you as a model when God blesses them with a family of their own. Steve Farrar suggests four tips in addition to hugs for helping men to develop a spirit of tenderness with our kids:

- Listen to them and respect their feelings.
- If you have been wrong or too harsh with them, be man enough to clearly confess and admit your wrongdoing and ask their forgiveness.
- Listen to the input your wife gives you about each child. Usually she is more in tune with their emotional needs than you are. She can be a tremendous resource, but you have to listen to her.
- Be in touch and dispense liberal encouragement to both sons and daughters (and don't forget your wife while you are at it.)

2. Be a dad of firmness. There is a balance between firmness and tenderness that all good fathers must understand. Firmness sets up boundaries, establishes parameters, and monitors performance, all of which are necessary for kids to enjoy a healthy respect for themselves and others. The guidelines for effective living are biblically based and embodied in the Ten Commandments. There are two ways to demonstrate firmness:

one is through discipline, the other is through admonition, teaching, warning, and encouragement.

3. Be a dad of principle. If you don't stand for something, your kids will fall for anything. Be a dad of moral and spiritual absolutes. Help your kids understand that most of the challenges in life will arise from "relative" thinking. God's Word creates absolutes, not suggestions; His words are immutable, not relative. He has no patience with situational ethics. The Bible does not say *try not* to have sex outside of marriage, *try not* to kill someone, *try not* to steal, or *try not* to do this or that. God speaks in absolutes. There are some things our kids must also see as absolutes, and these are the bedrock of solid, foundational thinking that will serve them well as they grow and mature in their relationship with you, each other, and ultimately their own families.

"The best homes are those in which parents combine love with strong guidance and clear values. In those homes the children will grow up to be self-confident and effective adults."

If You Do It Right

If we do it right, the rewards of effective parenting are priceless. If we do it right, we will one day revel in the glory of watching our kids be fully functioning, well-balanced adults.

Peter Blitchington observed: "Parents of highly self-confident children met three criteria: First, they were very warm and accepting of their children. They showed in every way that they genuinely liked their children. Second, they provided clear guidance for their children. They laid down specific rules and regulations, and they expected their children to adhere to those guidelines. Third, they were respectful of their children's initiative and endeavors. They didn't stifle their children whenever they showed independent actions. . . . The best homes are those in which parents combine love with strong guidance and clear values. In those homes the children will grow up to be self-confident and effective adults."[9]

225

When we parent the right way, we secure the next generation's health. I recently heard an interview with one of the greatest mentors of all time. Eighty-year-old former UCLA basketball coach John Wooden recounted the lessons his dad taught him. Wouldn't it be great to have your kids remember what you taught them so that late in their life they could still be teaching others?

- Be true to yourself.
- Make each day your masterpiece.
- Help others.
- Drink deep from good books, especially the Bible.
- Make friendships a fine art.
- Build a shelter against a rainy day.
- Pray for guidance, count and give thanks for your blessings every day.

What will your kids remember about you? What meaningful lessons will you have taught them?

On a snowy day long before the Civil War, Robert E. Lee took his eight-year-old son, Custis, out for a walk. The boy, wearied by the high drifts, began to fall behind his father. After a few minutes Lee looked backed and saw that Custis was behind him, imitating his father's every move and walking in the tracks Lee had left in the snow.

"When I saw this," Lee told one of his friends long afterward, "I said to myself, it behooves me to walk very straight when this fellow is already following in my tracks."[10]

What footprints are you leaving for your children to follow? Are they straight or crooked? Wherever you go, they too will travel. Men, it's up to us to help make the next generation into men and women of God—people who obey the rules, who live by our heavenly Father's precepts, and who choose to walk the path of righteousness. Whatever is past is past; whatever you have not done right to this point is water under the bridge. Forget it and move on. No matter where your children are—at home or on their own—it is never too late to start being the dad God created you to be. There is no greater feeling than to know you are creating a legacy for your children.

Plan of Action for Being the Father God Designed You to Be

1. What is keeping you from developing complete trust with your children? What will you do to get rid of these distractions?

    _____

    _____

2. What are your thoughts on how you might be a better leader in the home? How might your new approach to leadership affect your children?

    _____

    _____

    _____

3. List up to five behaviors you can begin to do to add value for your children:

    1. _____

    2. _____

    3. _____

    4. _____

    5. _____

4. What are the two most important things you have committed to start doing today with your children?

    1. _____

    2. _____

When you have completed
these four assignments,
go to my website at
www.toddduncan.com
for ten inspirational quotes
to help you be the dad
God created you to be.
See you on-line. —*TD*

www.toddduncan.com

Action Planner Notes

_____

_____

_____

_____

_____

_____

_____

_____

_____

_____

_____

_____

_____

_____

_____

_____

_____

_____

_____

_____

_____

_____

_____

_____

_____

Love What You Do... Do What You Love... And The Money Will Follow

---

A large percentage of America's working population does not enjoy the work they do! This is a profoundly tragic statistic considering that work consumes so much time in our lives. In a few brief decades, our working life adds up to be life itself.
Marsha Sinetar

I've never heard anyone on his or her deathbed say, I wish I had spent more time at the office. **Anonymous**

 arly that morning the speaker had said, "There are not many things you need to get the life you deserve. In fact, every one of you in this room possesses the ingredients for success. But more than any one thing, you must love what you do." Bull's-eye! Something happened that morning that caused me to act. It was the statement, "You must love what you do."

What I have learned since is that this attitude is the core of success: People must love what they do. When we pursue life with passion and focus, the vocation of our choice will bring fulfillment to our purpose.

Midway through the seminar, I approached the speaker, Tom Hopkins. I told him that he had inspired me that morning. We were walking together up the center aisle of the auditorium where more than two thousand people were preparing for the afternoon session, when I blurted, "Mr. Hopkins, I want to be a speaker. It is something I have wanted to do for years. I wonder if you could help me." Hopkins said, "See me after the seminar and let's talk."

As I waited in line later, every thought imaginable went through my mind. What would I say? What would he say? How would I respond? Thankfully, there were hundreds of people waiting for Hopkins to autograph a book he had written. It gave me time to think.

When I finally approached him, and before I could say a word he said, "So you want to be a speaker, do you?" Before I could even nod my head yes, he asked a second question, "When will you be one?" I looked at him, confused, and then he said, "Until you decide *when* you are going to be a speaker, you will never begin doing the things necessary that will lead you to becoming one. Without a vision, you will not succeed!"

I was ready to give him some sort of an answer, when he asked me again, "So, when will you be one?"

This was getting embarrassing. I thought quickly and said, "July 6, 1988. Yes, that's the date, July 6, 1988."

He said, "Okay, take out your planner and write down July 6, 1988. If I don't hear from you by that date, I will call you and ask you why you have not held to the commitment you have just made to yourself."

In that moment, I went from thinking about being a speaker to being committed to being one. Talk about a paradigm shift! I went from, Gee, it sure would be nice . . . to I am going to make this happen by July 6, 1988.

Our conversation reminded me of the story of the pig and the chicken walking by a bulletin board in front of the local church. On the marquee, the men's group of the church was announcing its annual ham and eggs breakfast. The pig and the chicken checked it out with great interest, after which the pig said, "You know, Ms. Chicken, for you, that's a day's work; for me, however, it is the ultimate sacrifice."

That is how I felt. I went from mild interest to sacrifice. In that moment, I realized why my work over the last eight years had not been as satisfying as it might have been. Now I had my assignment, but how would I do it? How could I make the transition financially, mentally, and physically?

Several months passed as I continued to think of my deadline. One weekend, Sheryl and I were walking through the local mall, and my eyes fell on a book titled, *Do What You Love, The Money Will Follow*, by Marsha Sinetar. I bought it and read it. Its pages gave me a new perspective on the meaning of success.

About two weeks before July 6, 1988, I telephoned Tom Hopkins. He was not in. A couple of days later he returned my call from the Atlanta's airport and spent the next forty-five minutes coaching me over the phone on how to become a speaker. He told me what to do to market myself, how to promote myself, and how to become sought after by clients. The most important thing he told me, however, was to never give up! At the end of our conversation, he said, "Todd, if you ever need me, feel free to call, and I will help you." There's more involved here about why he did this, but I'm not ready to reveal that until we get to chapter 11. Meanwhile, I found myself armed with a plan and some new thinking—accompanied by our savings—and so Sheryl and I decided this was the moment to follow my dream.

What Is a Livelihood?

You will always find the power to be your best in the context of doing your best at what you do best. Your basic capacity to do your best is already built into your biological structure. You can go to school, take seminars, listen to tapes, and obtain counsel; however, even if you did not have access to all that, you would still already possess enough to be your best. So what is the key to unlocking that door?

You will always find the power to be your best in the context of doing your best at what you do best.

Some of us are equipped to be more suitable for sales, for leadership, for art, for music, for writing, for speaking, for medicine, for research, or for a host of other callings. Doing something is the easy part. To understand that you already possess the skills to do it is another matter.

As you seek to put power in your vocation, you must choose a vocation that is best for you so you can do your best. This is the essence of livelihood. In her book, *Do What You Love,* Marsha Sinetar says:

> *Current research on child prodigies—youngsters who, from an early age, are mathematical wizards, virtuoso musicians, brilliant performers—tells us that they possess a burning desire to express themselves, to use their unique gifts. In a similar fashion, each of us, no matter how ordinary we consider our talents, wants and needs to use them. Right Livelihood is the natural expression of this need. Yet, many of us cannot imagine that what we enjoy doing, what we have talent for, could be a source of income for us or even a catalyst for transforming our relationship to work. Leaders in every walk of life (e.g. housewives, crafts persons, entrepreneurs, inventors, community volunteers, etc.) who have the drive, skill and compelling vision to advance their ideas, despite obstacles, need to exert their influence as much as their solutions, energy and enthusiasm are needed by others.[1]*

When I was a young boy, I noticed this pattern in my father. I still remember how I felt when I learned that he, at the age of twenty-seven and newly married, decided that corporate accounting was not his forte. Dad had spent the previous five years working successfully at Mobil Oil. One day, he began thinking about his life, his career, and what seemed to be a less-than-exciting future. Each day he would go to work aware that he needed to do something different to bring excitement to his life.

As you seek to put power in your vocation, you must choose a vocation that is best for you so you can do your best.

Several years later, the daily grind and the frustration of his work—along with the void he felt deep inside—pushed him to focus on a new career: medicine, dentistry in particular. Unfortunately, he flunked the "soap" test, a challenge to determine how good one is with his hands—an obvious requirement for dentistry. So no problem, right? Dad realized that failure was essential to success, so he determined to pursue a career in medicine, but instead of dentistry, it would be general medicine. He completed medical school with a specialty in radiology. Eight years later, he opened his practice at the age of thirty-eight. For the next twenty-seven years, Dad did what he loved and loved what he did.

I was so impressed with dad's commitment and focus that I decided I would also be a doctor. In my first year at college, I chose pre-med. I took all the chemistry and biology classes that were required and struggled greatly with every one

It was my first lesson in learning that a "wealth" that provides happiness is the greatest treasure of all.

of them. I remember having this sick feeling inside that I was doing all the wrong things for all the wrong reasons: to be like dad and to make a lot of money. After my second year in college, it became increasingly clear that medicine and I would soon part company. This decision was later confirmed when Dad said, "Todd, maybe medicine isn't for you. The most important thing in life is to be happy with what you are doing." It was my first lesson in learning that a "wealth" that provides happiness is the greatest treasure of all.

LOVE WHAT YOU DO...DO WHAT YOU LOVE...AND THE MONEY WILL FOLLOW

The Bible gives us considerable guidance in this area. It says, "Therefore I hated life because the work that was done under the sun was distressing to me, for all is vanity and grasping for the wind… And this also is a severe evil; Just exactly as [a man] came, so shall he go. And what profit has he who has labored for the wind?" (Ecclesiastes 2:17, 5:16). What is the message of these verses? Life is too short not to do what we feel we really want to do with our careers.

You will always find the power to be your best in the context of doing your best at what you do best. To do this is to give your life congruence. If the accumulation of material wealth is your goal, it will never be enough; it will never even get you close to the joy, freedom, and delight that comes from simply doing your best at what you do best.

When we do what we love, we not only get more done, but we do it better, more efficiently, and our rewards are enormous. When we live out that decision, money and security cease to be our only payments.

Shortly before his death, Malcolm Forbes was asked, "How much money do you expect to leave behind?"

"All of it," he replied.

You and I have a choice: We can spend our lives pursuing power, money, and fame—the most fleeting of all successes—or we can pursue a life of fulfillment by doing our best at what we do best. Remember the words of Sinetar: "Do what you love, and the money will follow." Don't confuse the sequence: It's love first, money second. The last time I checked they were still handing out prizes at the end of the race.

Choices or Conflict

Let me ask you a question: If money did not matter, what would you do with your life? Is it possible you might be happier doing something other than what you are doing now? If so, why aren't you doing it? This path of choosing a new direction in your work life, or living with the conflict that you would rather be doing something else, may be a challenge you have not yet embraced. To find and harness a dream and to feel what it is like to go for it at all costs are some of the toughest decisions you will make in your life. The transition, however, is generally made easier when your self-esteem and personal confidence are high.

Without an honest appreciation of the face you see every day in your mirror, without feeling you are trustworthy and deserving (discussed in chapter 5), the easy decision is to say, I think I won't change; it's too painful. When we feel good about our plans and ourselves, and when we feel confident about our direction, the change is much easier. When we do what we love, we not only get more done, but we do it better, more efficiently, and our rewards are enormous. When we live out that decision, money and security cease to be our only payments.

Here is the truth about new choices:

- A change in career or vocation is an important decision, but such a decision can give you the heightened level of fulfillment you have been missing for years.
- It takes power, confidence, courage, and faith to break ground in a new vocational direction. That is why we must be passionate about why we want to do it (the most important decision) as we acquire the skills of how to get it done.
- Usually, to choose to go in a new direction creates a considerable degree of fear, but since our decisions have now become value- and purpose-based, most of this borrowed anxiety will never manifest itself. Still, however, fear and loathing have a way of sneaking up on us. That is why we must not let fear develop a life of its own. If we do, it will inhibit us, control us, and render us helpless.
- In making a vocational change, we will invariably move out of our comfort zone. Generally speaking, after we make the change, we will ask ourselves, Why did I wait so long?

- We do not have to give up our day job to begin the journey of becoming what we want to be tomorrow. This is a skill called "double-tracking." I will show you a little later in this chapter how you can make this work for you.

Belief Esteem

While on a flight recently, the video playing was an episode from the television comedy *Third Rock from the Sun.* In one of the exchanges, John Lithgow, after posing nude for a portrait, said, "There are two types of people on earth: Those who accept their flaws, and those who pursue their talents."

What an interesting comment. I have helped hundreds of people to make career shifts, and in almost every situation there was either an enormous amount of doubt (Can I really do this?) or the confidence that they could do it (Watch out world, here I come!). Rarely did anyone say, Should I be doing this? The first key in making a shift into what you want vocationally is your "belief esteem."

We do not have to stop working in our job today to begin our journey of becoming what we want to be tomorrow.

Overall, self-esteem is the driving force of success in school, the workplace, and in our personal life. In a Gallup poll conducted in 1992, the pollsters interviewed 612 adults about self-esteem and found that 89 percent considered self-esteem important as the source of motivation for hard work and success in any enterprise.

There are two things at the heart of how we feel about ourselves: our self-respect levels and the trust we place in our Creator. Invariably, if we are in a vocation that we do not like or want to do, and we feel God does want us to do it, then each day we perform our work, we chip away at the intimacy we have with our heavenly Father and lose respect for ourselves. This truth runs through every area of our life. For example, if we go to a movie that we do not want to see, but go because we allow friends to overrule our decision, that lowers our self-respect. Going to a bar or a nightclub for the wrong reasons (someone else's reasons) does the same thing.

I admire my friend John who recently worked in Atlanta on a two-year project with MCI. He told me that his coworkers enjoyed going out to strip joints at night after work. He disapproved because he did not feel it was right for him to do this. After repeatedly voicing his refusal to go along with the gang, they finally stopped asking him. They did not stop working with him, because they realized that what was okay for them was not okay for John. Each time they asked and John said no, John's self-respect increased, as did his favor with God.

As I write this chapter, John is in the midst of heading down a new career path, one that he is passionate and excited about. Because he had the guts to live his life on-purpose in the "little things," he had prepared his heart and mind to make larger decisions. When it was finally time to make them, they were not nearly as difficult as he had imagined they might be. That is what living on-purpose is all about.

In almost every situation there was either an enormous amount of doubt (Can I really do this?) or the confidence that they could do it (Watch out world, here I come!). Rarely did anyone say, Should I be doing this?

If you decide to make a vocational move, you may expose yourself to two types of change. The first is you may have the option of doing something in your present company along with a new, more interesting, more fulfilling assignment. You will change elements of your environment, but you will stay where you are. The second is external. This form of change takes on two dimensions. First, you will leave your current employment to pursue a vocational path or focus that did not exist in your previous environment, and/or second, you leave your company to start your own organization to pursue a vocational path or focus that did not exist in your previous environment.

> **When we feel good about ourselves, we will make decisions with confidence.**

In either situation, the change will be easier for you when you have a dignified respect for yourself and for what God wants for your life. When we feel good about ourselves, we will make decisions with confidence. If we do not see ourselves as worthy, we may not decide at all, but to decide not to decide leads to a life of frustration, when a simple, right decision might have directed us toward the happiness we seek and deserve. Bottom line: When you do what you love, you will do it better, with a greater sense of commitment, more attention to focus, and with a stronger feeling of purpose and alignment.

In fact, it is harder to fail at something you love than it is to succeed at something you dislike. My question to you: If you were doing what you loved to do, what would give your life incredible fulfillment and meaning? To ask the question another way, What would you be willing to attempt if you knew you could not fail?

Over the years, I have collected the following questions that have helped shape and reshape the vocational decisions for thousands of people:

> **It is harder to fail at something you love than it is to succeed at something you dislike.**

1. What do I want to be remembered for? What do I need to start doing to move in that direction?
2. How much money is enough? If I do not have enough, what could I do to earn more? If I have enough, what purpose does my surplus serve?
3. How am I feeling about my job or career right now? What changes would I want to make if I knew I could not fail?
4. Where do I want to be vocationally in ten or twenty years?
5. What could I offer in the marketplace that is not now being offered?

6. How can I perform better in my current job and enjoy more fulfillment?
7. How can I add value to the products, people, and industry I work with and serve?
8. What have my customers asked for that is not available?
9. Am I a person in business, or am I in business as a professional?
10. What am I doing where I am at my best? How can I do more of this? What transition options seem to fit my personality and gift traits?[2] Should I: (1) Keep doing what I already do well, but change the environment? (2) Change the work but stay in the same environment? (3) Turn an avocation into a new career? (4) Double-track or triple-track in parallel careers? Keep on doing what I am doing past "retirement" age?

When you do what you love, you will do it better, with a greater sense of commitment, more attention to focus, and with a stronger feeling of purpose and alignment.

How can we feel good enough about ourselves to take decisive action? Our motives and motivation create action, but that is not enough. We need to know that the decision to change the way we work, where we work, or for whom we work will help us move closer to a purposeful, God-directed life. The best way to feel good about what you are doing or should be doing with your life is to remember that God wants to give you the desires of your heart.

The apostle Paul writes: "For we are [God's] workmanship, created in Christ Jesus for good works, which God prepared beforehand that we should walk in them" (Ephesians 2:10). Will God allow you to fail at what He wants you to do? The answer is of course no. Paul continues, "[I am] confident of this very thing, that He who has begun a good work in you will complete it until the day of Jesus Christ" (Philippians 1:6). Logically, if God is for us, who can be against us? If our vocational path and focus are in concert with God's "nudging," there is no way we can fail. We will have setbacks and challenges; however, if we stay the course, He will direct our paths. That, my friends, is the best motivation you and I will ever receive in this life!

Loyalty or Fear: The Saboteurs of Life

Often we live under the illusion that we "owe" someone our loyalty for the opportunities they have provided us. While I do not advocate an attitude of ingratitude, I have seen too many people remain in their vocational jungle too long because of misplaced loyalty. You must break free to be your best. Listen to the words of the provocative David Viscott, from his book *The Language of Feelings*:

There is yet another trap: fear. Think about it. If you do not love what you are doing, and I ask you, "Why, then, are you doing it?" Your answer would most likely be that you are afraid of failing at something new. What most people do not realize is that to avoid failure is to avoid all chance for success.

> *Your ultimate goal in life is to become your best. Your immediate goal is to get on the path that will lead you there. Why should you feel guilty if you refuse to be intimidated by [someone] who persists in standing in the way of your being that best self or who is "hurt" when you finally manage it? The highest love a person can have for you is to wish for you to evolve into the best person you can be. No one owns you, no matter what your relationship. You are not here on this earth to fulfill the unmet dreams of a frustrated parent or to protect another person from facing the reality of himself or the world. You are here to develop and grow.[3]*

There is yet another trap: fear. Think about it. If you do not love what you are doing, and I ask you, "Why, then, are you doing it?" Your answer would most likely be that you are afraid of failing at something new. Welcome to the club. What most people do not realize is that to avoid failure is to avoid all chance for success. If you are afraid, your fears will make it impossible to alter your career course. The word *fear* has appeared many times in this book, and it is no different in this "vocational change" context. What will happen to you in the midst of your change is less important than the change itself. If you want to do it and God is for it, you should go for it!

When you are doing what you love, it is never a matter of if you succeed but when.

Let me illustrate this process with another story from my own experience. My decision to become a professional speaker had been a nudging from God for the better part of three years. I began to see this potential in myself when I realized I could add value to my clients by doing seminars for them. What began as five-minute presentations grew to thirty-minute sessions once a month. While on the job, I was "double-tracking," doing what I loved while doing what was required of me on the job. I incorporated my "true desire" into my daily job description.

Before long, my company recognized my abilities in this area of communication and asked if I would start teaching the other salespeople how to sell. For three years, I did seminars for my co-workers in an area apart from that for which I had been hired originally. Soon, several colleagues asked if I had considered speaking professionally. After hearing that suggestion repeatedly, I began to build some confidence in the safety of my "regular" job that said, Hey, Todd, maybe you should do this full time.

What most people do not realize is that to avoid failure is to avoid all chance for success.

So I found a company in the same industry where one of my primary jobs would be to develop sales-training curriculum. That was another confidence builder. After a year, the nudging became stronger. I made the decision to set up my own company while still working full time for the group that had hired me to develop curriculum. I "double-tracked" again; I worked full time for someone else while building my own company on my own time, which was another boost to my confidence.

I started speaking gratis on weekends. Eventually, I started sending invoices for my presentations. Before long, I realized it was time for me to fly. That is when I attended the seminar where I met Tom Hopkins. Within six months, I was self-employed and doing what God had given me the gift of doing: speaking. It took five years from the first thought to the final move.

As I share this story with you, I am now preparing to take the same gift and use it in yet another way. This will produce the same challenges the first move did. The difference is that this time I have more confidence than ever. You can also have this kind of confidence if you learn the fine art of double-tracking. When you are doing what you love, it is never a matter of *if* you succeed but *when*.

The Secret of Success—Power

To be your best in the midst of a career shift, you need power! As you begin to venture down this new path—whether within your current environment, in a new environment working for someone else, or by starting your own business—without the right kind of power, you will never be your best. Here are some tips to help you make the transition to one of the most exciting periods of your life in the form of an acrostic for POWER.

Passion is behind all forms of excellence: sports, relationships, business. Passion is everything. What emotion comes to mind when you think of passion? Do the words *excitement* and *enthusiasm* come to mind? These may be two components of passion, but they are not the most important. Actually, a root definition of passion is suffering, specifically, the suffering of Christ between the Last Supper with His disciples and His crucifixion. While I cannot begin to understand the suffering Christ experienced on the cross, I do know if we are to live the life we have imagined, it will always require suffering before we succeed. It was the same with Jesus. He was living the life that God has chosen for Him, and He suffered greatly as the purpose of His life unfolded.

While I cannot begin to understand the suffering Christ experienced on the cross, I do know if we are to live the life we have imagined, it will always require suffering before we succeed.

Suffering. Passion. Doing up front what is right. Recognizing that our greatest rewards come at the end of the race. Ironically, when our suffering leads to success, the other, more common definitions of passion begin to kick into high gear: excitement, enthusiasm, a burning-the-midnight-oil behavior, and a never-say-die confidence. First things first. If you are not suffering or paying the price in your vocational transition, you are not really succeeding.

Opportunity. The great Wayne Gretzky summed it up in ten words: "You'll miss 100 percent of the shots you don't take." You have several choices: You can watch things happen, make things happen, or be dazzled with the success of others and later ask yourself what happened. It is your choice. If you know what you are aiming for, you will seize the moment when the time is right and you will make it happen.

Imagine if Harriet Tubman had not seized her opportunity:

Harriet Tubman was born a slave in Maryland. She yearned to be free. In 1849 she made her escape to Pennsylvania through the secret Underground Railroad. She then used that route 19 more times, returning to the South to lead more than 300 slaves to freedom. As the years passed, Tubman became

LOVE WHAT YOU DO...DO WHAT YOU LOVE...AND THE MONEY WILL FOLLOW *known as the "Moses" of her people, directing them out of the enslaved land. During the Civil War, she served the Union Army as a nurse and a spy. Following the war, Tubman raised funds to construct schools for ex-slaves. She labored for female suffrage and, in 1903, established a shelter for poor, homeless blacks. Today her legacy is that of an extraordinary humanitarian.[4]*

Willingness. It is one thing to see an opportunity, but to do something to make an impact on your life and the lives of others you must take action. To succeed, you must have a willingness that transcends procrastination. "Some day" is "none day." If you are unable to cut through your barricade of excuses for not doing well, you will make yourself settle for mediocrity.

If you do not change today, you will still be where you are now, only later. If you change now, you will be where you have always dreamed of being, and you will look back on your accomplishments in amazement.

In 1960 Wilma Rudolph earned three Olympic gold medals in track and field. What makes her accomplishment especially remarkable was that she had been stricken with polio at an early age. She observed, "Sometimes it takes years to really grasp what has happened in your life."[5]

I can almost hear her speak those words as I write them—words that have two possible meanings. First, if you do not change today, you will still be where you are now, only later. Second, if you change now, you will be where you have always dreamed of being, and you will look back on your accomplishments in amazement.

What is the secret to getting the job done? It is to get moving, to do it now. Do not wait for your ship to come in, and do not expect someone to come alongside to lend you a hand. The greatest helping hand available to you is the one at the end of your arm. Here are some thoughts to help you become more proactive now:

- Review your value system every day and determine what you will miss if you do not act on one or more of your values.

- Talk to someone who has already done what you are thinking about doing. Your confidence will increase in direct proportion to your willingness to act.

- What one thing can you do today that will have the greatest impact on your career direction? Schedule time to address this issue and link your future rewards with the decision to act now.

- Reframe your concept of FEAR: **F**alse **E**xperiences **A**ppearing **R**eal. Do not give your power away to an event for which the outcome has not yet been determined. Seek correct knowledge. Learn from the successes and failures of others, and you will be less likely to delay the major decisions that are about to impact your life.

- Ask "what if?" What if I take this class? What if I start this business? What if I see my boss about another job in the company? What if I become so happy I cannot stand it? Make a longer list of your own. Keep adding to it. Your list of "what ifs?" will motivate you to be your best.

Energy. You must be energetic to have energy, that's just the way it works. In the "vocational change game," this is axiomatic. For example, what you do to your body and what you put into your body will dictate your level of energy and stamina. Coach Vince Lombardi noted, "Fatigue makes cowards of us all."

Do you have an exercise program? I remember hearing Zig Ziglar describe his workout program: "I fill the tub, take a bath, pull the plug, and fight the current." That may be vintage Ziglar, but he hardly describes a program that will increase one's heart rate.

Energy is released by increasing it and getting more of it. That is why after a vigorous walk, run, cycle, or workout, you

> *As we make these shifts, however, we must evaluate our progress and make changes preventively. Gerber refers to this as the "on" part of working. The "in" part is the actual doing. Doing it right is imperative.*

feel better for hours. You have released the energy stored inside of you. The experts claim that you will increase your energy levels and live longer if you exercise for thirty minutes three times a week, pushing your heart rate to its aerobic target. You can calculate your target rate by subtracting your age from 220 and multiplying the result by .75. (This formula is also printed on most exercise bikes and treadmills for easy reference.)

Limiting your alcohol consumption is paramount. Spreading your food consumption over at least five intake periods during the day will keep your brain and body working at peak capacity. To do otherwise is to deplete your energy. Everything in moderation says the good book, plus: "Do not mix with winebibbers, or with gluttonous eaters of meat; for the drunkard and the glutton will come to poverty, and drowsiness will clothe a man with rags" (Proverbs 23:20–21). Sounds like good advice for the person on the cusp of reinventing himself or herself vocationally. Sir Thomas Buxton had a profound thought on the subject, which I memorized many years ago and continue to reflect on to this day:

> *The longer I am alive the more convinced I am that what makes the difference between one man and another, between the great and insignificant is energy, that invincible determination, a purpose once formed, nothing can take away from. And I am convinced that anything on this earth that was meant by God to be done requires energy and no training, opportunity, or circumstance will make any man without it.*

Results. The last element of our acrostic is *results*. We often move too quickly to change a vocation. This can be deadly because it will not yield the results we want. The worst thing you can do is to make a change without a sober evaluation of what that change will produce. Best-selling author Michael Gerber introduced the principles of working "in" our jobs and working "on" our jobs in his book *The E-Myth*. If you are considering a vocational move and if you want to end up truly loving what you do, then your present business or job must be done as efficiently as possible to produce the most profitable results.

How often have you seen someone operate out of panic when making a change? There is that which is urgent and that which is important. They are not the same. A successful vocational shift requires proper planning and the right amount of focus on the important issues and activities more so than the urgent. If you make a vocational decision based on your values, gifts, and what you feel God wants you to do, then it will work out. As we make these shifts, however, we must evaluate our progress and make changes preventively. Gerber refers to this as the "on" part of working. The "in" part is the actual doing. Doing it right is imperative. How do you do that? Let's go back to school, only this time we will study a different set of the Three Rs.

Reflect. What's working and what is not working with your work? Be brutally honest with yourself. Take a sheet of paper, draw a line down the middle. On the left write the word *working,* one the right *not working.* Now write your responses.

React. What will you do differently to change your results? Write these down. Unless you put pencil to paper, you will not have what I call an "accountability list." Ask the "what if" questions we referred to earlier. They will help you to compare your present state with your potentially better, brighter future.

Restart. Review your professional value area and your clarifying vision statement. Look at your short- and long-term lists of goals. Review your affirmations and go!

Evaluation is your cornerstone for vocational change. Many changes do not pan out because there is limited attention to the efficiency of the process. Whether it is speaking, writing, painting, sculpting, constructing, building, designing, selling, managing, directing, policing, cooking, driving, or cleaning, to be your best, you have to do your best at what you do best.

Launch Your Dream

When you take a new path that is leading you in the direction of your dreams, you will need massive amounts of fuel, figuratively as much as is required to launch a space shuttle. Keep the space shuttle image in your mind. You must back all your plans and plan all your future events with the knowledge that you will need enormous power to blast away from what has been grounding you up until now. Here are the components with an acrostic for *Blastoff*.

Believing Is Seeing. All your life you have heard the phrase "seeing is believing." In the world of vocational shifting, however, I suggest you turn this phrase on its head. The power to be your best begins when you see your outcomes before you hold them in your hand. This is not a new concept. All great performers demonstrate a believing attitude in advance of their next accomplishment. Tiger Woods sees the ball in the cup before he tees off. Mark McGwire sees the baseball being propelled far beyond the center-field fence before the pitcher starts his windup. Best-selling author Toni Morrison sees her completed novel and millions of readers reading it before she starts writing. These mind-sets are what separates the winners from the losers. It is how they have wired themselves. Believing is seeing! These champions do not own the concept; it can also be yours!

Every great inventor, all successful entrepreneurs, and each polished actor or performer sees the end result first. It is this "believing is seeing" frame of reference that gives them the energy to make it happen. When it does happen, for them it is déjà vu. They have already been there in their minds. Imagine if President John F. Kennedy had not believed that putting a man on the moon was possible. If Thomas Edison had not believed he could generate power for electric lights so we would no longer need candles? What if Fred Smith had not believed that an overnight package express was an option? What if Jonas Salk had not believed there could be a vaccine for polio? Imagine if Henry Ford had not believed there could be a Ford in your future, an alternative (laughable at the time) to neighing, four-legged transportation.

Imagine what you might be able to do if you could believe for even one fleeting moment in your dream and see its complete fulfillment now! My friend, you have no circumstances, only dreams and opportunities. Stick to your convictions. Do not make wrong assumptions. As one homespun thought suggests, Keep your heart believin' and your eyes a'seein' and before long, you'll be achievin'. Trust me. You can make it work for you. There is no other way to be your best and live the life you want and deserve.

The more you know about what you are doing, the more likely you are to get positive results. As those favorable results increase, you will find more enjoyment in your life and gain greater fulfillment from your work.

Learn It to Love It. "With all thy getting, get understanding" (Proverbs 4:7, paraphrased). One of the keys to success in your vocational shift is to become an expert in what you do. I recall listening in my early twenties to a recording by Brian Tracy entitled *The Psychology of Success*. On one of the tapes, Tracy suggested that if you studied a topic for one hour each day for three years, you would be among the most knowledgeable people in the world on that subject. I am glad I heard that tape. I am even happier that I chose to put his words into action.

One of the greatest fibs of all time is that when we graduate from high school or college, we have somehow completed our learning. That is not the meaning of commencement. Commencement means to start, not to fold one's tent and slip quietly away into the sunset. To love what you do—really love it—you need to know your purpose and then pursue it with every skill you can muster. Only then will life's true excitement begin for you. Your purpose, however, must be laced with a thirst for learning—the right kind of learning that prepares you to deal positively, productively, and persuasively with the issues necessary for your growth and advancement.

The more you know about what you are doing, the more likely you are to get positive results. As those favorable results increase, you will find more enjoyment in your life and gain greater fulfillment from your work.

Accumulate Knowledge. Knowledge is power. Have you heard that before? Do you agree with its premise? Well, it is both true and false. Knowledge is the prelude to power, but only when knowledge is put to use will it place power in your hands and in your heart. If, for example, I take a straight pin and gently toss it at your bare arm, you will hardly feel it. It may seem like a fly landed on you and then flew away. If I take that same pin, weld it to a five-pound iron bar, and strike your bare arm, you would not mistake it for a fly. It will, on the contrary, cause major damage. Same pin; different source of power. It is the same with knowledge. Knowledge is the "pin"; power is the five-pound iron bar.

What are you doing to keep your mind filled with the kind of knowledge to become the person you were created and designed to be? It really does all start in the mind, you know. Here are some ideas I have gleaned from the hundreds of interviews I have done with high-performance people:

• **Go back to school.** Take classes that feed you with the knowledge that will take you to the vocation of your dreams.

• **Ask Questions.** Go out of your way to find people who are doing what you want to do and interview them. Perhaps their handshake has put them over the top. Maybe it is the way they listen or ask questions. Success always leaves clues. Be a sleuth. Be the Sherlock Holmes of your own destiny. The cases you solve (your own) will absolutely amaze you.

• **Read books.** What is the last book you read and what is the next one you will complete? The incredible, one-of-a-kind motivational speaker Charlie "Tremendous" Jones has told audiences for years you will be the same person you are today except for the books you read and the people you meet. Are you on speaking terms with your library? What does your library, in fact, look like? Are its shelves littered with questionable pulp or are its pages filled with the gold you are mining daily in your quest to be your best?

• **Audio Books.** If you choose not to make time to read, then listen to good books on audiocassette or CD-ROMs that feed you with critical knowledge. Never has the accumulation

252

THE *POWER!* TO BE YOUR BEST!

of information been more accessible or less costly than it is today. You can learn a language in two months while you are stuck in traffic. You can "hear" a book in few hours that just may change your life. Turn off the car radio (except to keep tabs on the weather and road conditions), insert a tape or CD and make your car your own personal university on wheels.

- **Book Summaries.** If you do not want to read books or listen to motivational tapes, I encourage you to subscribe to a monthly summary of the latest books. Executive Book Summaries is an excellent resource to feed your knowledge base. Call this company today and start reading scaled-down versions of today's bestsellers. Their number is (800) 521-1227.
- **The Internet.** Use the Web to gather information on your present or proposed new vocation. Find out what is happening in your field of expertise by working with user groups that can help you expand your knowledge base.
- **Television.** No trash. No tawdry afternoon "peep" shows. If you watch television at all, go for the educational, nature, history, and success channels. Your local listings will tell you what is available in your market.
- **Conferences and Seminars.** Save your money and attend conferences and seminars on subjects in your field. Network with people who have interests similar to yours. Your future is at stake. Order a thousand business cards and then get rid of them as quickly as possible. I once heard the story of a Cadillac dealer in a midwestern town who would go to local high school football games every Friday night. He would start the evening by sitting in the bleachers in front of the twenty-yard line. When the home team scored a touchdown, he would jump to his feet with the rest of the fans, and as he did he would let fly a couple hundred business cards. A few minutes later, he sat himself in the seats in front of the fifty-yard line where he did the same thing. By the end of the game, he was seated at the other twenty-yard line tossing his business cards into the air with every score until he was out of cards. Would it surprise you to learn that he was the most successful Cadillac dealer in the county? Customers probably came by just to see this crazy person! Make yourself known. Be friendly. Get creative about your self-promotion. Seminars and conferences are some of the best

places to learn your new craft and to dispose of your business cards!

Sigmoid Has It Right. The greatest lie in the world is "It will be different tomorrow." The truth is it will only be different if you change what is causing it to be not right for you today. Your life is not a singular growth curve at which you peak once, only to start the downward path to your final demise (see diagram 1).

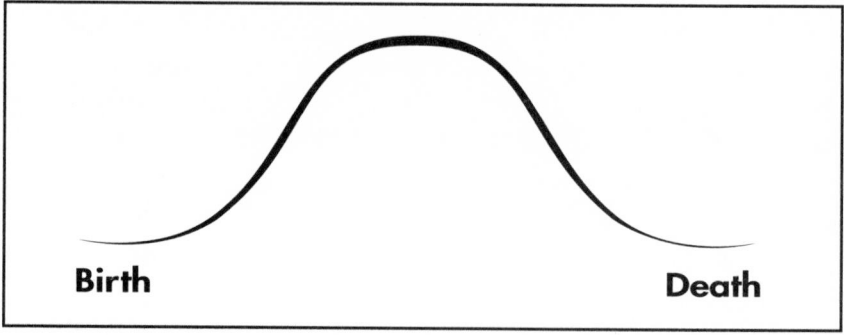

Birth **Death**

DIAGRAM 1

That would be too easy. Enter the sigmoid curve—an S-shaped "squashing function" that maps a more honest value. Vocationally, for example, your life is an ongoing series of growth curves, one after the other (see diagram 2). When you overlap the two diagrams (see diagram 3), you can see that when you do not change your pattern early on, but wait to alter your behavior only when it is more convenient, the "lag"—or cost of energy, money, and time to you—will always be greater. Moreover, you never really grow; instead, you are always playing catch up.

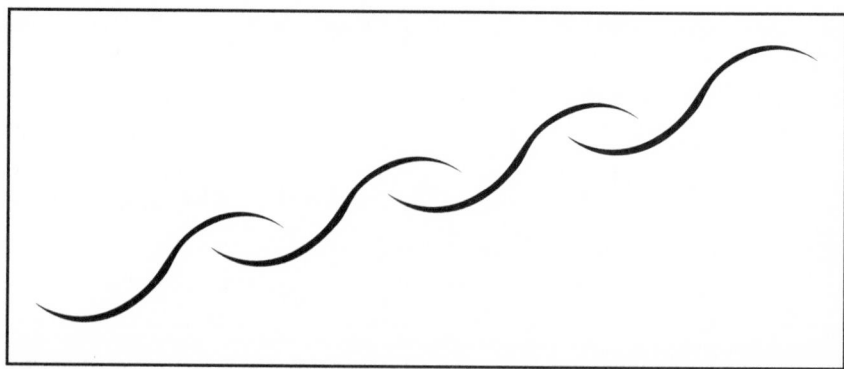

DIAGRAM 2

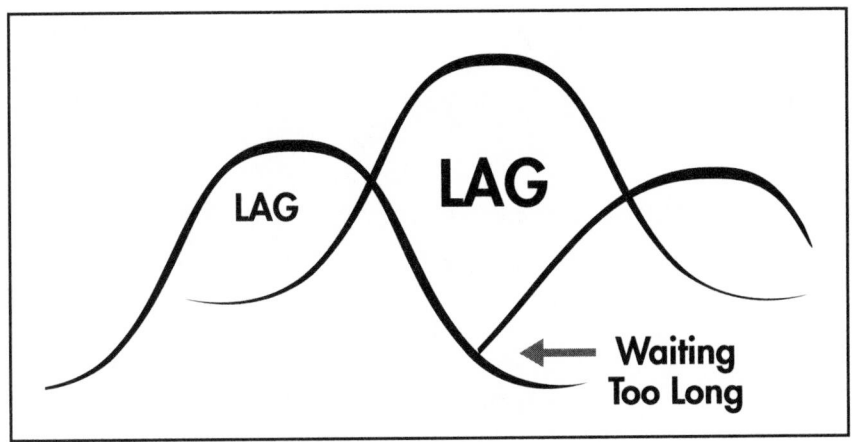

DIAGRAM 3

The solution: Get into the habit of creating change as you grow. By doing so, you will leverage your momentum.

Tenacity Is Your Friend. The great college basketball coach Jim Valvano was one of a kind. A reporter once said that Damon Runyan would have loved him. Valvano was the choirboy who hid the matches, the fellow who'd shake your hand then hand you your watch. He was, by his own admission, a rogue, and he thrived on it. An honest con, the reporter said lovingly. Valvano once agreed to wear a microphone during the game for a feature that was going to run on the six o'clock news. The sports editor later said that there was so much material, he could have composed a sitcom from the outtakes of this colorful coach from North Carolina State.

Valvano, in one of the most inspirational speeches of all time, given just a few months before he died of brain cancer, looked his team in the face and said, "Guys, never, ever give up!" Churchill once gave a similar speech to spur his countrymen on during the darkest days of World War II. Now it is time that you give yourself that same speech. There is no better counsel or therapy available than those words that have the power to keep you in the thick of your dreams when facing the most daunting challenges of life if you will only apply them to your life. Remember that the purpose of your life is to live a life of purpose. Your purpose in making a vocational change is your motivation to stay the course. Everything that is new takes time to perfect. Every time you do it, you are one step closer to being your best.

Oh, the Status Quo. When Denis Waitley was research-
ing material for his bestseller *The Psychology of Winning,* he
came across a study of a South American tribe whose people
had been dying prematurely for generations. The cause of the
illness was a rare disease that scientists finally discovered was
carried by an insect living within the walls of their adobe homes.
The tribe had several solutions: (1) they could destroy the in-
sects with a pesticide; (2) they could tear down their homes and
rebuild them; (3) they could move to where the insect did not
live; or (4) they could do nothing and continue to die young.[6]

In the end, they chose the last alternative. What do you
make of their decision? Given the choice to live or die, if one
could live happily, why would anyone choose to die? Yet I see
thousands of students in my seminars every year are who are
"dying." Although they have the smarts and the wherewithal to
move, relocate, choose a new profession, even "kill" the plague
of pests that keeps them from realizing their dreams, they still
choose the only thing familiar to them: the binding comfort of
the here and now, when, in fact, a life of fulfillment may have
been but a few blocks away.

Fun Is Your Imperative. I was on my way to do a
seminar in a branch office of one of my clients. This was to be
my third session with the group in the past two years. I dreaded
leaving for the assignment, because the last two times I was
with them had been like a visit to a morgue or to a dentist.
Standing before this group was like having a flat tire on a snowy
night with no flashlight and a flat spare. Who needed these
people! By the time I arrived at the meeting, my attitude had not
changed. I just wanted to get in and get out. Speak and split.

Sure enough, there they were, seated in their boring seats,
thinking boring thoughts, daring me to motivate them, forever
comfortable on their plateaus of mediocrity—or so I thought. To
my surprise, I soon learned that the manager had been fired and
had been replaced by a leader with a winning attitude. Not only
was he a winner, the audience was incredible. They laughed
with me, leaning forward and hanging on my every word. They
took notes, applauded, and as the old masters of vaudeville
used to hope for, they seemed to want even more!

What had happened to my dull, boring group? At the close of the session, Phillip, the new manager, told me the secret: "We made some changes here, as you've no doubt noticed. One thing in particular, we told our group there was only one requirement to remain employed here: You've got to have fun!"

What a concept! What a difference the paradigm shift to "having fun" made for them, for their clients, and for me. I later learned that their business was up 25 percent, and their turnover had fallen by 50%.

Faith Is Your Guarantee. Few people get into their cars wondering if they will be able to drive. They just step on the gas and go. An accomplished snow skier turns fear into powder as he or she flies down an expert run. A racecar driver can go 225 miles per hour and know he is in complete control. Previous experience has given these experts the faith to make a difficult task look amazingly simple.

The good news is that the situation can be the same for you. Do something a few hundred times, like drive a car or ride a bike, and you cannot help but get good at it. Speak a few hundred times on a difficult subject and people will think you are a genius. Change course vocationally and over time you'll be great at it and happy. As your accomplishments increase, so will your confidence and certainty, instilling within you an attitude that propels you to new levels in your quest to be your best. All these elements are critical to helping you *blastoff* into a new or revised vocation. As you make your move, you will need all the power you can get, power that is available to you just for the taking.

The twelfth chapter of the Book of Hebrews talks about the power of faith. The Bible heroes listed in this "hall of fame"— Abel, Enoch, Noah, Abraham, Sarah, Jacob, Joseph, Moses, and David—all had tremendous faith: faith in themselves, faith in God, and a boundless faith in their own future. If you want to read how faith alone can shape you and give you the power to be your best, take a few minutes and read this chapter. You will get the idea.

Put Your Signature on It

Pablo Picasso created many masterpieces. His commitment to quality was unparalleled, but he only signed the paintings he felt measured up to his lofty standards. It has been said that long after he had created a masterpiece, he still longed to make it better. This was obvious when, in the last years of his life, he was caught breaking into art galleries where he would try to improve on his great works of art.

Antonio Stradivarius, the Italian violin maker, had a similar passion for excellence. When he died at the age of ninety-three, he was still making violins. He was a man possessed, putting his heart and soul into every violin and viola he crafted. Only after he completed a piece that met his high standards, did he put his signature on the instrument. Both Picasso and Stradivarius have been dead for years, but their masterpieces still sell for millions. It is the price people are willing to pay for a signed product of excellence. How about you? Are you proud enough of your work to sign it? It is something to think about.

It's Time to Fly

When I reviewed this chapter, I wrote this poem for you to put the final touch on this important subject.

It's time to lift your head! Forget the boundaries of your nest.
Calmly let the mighty wind breeze hard against your chest.
Now's the time to spread your wings and raise them wide and high.
Your time is here, it has arrived, jump now, it's time to fly!

The future is in your hands. The decisions to be made are before you. At the most, I can only encourage you to evaluate your present situation and then look toward something that offers more—more happiness, more fulfillment, more satisfac-

258

tion. The only person who can instill the desire to accomplish more in your life is you. In this chapter you found the tools to help you, the source of energy you need to bring about this change in your life and the actions you must take to launch yourself toward that goal. At best, I can only be your number-one fan and cheerleader. I know you can do it. The secret to achievement now is that you need to know it too.

Plan of Action for Vocational Fulfillment

1. Review all the questions on pages *238–239* and journal your response to each question.

    _____

    _____

    _____

2. Review the **POWER** acrostic. In the areas of *passion, opportunities, willingness, energy,* and *results,* determine where you need to focus immediately to get closer to the life you desire.

    _____

    _____

    _____

3. Review the **BLASTOFF** acrostic. In the areas of *belief, love, accumulating knowledge, Sigmoid's curve, tenacity, oh the status quo, fun,* and *faith,* write what you need to do to take immediate action to gain the power to be your best.

    _____

    _____

    _____

4. What two steps can you take today to begin moving in a different vocational direction, a direction you know is right for you?

    _____

    _____

    _____

When you have completed
these four assignments,
go to my website at
www.toddduncan.com
for a fifteen-minute
motivational exercise on
vocational coaching.
See you on-line. —*TD*

www.**toddduncan**.com

Action Planner Notes

The Power
of Promises

The future is not some place we are going,
but one we create. The paths are not found,
but made, and the activity of making them
changes both the maker and the
destination. **John Schaar**

---

o be successful and to achieve our desires, we must
raise the standards in our personal life. By pursuing an
enriched-values lifestyle, we daily place our integrity at risk. In
achieving our goals, we make promises to ourselves and others.
From this point forward the richness of our lives is a reflection
of those promises, and our success is based upon our keeping
them.

By this time, you no doubt have already committed to
some new courses of action in your life. When you choose a
new direction, by definition you jettison other directions no longer
acceptable to you. As you do this, you first must investigate how
you have performed in the past. Ask yourself these next questions to help you think in this direction:

- Are you a person of integrity?

- Are you a person who keeps your word to yourself and others?

- How would you do in a *60 Minutes* interview?

- Is there anything in the private areas of your life that should not be there?

These are the kinds of questions I heard resonate from the heart of a man of unquestioned integrity, Chuck Swindoll. These personal inquiries forced me to look into my own life and ask, Am I a person of integrity? Would I pass the scrutiny of the outside world?

I know I do my best to keep the promises I make to others. If I say I will be home at a certain time, I am. If I have promised to spend the day with my sons, our time together is nonnegotiable. If I have a date with Sheryl, the only time it gets canceled is if we both agree to it. If I tell a customer I will do something for him, I do it.

Where I am most vulnerable is never in my outside world but rather in the privacy of my own world. If a private investigator were to follow me for a few days, what would he or she find that I would not want anyone else to know or see? Just thinking that gives me pause. What does that question do for you? Yet there is someone watching me every day; God sees my every move in the marketplace, at home, when I'm traveling, and when I am alone. He knows my motives and reads my heart. Knowing this, my motivation to be a person of integrity has grown out of my desire to serve and honor Him. Here's what the Bible says about the importance of integrity:

He who walks in integrity walks securely, but he who perverts his ways will be found out. **Proverbs 10:9,** NASB

The integrity of the upright will guide them, but the falseness of the treacherous will destroy them. **Proverbs 11:3,** NASB

A righteous man who walks in his integrity—how blessed are his sons after him. **Proverbs 20:7,** NASB

Integrity is defined as an unimpaired commitment to personal, moral, and absolute standards. To live a life of integrity signifies that you say what you mean and mean what you say at all times—without compromise. In your quest to have the power to be your best, integrity will be your most important trait.

Integrity is defined as an unimpaired commitment to personal, moral, and absolute standards. To live a life of integrity signifies that you say what you mean and mean what you say at all times—without compromise.

Where Are Your Cracks?

Sheryl and I had just purchased our second home and had spent the better part of three months getting it remodeled so we could move in our expanding family—our second child had just been born. After weeks of delays, moving day finally arrived, and we were in.

A few weeks later, I noticed a crack in one of the walls. A couple days later, I noticed a crack in the ceiling. Another several days went by, and I noticed another crack on a different wall. I was starting to get frustrated. Here we had spent all this money, and in less than one month our walls were cracking. I went to the garage for some filling compound and some leftover paint and then went from room to room, filling the cracks and painting them. When I finished, I breathed a sigh of relief and pronounced our new home to be as good as new. The cracks were gone—or so I thought!

Several weeks later, I noticed the cracks had reappeared. Again, I pulled out the filling compound and paint and re-treated them. That, however, did not solve my problem. In less than a week, the cracks reappeared. Then it hit me! The cracks were not the problem, it was the foundation! If the foundation of our home was not firm, the cracks would continue to reappear. If the foundation were solid, unmovable, the cracks would be less likely to occur.

The same thing is true with our lives. If our foundation is not built on a solid, uncompromising foundation, our external actions will have "cracks" that the best treatments of positive thinking and years of therapy will not touch. What is that foundation? Our foundation is our integrity—the one component that helps us weather the storms of life, keep our promises, and make us become the people God designed us to be. Earlier I shared with you God's words on integrity. Here is what His Son said some seven hundred years later:

Therefore whoever hears these sayings of Mine, and does them, I will liken him to a wise man who built his house on the rock: and the rain descended, the floods came, and the winds blew and beat on that house; and it did not fall, for it was founded on the rock. But everyone who hears these sayings of Mine, and does not do them, will be like a foolish man who built his house on the sand: and the rain descended, the floods came, and the winds blew and beat on that house; and it fell. And great was its fall. **Matthew 7:24–27**

What Jesus is saying is really quite simple: Your foundation is either strong or weak. The promises we make and keep are the foundation that sets us up to go the distance, to run the race, and to cross the finish line with joy and a sense of fulfillment that alludes most of the human race.

Promises for the Second Half

I wish I could have a conversation with you at this point in the book; I imagine it might last for hours. Lacking that kind of one-on-one exchange, I can only pose some thought-provoking questions and you will have to engage in some serious self-evaluation. Chances are good that you are either a baby boomer or a Generation X'er. This means you are probably asking, Is what I'm doing really all there is to life? In fact, you may already be framing your question along the lines of, What is success? and What is significance? Perhaps you began to feel your mind dealing with this transition as you read the last chapter. Although you have attained a level of vocational and monetary success, you may feel it is not providing the level of satisfaction for which you had hoped. This creative tension is good, because whatever changes you are making or contemplate making will usher in a series of "promise making" to yourself and to others. How you articulate and keep your promises will be the unalterable keystone for every success you will enjoy for the rest of your life. Conversely, not to keep your promises will have its own unsavory effect.

I mentioned Bob Buford and Mike Kiami in chapter 1. Mike was a strategic planning consultant who helped Bob determine what his "mainspring" in life was going to be. This transition is what Bob refers to as halftime or "what's in your box?" The metaphor is quite simple. Select any sport that has two periods of play separated at the half. The purpose of halftime is to ensure that the second half is more significant than the first. Halftime is when we look at what we've just done. It is a time to make both major and minor adjustments. If we are "losing" in the first half, halftime gives us an opportunity to review the tapes, check with outside observers, and look deep inside so we can set ourselves up to "win" in the second half. If we are already "winning" in the first half, halftime helps prepare us to keep winning. It is not how we start, but how we finish that counts.

> *If we are "losing" in the first half, halftime gives us an opportunity to review the tapes, check with outside observers, and look deep inside so we can set ourselves up to "win" in the second half. If we are already "winning" in the first half, halftime helps prepare us to keep winning. It is not how we start, but how we finish that counts.*

This concept, when it is expanded and applied to us individually, means that during any period of your life you could be playing a "game" with four quarters. You may make one, two, or even three transitions in your game plan to finish life in a winning position. Whether you use the halftime or a "quartertime" analogy, you can afford to make less and less mistakes as the game progresses and the clock winds down. How you play and what you play for becomes increasingly important. For example, had John Elway and the Denver Broncos not won the Super Bowl in 1998, Elway's chances to win a Super Bowl would have become statistically more difficult. Ten years ago, after losing in three trips to the great game, there was still enough time for Elway, his teammates, and his coaches to perfect their game and improve their skills until victory was finally theirs.

The premise behind this concept is this: As you go and grow through life, you are always looking at where you are and toward where you want to go. You make commitments and promises to yourself, your family, and to others you care about. Your promises, and whether or not you keep them, determine how you will finish the race. Furthermore, they will also dictate your emotional balance—or lack of it—along the way. As you progress, each decision and promise you make becomes the platform for the development of your character.

Whether you are in your twenties, thirties, forties, fifties, sixties, or beyond, there is an opportunity for you to pursue intentionally that which can give you a sense of true fulfillment. Once determined, you also give yourself the option to approach whatever changes and subsequent promises may be necessary with an unwavering sense of commitment. Here, however, is the hard part: If you are not transitioning to the end, you are dying en route and just refusing to fall over.

As you continue to change, transition, and move closer to the person God designed you to be, you will need to focus on what I call the "really big question." This question will help you clarify how you can ensure that you are choosing to do the things in each of your value areas that will produce the greatest possible results for you and those with whom you interact. It is the question that ultimately will create your legacy. The question is this: If my life were perfect, how would it be different? Ponder this question because it has within it the guidance system that can help direct you to the life of joy, fulfillment, and service you have always imagined. George Bernard Shaw said it this way:

> *Your promises, and whether or not you keep them, determine how you will finish the race. Furthermore, they will also dictate your emotional balance—or lack of it—along the way. As you progress, each decision and promise you make becomes the platform for the development of your character.*

This is the true joy in life—the being used for a purpose recognized by yourself as a mighty one, the being a force of nature instead of a feverish, selfish little clod of ailments and grievances, complaining that the world will not devote itself to making you happy. I am of the opinion that my life belongs to the whole community and as long as I live, it is my privilege to do for it whatever I can. I want to be thoroughly used up when I die, for the harder I work, the more I live. I rejoice for life for its own sake. Life is no brief candle to me. It is a sort of splendid torch which I've got a hold of for the moment, and I want to make it burn as brightly as possible before handing it on to future generations.[1]

As much as we would like to relive and redo elements of our past, it is obvious that what has been done is history. We cannot live our life on "rewind." The only day we can ever live is today, and for that reason we must know that today we are moving toward and living in accordance with what we know promises true and lasting joy.

The Power of a Promise Made

Keep asking yourself, If my life were perfect, how would it be different? What are your tentative answers? Do your answers surprise you?

Do you see how the promises you make to yourself and others help you answer this question? Would you agree that "living your promises" has a bearing on whether or not you live your life to its fullest? I am interested in your answers and that's why I've included my website address at the close of each chapter. I want our future conversations to be a dialog.

In 1994 I attended a conference at

> *If you are not transitioning to the end, you are dying en route and just refusing to fall over.*

THE *POWER!* TO BE YOUR BEST!

which John Maxwell was the speaker. He began his speech by pointing to three chairs that had been placed on the stage. I was not sure where he was going with this, but I can tell you that where he ended up changed me in more ways than I would have imagined.

Maxwell said that chairs played a significant role in his life as he grew up. For example, at dinner, dad always sat at the head chair. On the basketball team, the sixth man had a specific chair—the one right next to the coach. In the band, soloists had specific chairs. At graduation, the students with the highest grades and honors sat in special chairs.

I started to understand what he meant. Whenever I fly, I always have my favorite seat. When I go to a restaurant, I always like to sit at the end of the table if it is an option. At home, I have my usual dinner chair. In our sitting room, I have my chair and Sheryl has her chair. My two sons have their special chairs.

As I recall the story, Maxwell then pointed at the chairs indicating that there was number-one chair, a number-two chair, and a number-three chair. As I think about this experience today, I am still moved because of what came next. He said that chair number one was hot, chair number two was warm, and chair number three was cold. He then related the three chairs to our relationship with God.

Maxwell said something like this: Our relationship with God is either hot, warm, or cold. I also know that for many of us, our life in general is either hot, warm, or cold. We are either living our life with the sense of commitment and integrity that supports God's goals for our life, or we have "backslidden" a little and are a little off-purpose. Or we have completely stopped living life as we once had hoped and have settled into an almost numbing existence of mediocrity and complacency.

Do you get the picture as I got it that day? No matter which chair is yours, you will always have a tendency to slide. It is easy to relax a little in chair number one. Take life for granted. Assume your comfort. If you do that for any length of time, you will find yourself somehow suddenly sitting in chair number two. This is the pivotal chair, because your attitude determines

> *The goal of a marriage is for both partners to be in chair number one.*

whether you will go back to chair number one or fall further behind and end up in chair number three. The amazing thing about this illustration is that it works in all areas of our life.

Take marriage. We start out in chair number one. We are hot for our spouse. We say "I do" until death do us part. We are fired up. Hot! Hot! HOT! We do the things that keep the marriage fire burning. Then we start to take our spouse for granted, lose interest, and forget our promises. The result is that we slip over into chair number two. It was not our goal, and it does not mean the marriage is necessarily in trouble. What it does mean is that we are in a pivotal position, and what we do next, the promises we make, will determine whether our marriage will not only survive but also thrive. If it continues to slide (and begin looking for chairs four, five, and six), it may lead to separation and even divorce. The goal of a marriage is for both partners to be in chair number one.

Take a career. When we began our intended vocation, we started out in chair number one. We were committed to success. We did not plan to fail. We wanted to become the epitome of success, so we did the things that created more-than-average results. If we were in selling, we prospected like there was no tomorrow. We filled the pipeline with future business, knowing that even the best cannot win them all. If we were in leadership, we did those things that created goodwill with our new team. If we were starting our own business, we were relentless in doing that which would launch our work and make it a success. All this is chair-one stuff. Then something happens. We began to enjoy the chair. We settled in. We decided that comfort was more desirable than challenge. We started taking our prospects and our employees for granted. We no longer led as we once did. We began to regress in attitude, spirit, and actions. Voila! We suddenly found ourselves in chair number two—the not-so-hot chair.

What we do at this precise moment determines whether

or not we can get back to chair number one or if we continue the fall and revert to chair number three. This is subtle and will happen to the best, but awareness of the problem is the problem half solved. Where do you want and need to be? In chair number one. You will not get there by accident.

Take our health. While growing up, we didn't have to worry much about staying in shape. We ate whatever we liked, and we survived. We stayed out late, engaged in lifestyles that somehow did not destroy us—although you and I know how we pushed the envelope! Then it happens. We start to tear off another page from the calendar. The bones begin to creak. We cannot run as fast or as long as we once did, and now we realize we have to work at staying healthy. It's tough to stay in chair number one at this time of life. It's easy to slip over to chair number three. We miss the gym for a few weeks. We eat too many fatty foods. We become "couch potatoes." Bingo! The slide begins, and we find ourselves in chair number three. The longer we sit there, implacable and immovable, the tougher it is to make a change.

Take churches and organizations. Most start out with a mission that takes on the world. The vision is clear. The message is strong. Parking lots are full. Staff is hired. Everything is working just fine and then—Whamo! There is the inevitable slide from chair one to chairs two and three. Why? We strayed from our first love, our first commitments, our first promises—all the vital ingredients necessary for our organization to grow and to make a difference in people's lives. Life is in chair one; chair two symbolizes a slide in the wrong direction; chair number three is all about death and a hardening of the attitudes that brings on our physical and spiritual demise.

What chair do you want to sit in? How do you want your life to operate? Do you want to be in chair number two, living a life of mediocrity? Do you want to be in chair number three, living a life of progressive failure? Chances are your answers to these two questions is no. If that is true, then it is also true that unless you promise yourself that you will live your life in chair number one, you will by default settle for chairs two and three.

Maxwell was speaking at a Christian conference, so his

remarks had to do with faith in God. During his talk, he developed the theme that dads have sons who have sons who have sons. Each generation has an opportunity to create the environment for the next to be in chair number one, committed to faith in God. The primary requirement is that the previous generation demonstrates its commitment to be in chair number one over numbers two or three.

Maxwell said that it was the responsibility of the parents to live their lives in such a way that their children would grow up to be in chair number one. By so doing, there is a strong possibility that they will raise their sons and daughters to be in chair number one also. If you have kids and you understand this progression, I hope you feel the power of where Maxwell was leading us with his illustration of the three chairs.

Toward the end of the speech, Maxwell asked the fathers in the audience who were committed to raising their children to be in chair number one to stand up. He then asked the pianist to start playing. He said if we promised in our hearts to do this, that when the music stopped, we were to sit down, and when we did, we would be in chair number one having forever promised not to be in chairs two or three. With my eyes closed, and the soft music playing, I found myself emotionally moved.

I want my kids to be in chair number one. I want them to love God and to grow up to have faith in Him. I want to be a dad of authenticity. I want to be the model they would want to follow. The time had now come, and I prayed with about forty-five thousand other dads. I made the promise. The music stopped, and I sat down.

A month later, as Sheryl and I were watching a videotape of this speech, to the surprise of both of us, the camera panned to me, standing there with tears running down my face. The camera caught me in the midst of making my promise. My promise and commitment was caught on tape. One day, when my boys are older, I plan to play that tape for them. In that future moment, I want them to say to me, "Dad, you kept your word. Thank you for putting us in chair number one."

Where do you need to make some promises? What needs to happen in your life as you journey in the direction of your

274

> *We all make mistakes. We have all messed up. Although we cannot start over, we can start fresh. The even better news is that we can make a brand-new end.*

goals and dreams. Are your promises driving those dreams? Are you sitting down when the music stops? What are the issues in your life that need fixing? If your life were perfect, what promises would you have made to arrive at your stage of perfection? We all make mistakes. We have all messed up. Although we cannot start over, we can start fresh. The even better news is that we can make a brand-new end.

The way to engineer new, better, more promise-directed results is to return to your purpose. Ask yourself, What's in my box? What is one thing around which you promise to center the rest of your life? What can you do today to help propel you to the most successful, focused, values-centered level possible? What promises can you, will you, make that will provide you with the desires of your heart?

Five years ago, I asked myself that question. I was on my rock in La Jolla, reviewing my answer to "What's in your box, Todd?" I decided my answer was Jesus Christ. My heart dictated my response, and I knew I needed to revisit my goals and my priorities. I would have to change my course of action and behaviors. I had to make some new promises. Before you read these promises I want you to know that you do not have to be "religious" to make the "Promise Principle" work for you. It is not my intent to preach to you. I share this with you so you can make two observations: (1) to demonstrate how each promise touches on one of my value areas, and (2) to show you how my purpose of making a difference is embedded within each promise. On that basis, here are the promises that govern my life.

My Life Promise: I will be devoted to energizing people's passion and commitment to Jesus Christ; through active discipleship, I will do my part to help build His kingdom, glorify His name, and make a difference for eternity.

My Daily Promises:

1. I promise to be totally committed to Christ and to use the gifts He has given me fully in service to Him.

2. I promise to be committed to a vital marriage until "death do us part."

3. I promise to be committed to transferring Judeo-Christian values to my children as a model of love and respect.

4. I promise to commit the majority of my time to developing seminars, products, and books that transfer vital information to churched and unchurched people alike.

5. I promise to be committed to praising God regularly and to be an effective steward of all resources entrusted to my care.

6. I promise to be committed to the physical well-being of my body so I may maintain my stamina to serve God.

7. I promise to be committed to responsible fiscal management so I can be financially free to serve the kingdom of God.

8. I promise to be a mentor or accountability partner to at least five other people. (More on this in the next chapter.)

9. I promise to be committed to reading at least three books each month that expand my knowledge. This is one way for me to develop the tools necessary for personal, spiritual, and professional growth.

10. I promise to be committed to fostering deep relationships with those in my life who share my commitments and values.

These promises are the core of who I am trying to be. In the spirit of integrity, I am driven daily to live my life in accordance with them. They undergird my behavior and the decisions I make 365 days a year. They are the core of who I am and how I operate daily. They are the source of huge levels of power. As I continually review how they affect my life, I am struck by three main things:

• **Promises eliminate confusion.** When you make a promise, it helps you focus. There is less difficulty in seeing what you should do and what your motivations are in doing it. Promise making creates a more natural pull to the activities that you know will give you the life you desire.

- **Promises negate compromise.** It is hard to be out of sync with your promises for any length of time. The promise will always bring you back to the central behavior and action that is critical to success. You are more unwavering and dogmatic with your time and the way you go about making sure the important things get done.
- **Promises increase commitment.** When you make a promise that is values based, it is easier to have the commitment to live in chair number one and be "hot" for that promise. The more you execute the promise, the more momentum you develop for other growth tasks.

I can say that, without reservation, the most powerful thing we can do with our life is make the kinds of promises that have a major impact on governing our decisions and our actions each and every day. There is no other more critical, character-building principle than to make promises that affect your future. The only danger is in not keeping them.

The Power of a Promise Kept

Where are you? Are you living a life of authenticity? When we live and keep the promises we make, we have and demonstrate real authenticity. This is the well from which our real power and velocity in life spring. If we focus our life on the keeping of promises, we end up living every day with the power to be our best. I do not want to say here that this is easy—if it were, more people would have inner peace—but it is probably one of the most important issues we need to discuss.

We cannot live our lives in a lie. We have to be honest with our assessments of where we are, where we want to go, who we are, and where the gaps are in our lives. We've spent a whole book helping to define that for you. We now focus on the real essence of commitment or promises and how your character is a result of whether you are living in accordance with those promises.

Moses said to the heads of the tribes of Israel: "If a man makes a vow to the LORD, or swears an oath to bind himself by some agreement, he shall not break his word; he shall do according to all that proceeds out of his mouth" (Numbers 30:2).

Our life is a masterpiece, a work in progress. You are the architect and you are the builder. Each time you make a promise, it is an addition to the work in progress. Your masterpiece, the life you are designing, will become easier and easier to build as you keep more and more of the promises you make. Since each of your promises is tied to the values you hold dear, you run little risk in ending up with something you don't like. The key is momentum, thus the value to keeping your promises is that you continue to build momentum. The more you have, the easier it is to advance to the next level. The better you feel about you, the more likely you are to continue the journey.

I asked you some questions at the start of this chapter:
- Are you a person of integrity?
- Are you a person who keeps your word to yourself and others?
- How would you do in a *60 Minutes* interview?
- Is there anything in the private areas of your life that should not be there?

To make a promise is to take a risk. Look at the areas of your life in which you are not maintaining uncompromising integrity. What new promises should you make? Look at areas of your life where you are not keeping your word to yourself or others. What new promises should you make? If a sixty-minute interview were done about you tomorrow, what would they find that you would not want anyone to know about? What should you do in those areas now? To make promises is to risk, so the obvious question we need to ask is, Is it worth it? What's the payoff for making and keeping promises? I'd like sharing with you some of my notes from a seminar that I attended about five years ago. The speaker was Chuck Swindoll:

> *Keeping a promise creates substantial cultivation of our character.* You and I live our lives in a way that makes us either character killers or character builders. Therein lies the risk. Every time we

When we live and keep the promises we make, we have and demonstrate real authenticity. This is the well from which our real power and velocity in life spring.

THE *POWER!* TO BE YOUR BEST!

make a promise, we set the stage for one of these eventualities to occur. So when we make a promise, we have to make sure that it is genuinely a promise that we are likely to keep. The motivation to do so lies in matching the promise with our values. If we don't link promises with our values, we are not likely to live up to our promises. When that occurs, we take equity out of our personal character, and over time, if this behavior is repeated, we not only stop keeping our promises, but we stop making new ones. The great reward is in making sure that the central theme to every promise you make is values-based so that your character equity increases. Every time you do what you've promised, your reward goes up!

Keeping a promise gives us continued relief of clear conscience. You and I need to have a clear mind always. This is so critical in living life on-purpose. Every time we keep a promise, it relieves our conscience from talking negatively. As that happens, we feel better about the why behind why we are doing something. Simply by keeping our promises, we avoid beating ourselves up. We can live healthy, having a good outlook on our performance and building the subsequent motivations to do it again.

> *The key is momentum, thus the value to keeping your promises is that you continue to build momentum.*

Keeping a promise creates personal delight in our intimacy with God. On the spiritual plane, if our goals are God's goals, than our promises honor Him. When we live life in this way, He gets pleasure from seeing us follow through. We are told to seek first His kingdom (His goals) and His righteousness and all these things will be added to us (Matthew 6:33). The apostle Paul said that we are to conduct (keeping our promises) ourselves in a manner worthy of God (Philippians 1:27). If we believe this way, then we should strive every day to make and keep promises in accordance with His word. The manifestation of His power will come through us as we live these promises.

Keeping a promise gives us the pricelessness of the inheritance of a lingering legacy. You can't buy a legacy, you have to earn it, and when it's over, it's over! How will you be remembered? What will you have represented while here?

The unfortunate truth is that we can never really plan when the game is over for us. If your life ended today, what would others say about you? What would they say about me? We must create our legacy every day by making and keeping our word, and we will always be guaranteed that our absence will be felt long after we have departed. Our legacy is created mostly by what promises we make and keep to others. It is the investment of our time and talents in other people and other causes. This legacy is rooted in our keeping the commitments we make to others and to the causes we claim have some importance to us. A legacy requires time to create, but we should never wait to begin creating ours. If we do it right, we will be remembered for a long, long time.

Keeping a promise gives us the rare privilege of remaining a mentor. One of the great things about keeping promises is that as your character develops, your judgment and discernment develop. At that point in life, you go from learning to teaching, and you invariably become a mentor to someone else. This important responsibility can only be yours if your integrity is solid. Yet, as we make promises, one of the great ways we can be encouraged to keep those promises is through a relationship with a mentor or an accountability coach. You and I go through life needing motivators, models, and mentors. As we mature by making and keeping promises, we go from needing those three to becoming those three.

Keeping a promise gives us the crowning reward of ending well. Each of us will one day cross the finish line. One day our journey on this earth will end. There is no better way than to go through life now than by looking at it from the perspective of the finish line and deciding how you will run the race. The apostle Paul says we must forget what lies behind and reach forward to what lies ahead. If we do that now, we will finish strong, which is the most important part of the whole game of life.

Promises are the critical hinge on which our success is dependent. Are you a promise maker? More importantly, are you a promise keeper? There is no better choice for you to make in this moment than to be the latter. The only alternative is to be a promise breaker, and that's the fast track to chair number three.

Plan of Action for Promise Making and Promise Keeping

1. Look at the areas of your life that lack uncompromising integrity. What new promises should you make?

   _____

   _____

   _____

2. Look at areas of your life where you are not keeping your word to yourself or others. What new promises should you make?

   _____

   _____

   _____

3. If a sixty-minute interview were done on you tomorrow, what would they find that you would not want anyone to know about? What should you do with those areas now?

   _____

   _____

   _____

4. What are the top three benefits you would experience by making and keeping new promises?

   _____

   _____

   _____

When you've completed
these four assignments,
go to my website at
www.toddduncan.com
for a fifteen-minute motivational
message on promise keeping.
See you on-line. —TD

www.**toddduncan**.com

Action Planner Notes

The Power of a Mentor

As iron sharpens iron, so a man sharpens the countenance of his friend.
Proverbs 27:17

Two are better than one, because they have a good reward for their labor. For if they fall, one will lift up his companion. But woe to him who is alone when he falls, for he has no one to help him up.
Ecclesiastes 4:9–10

lympic gold medalist Michael Johnson has one. One of the greatest Olympians in history, Bonnie Blair, has one. The winners of the Ironman Triathlon, Thomas Hellriegel and Heather Fuhr, both have one. Arguably the greatest basketball player who has ever lived, Michael Jordan, has one. The first and youngest player on the PGA ever to win over two million dollars in a single year, Tiger Woods, has one. Leaders of some of the greatest companies in the world have one. Increasingly, thousands of individuals like you and I each year are bringing

one on board to help us gain and maintain the life we know we deserve. Behind every great accomplishment stands two people: the one who teaches and the person who executes what is taught. Enter the *mentor.*

One of the most significant things we can do with our life is to engage the service of another person or persons to act as our lighthouse in a stormy sea. This person is our beacon who helps us avoid the rocks and shoals, gives us counsel, and provides the encouragement and hands-on assistance for us to make the right decisions on this journey called life. This is not a go-it-alone process; to believe it is, is to struggle through a half-life. To build quality relationships with others is what gives our time on earth significance. The stronger our alliances with others, the better our decisions, and the better our decisions, the greater our confidence and certainty in what we do.

The History of Mentoring

There are many ways to make progress in the vocation of our dreams. We can read books, listen to tapes, go to seminars, and engage in the other normal methods of instruction—all of which are good, wise, and important. The fastest way to making right decisions in our work and life, however, comes from the influence and accountability of a mentor. This is not a new concept. Mentors have been around for a long time.

For thousands of years, influential men and women have been making profound impacts on the lives of others by being their mentors. One of the earliest examples of mentoring can be found in Homer's story of *The Iliad*. When Odysseus, one of the Greek heroes, left home to fight in the war against the Trojans, he approached his trusted friend, Mentor, and asked him to act as teacher and father to his son, Telemachus, while he was away. When young Telemachus wanted to learn the art of hunting, he spent time with Mentor. He watched and asked questions until his mentor believed the young man's skills were adequate to the task, after which he gave the boy the opportunity to hunt.

Another example of mentoring is apparent in the teachings of Jesus. For three short years He mentored a handful of disciples by teaching them the most effective way to live and how to teach those same principles of daily living to others. By His own spirited example, Jesus showed His followers how to deal with the angry, heal the sick, feed the hungry, and provide drink for the thirsty—physically and spiritually. The followers of Jesus could see firsthand how the Master handled material things, how He strove for intimacy with His Father, how He faced up to an ever-present opposition, how He treated women, and how much He loved children. It was a watch-me-do-this-and-then-you-go-and-do-likewise relationship.

Although Tiger Woods is one of a kind, one has to conclude that he probably would not have achieved his present level of greatness alone. He needed a mentor.

A more recent example of mentoring is Earl Woods, father of the golf phenomenon Tiger Woods. For years, Earl mentored his son simultaneously in the game of thinking and in the game of golf. Tiger's talents were shaped by his father, the key to making him among the best in his chosen field. Although Tiger Woods is one of a kind, one has to conclude that he probably would not have achieved his present level of greatness alone. He needed a mentor.

The Attitude of the Mentored

One of the great mentoring stories of all time is found in the Old Testament—a story that is as fresh in its insights today as it was when penned by the prophet Joshua. The players are Joshua and Caleb. Read these words and see if you can determine the attitudes of the mentor and the mentored.

> *7: I was forty years old when Moses the servant of the LORD sent me from Kadesh Barnea to spy out the land, and I brought back word to him as it was in my heart. 8: Nevertheless my brethren who went up with me made the heart of the people melt, but*

I wholly followed the Lord my God. 9: So Moses swore on that day, saying, "Surely the land where your foot has trodden shall be your inheritance and your children's forever, because you have wholly followed the Lord my God." 10: And now, behold, the Lord has kept me alive, as He said, these forty-five years, ever since the Lord spoke this word to Moses while Israel wandered in the wilderness; and now, here I am this day, eighty-five years old. 11: As yet I am as strong this day as on the day that Moses sent me; just as my strength was then, so now is my strength for war, both for going out and for coming in. **Joshua 14:7–11**

Verse 7 says that Caleb was forty years old when he did what Moses told him to do. This is a key point: There is never a time in your life when you will be either too young or too old to be mentored. In either case, you have to be willing to be *sent* and willing to *submit*. As we move through this discussion of the mentor and the mentored, ask yourself if you are willing to submit to another's leadership, knowing that it will, in the end, be for your own good?

Another principle of mentoring is found in the next two verses. Caleb followed the Lord fully. Moses had already created the background and the context for the people of Israel. They had been taught one thing repeatedly: to follow God alone. In this ancient situation, to be mentored meant to follow, to submit quietly and graciously, and to do it with joy. If you would be mentored, you too must spend much of your time in silence, taking notes, letting the wisdom of another soak in. To be mentored is always to submit fully as a servant to another. What sense would it make to seek the advice of a mentor and not follow his or her counsel? To be mentored is to engage in the fine art of *followership*. That is why it is so important to select the right mentor for you.

In the last two verses, we note that one of the requirements to being mentored is to have adequate physical and emotional stamina. Read these verses again and you will see that forty-five years had passed from the time Caleb began to follow until the time his followership was rewarded. If it took your mentor a lifetime to understand the key principles she or he is teaching you, that should be all the more reason to remember that it may take you a long time to understand fully and implement what you are learning.

In this biblical scenario, notice how Caleb's strength was as strong as when he begun. If you are a good student, being mentored will bring you an incredible sense of fulfillment. Not today, tomorrow, or even next year, but in the end, you will be strong, wise, and eternally grateful to your mentor. To do so, however, you must be strong coming out of the gate—mentally, physically, and spiritually to do what your mentor, model, and motivator tells you to do. Unfortunately, in a world where *submit* is often perceived as an unkind, politically incorrect word, not everyone will jump at a mentor-mentored relationship. To be pigheaded and to assume you can successfully go it alone is to flirt with disaster. It would be like Tiger Woods saying to his father, "Dad, just give me a club. I know what I am doing."

> *Your mentor will know how to share alternatives to your present course of action, warn you of the potential pitfalls, and give you the method and motivation to change course if necessary.*

The Art of Finding a Mentor

A good mentor will facilitate your growth, encourage your development, and provide a model and a method for you to follow. A mentor will walk you through the necessary steps to help you reach your goals. As you continue to pay attention to the promises you are making and as you focus on the visions you have set for your life, your mentor will be the one person who can do more to help you arrive at your destination than anything or anyone else. Your mentor will know how to share alternatives to your present course of action, warn you of the potential pitfalls, and give you the method and motivation to change course if necessary. Successful people report that the guidance they received from a mentor invariably made the difference in their business and personal success.

The biblical book of wisdom, Proverbs, talks at great length about the importance of mentoring. One verse states, "As iron sharpens iron, so a man sharpens the countenance of his friend" (Proverbs 27:17). What does this mean? Simply that if you want to make measurable progress in reasonable time, to go the distance, to accomplish greatness, and to maximize the time it takes for you to get there, then you best have a mentor in your life.

A mentor relationship helps you make a clearheaded assessment of your present situation and assists you in determining what new skills may be most beneficial to you as together you design a plan to acquire them. You and your mentor use your hours together to focus on plan completion, knowing that, en route, you can go always return to your guide for new information and new answers to new problems.

Mentors know they are also accountable to you as they make regular evaluations on your progress. Mentors must work as hard as you do. They must commit to give you new information, integrate it into the plan, and then work the process until you come out on the side of success. This is the most effective way to streamline your approach to the life you desire. With a mentor, you will get to your destination faster, smarter, and with fewer wounds. With a mentor, you will experience the joy of traveling with someone who believes in you, who will never let you down, and who will always have your best interests at heart.

All of this is prologue to the question How do I find a mentor? Here are some observations I want you to consider:

- Who do you know and respect who has attained a level of success and whom you would like to model? Call that person and request an appointment to speak with him or her about a specific issue.
- Determine who you might know who knows someone you could contact. Call that person and arrange an appointment to speak with their referral.

- Praise someone who has accomplished what you want to accomplish. Call him and offer your congratulations for something he is doing or accomplishing. Ask if he would be kind enough to share some ideas with you on how he does it. As time passes, such an individual may take on the role of mentor.
- Hire a mentor. There are many companies today who specialize in the mentoring and coaching business. You might seek out an organization of this type for the specific purpose of being coached by someone who has expertise in what you are trying to do.

These are four proven, time-effective ideas to help you initiate a mentor relationship. The key for you is to reach out and make it happen.

As you pursue your mentor relationship, do not limit your options. You may discover it is best for you to have more than one mentor at a time. You may engage the wisdom of a financial mentor, a health or personal-trainer mentor, a spiritual mentor, and a business or professional mentor. It is your life, and it has many facets that need specific attention. You may never have a one-mentor-fits-all relationship. The key is to look at what you want for your life and then travel that path by reaching out to those who can help you get to where you want to go. In my travels, one of the most interesting questions I hear is Why would someone want to mentor me? What a good question. The answer is simple: You are worth being mentored. You have tremendous untapped potential that may only emerge if you can believe that someone believes in you.

Earlier I introduced you to the concept of sowing and reaping. This law is the catalyst that evokes reciprocity. At some

In my travels, one of the most interesting questions I hear is Why would someone want to mentor me? What a good question. The answer is simple: You are worth being mentored.

point in his or her career or life, the person you may ask to be your mentor was mentored by someone else. The Bible says, "Let him who is taught the word share in all good things with him who teaches" (Galatians 6:6). We are teachers and we are students. One of the reasons you deserve to be mentored is because, down the road, someone is waiting to be mentored by you. If you have been taught something of value, you have a responsibility to share what you have learned. That is the ultimate meaning of a win-win relationship.

The Job Requirements of Being Mentored

If you want to travel the path of getting everything you want in life, you must understand what it means to be mentored. I have a very close friend who in some ways is my mentor. His name is Daniel Harkavay, president and head coach of Building Champions. Here are several of the character traits he and I have seen in the thousands of students we have worked with and mentored over the years:

1. A passion for excellence. At the center of the mentoring relationship lies an uncompromising commitment to excellence. This means you will no longer accept mediocrity or a mind-numbing allegiance to the status quo. If you would be mentored, you must first understand that you were designed to be the best. You are made in God's image, and He has great plans for you. Excellence is an issue of the heart, not the head. You must first believe that you deserve a better life, better circumstances, and better outcomes. You must believe in your untapped abilities. You must recognize that you may never operate at peak efficiency until you submit to the direction of someone who can help you get there—your mentor.

2. A teachable spirit. Kids have a teachable spirit. Nothing stops them. If they meet an obstacle, they pick themselves up and start all over again. They hunger for knowledge. They want to explore everything. Their curiosity drives adults crazy, but it is how they learn the lessons of life. As they get their

THE *POWER!* TO BE YOUR BEST!

answers and progress into adulthood, however, something terrible happens along the way: quest for knowledge slows down. That is why all of us need to "go back to the womb." A teachable spirit is when you admit you do not know it all. You are teachable when you maintain a spirit that subordinates your ego and pride to your quest for more knowledge. A teachable spirit means that learning never stops and that being mentored is a long-term contract. A teachable spirit means you know that commencement ceremonies are your signal that the journey has just begun.

3. Willing to experience short-term pain for long-term gain. This is also called delayed gratification. I hate it as much as you do. We want what we want now. Have you ever said something like "I've learned my lessons, now give me the good stuff." Sure you have, and so have I. The trouble is that effective living must push this line of short-term thinking aside. Getting what you desire will take time. New outcomes require new, carefully designed paradigms that will move you from your comfort zone (chairs number two and three) into the risk zone (chair number one). What worked for you in the past is no guarantee that it will work for your future benefit. In fact, you may have to jettison some of your cherished past options to create your new and better future. Whatever brought you to where you are today may *not* be enough to keep you there and help you to grow. New outcomes require new choices. This is sweaty palm stuff because it involves risk and the dissonance that makes your life uncomfortable and difficult.

Whatever brought you to where you are today may not be enough to keep you there and help you to grow. New outcomes require new choices. This is sweaty palm stuff because it involves risk and the dissonance that makes your life uncomfortable and difficult.

If there is to be long-term gain, short-term pain is inevitable. It may be the challenge of learning to pray with your spouse. It may be the difficult task of calling on former customers. It may be standing on a stage to give a presentation. It may be having the courage to engage in an unembarrassed conversation about sex with your kids. All of these are important tasks, and all of them are difficult in one way or another. Why do them? Because you will end up in a better place when you seize the power to blast through the immediate pain for what you know in your heart is ultimate gain. You say you cannot do it alone? Good. That is why you need a mentor to help show you the way.

4. **Willingness to be authentic.** To go forward, you must be truthful in assessing where you have been and where you want to go. Shakespeare says the wisest thing we can do is "to thine own self be true." If we want to arrive at the destination of our dreams, we must "come clean" with our mentor. We must be willing to explore why we are doing what we are doing to get what we think we want, when in reality what we need is something quite different. Former NFL head coach Don Shula said, "The mentor is someone who tells you what you may not want to hear in order for you to see what you may not want to see so you can be all you have always wanted to be." That may be the best counsel you will ever receive.

> *Former NFL head coach Don Shula said, "The mentor is someone who tells you what you may not want to hear in order for you to see what you may not want to see so you can be all you have always wanted to be."*

The Responsibilities of a Mentor

A mentor offers guidance, wisdom, and experience. He or she works with you to help you create a track on which you can run your race with confidence. Daniel Harkavay and I agree that the most effective mentors have the following seven characteristics:

1. They have the passion to see others succeed. Effective mentors have a loving heart that positively affects the lives of others. Their goal is to pour their energy and knowledge into another person for the improvement of that individual's life. Their defining moments are when their students win, because that is also when they win.

2. They have the humility to allow their students to take the spotlight. An effective mentor takes no credit for what he or she does. Mentors assume an unselfish, humble spirit, knowing their primary duty is to equip others for success. When the student does well, that is the successful conclusion of a predetermined and hoped-for outcome.

3. They have a commitment to being a life-learner. Gain knowledge, the Bible says. "A wise man will hear and increase learning, and a man of understanding will attain wise counsel" (Proverbs 1:5). Mentors never quit learning, not if they want to retain their influence. They read books, study trends, and listen avidly. They become adept in learning to read body language. Most importantly, mentors never feel that they have arrived themselves.

One of my mentors is Mike Vance. He is the former director of training for Disney University. From 1956 to 1964, Mike helped Walt Disney shape the future of the Disney Corporation. He did the same thing with GE and with Apple computer in their early stages of development. Mike and I were recently having dinner when he said, "One of the ways I am always coming up with new ideas is I read." He reads four to five books every week. The most impressive thing is that Mike, now seventy years old, is still totally committed to gaining knowledge—and this is a man who has undoubtedly forgotten more about business and training than many of us will ever know. Why does he do it? Because he made a decision long ago to commit himself to the wisdom business.

4. The boldness to confront when the mentoree's actions are not congruent with an established purpose. It takes great skill to keep calling the shots when the person being mentored has gone off-purpose. The mentor is the model and the motivator, and in that role, he or she must be the driving force when the student engages in spurious thinking and/or inappropriate behavior. Recently I experienced this with one of my mentorees. He was on the verge of destroying some of the equity he had created in his marriage. His wife wanted to go to a particular restaurant alone with him, and he wanted to go with two couples to a different place. Simple as this may seem, I saw the interaction as a potential land mine in their relationship. I took my friend aside, and as his mentor, I held him accountable.

He had long since established that his wife was more important to him than any other earthly relationship. It was my duty to remind him of the promise he had made. This meant—even in such a mundane decision as going to a restaurant—that he needed to change his course. When he did, this simple act sent a powerful message to his wife that indicated his true commitment to her. Had he not made the right decision, his actions would have confused that bond.

> *Further, if mentors want to retain their near sacred roles, they must continue to do what they teach to keep their relationship with their students dynamic and alive. Mentors keep up.*

5. They must have credibility. The mentor's past experiences must be translated into the kind of wisdom that makes him credible. Some people have fifty years of experience; others have one year of experience fifty times. There is a difference. Age does not necessarily equal experience, nor does experience guarantee wisdom. It is what one learns and applies to his or her own life during that fifty-year span that matters. Further, if mentors want to retain their near sacred roles, they must continue to do what they teach to keep their relationship with their students dynamic and alive. Mentors keep up. If they do not, their credibility begins to fray. When mentors continue their own quest for wisdom, as does Mike Vance, they will be forever sought after. Furthermore, they will create a legacy they never could have enjoyed had they decided to go it alone. Mentors know that the greatest force on earth is the power of duplication—and this is their job: to stand in the shadows as they pour themselves into the life of another.

6. *They must be modular thinkers and modular communicators.* Mentors must think and communicate compartmentally. The ability to take gray matter and make it black and white is the essence of mentoring. In the pursuit of doing, the mentoree often gets too close to a solution and begins to move on that fresh new data. The student, however, may move too quickly. The successful mentor slows the student down then removes and reconstructs the building blocks so the student can refocus. This skill is crucial for mentors since outcomes are never the result of one behavior alone, but the aggregate of many collective actions.

7. *Mentors must motivate and inspire.* When mentors motivate, they rely on personal experience to excite students. That is the mentor's stock in trade. Inspiration, however, is when the mentor so connects with the mentoree's values that movement toward a desired goal occurs over time without the mentor's constant involvement. In other words, good mentors are always trying to work themselves out of a job. The key to effective mentoring is to teach the student the Law of Alignment. Here's the amazing part: There will always be less need to motivate when students are inspired because they want to accomplish a specific task. Behaviors enjoy a longer life span when students are "pulled" to a task rather than "pushed" to perform it.

To be a mentor is to receive one of life's greatest gifts. That is why I call it a near sacred privilege. It is an honor to be one and a joy to remain one. Mentors never stop working. They never stop thinking about their students. They care about their charges and will do what is necessary to help them succeed, just as a mother and father will do all they can to help create the right learning environment for their children. If you are a mentor—and live your life right—you can earn the privilege to help others live their lives right as well.

The Value of a Small Group

In their book, *The Hidden Value of a Man*, Gary Smalley and John Trent reminded us of another kind of mentoring. They write, "From the time that Jesus left us to live out the Christian life, He put us in small groups, small centers of support—yet big enough to give us the help we desperately need during times of trouble, and major encouragement for positive growth."[1]

I know from firsthand experience that small accountability groups can change your life. About two years ago, several men from my church and I decided it would be beneficial to meet together on a regular basis. We knew it would be a challenge to find a regular date to meet since our jobs required extensive travel, but we all admitted that we constantly encountered situations on the road that demanded some form of accountability. For many of us, the bottom line was that we wanted our marriages to continue to grow and thrive, and for that to happen, the temptations of being on the road had to be held in check. Our needs to get together for fellowship and sharing were so strong that, in the end, a time to meet was the least of our problems. We decided that Saturday mornings would be the best time to get together, and we decided to read a book that focused on the challenges men face today. We were to read a chapter every two weeks and come prepared to discuss what it meant to us and how we planned to apply its principles to our lives. At the close of every session, we agreed on the next meeting time—if it needed to be changed— and what our assignment would be.

What an incredible feeling to know that a few great men are an integral part of my life. I can call on them day or night and every one of them will be there for me.

The results of our commitment and accountability to each other have been amazing! Over the last two years we have grown together in almost every area of our lives. We are all mentors to each other. We have learned to listen, care, confront, laugh, and cry. What an incredible feeling to know that a few great men are an integral part of my life. I can call on them day or night and every one of them will be there for me. More importantly, we are compelled to be accountable to each other—one of the most important things a mentor can advise his student. In our group we are both mentors and students. While our group is composed of five men, there is equal value when couples are involved in small groups. Sometimes, the results will be even more dramatic. This is illustrated beautifully with a story told by Smalley and Trent.

All of us face storms in life, but not everyone has a shelter from the storm. Thankfully, Kyle and Ann did. And if that shelter hadn't been there for them to run to, their marriage and family would have been shattered on the rocks.

Kyle and Ann live in a typical suburb in Southern California. They have two children, two cars, and the typical struggles that every couple faces. But what isn't typical is something Kyle and Ann committed themselves to several years ago that saved their marriage.

For 15 years, Kyle and Ann had weathered life's storms together. At times, their problems were like gale force winds, but their marriage had never come close to capsizing—that is until recently.

In the midst of financial and extended family problems, Kyle finally felt he'd reached the breaking point. Tired of the storm winds and of being driven emotionally night and day, in a tirade, he decided the only option he had left to him was to desert his wife and family.

Kyle tried to jump ship, but tied around his life was a line of support and accountability that kept him from going under…and his family from running around.

Without realizing it, Kyle and Ann had made one of the most important decisions of their married life when they joined a support group of other couples. Over the months, they had strengthened their support lines to the point that when Kyle began packing, Ann went to the phone and immediately called Terry, another man in the group. Within minutes, Terry had called Mike, yet another man in their group.

Like a 9-1-1 alert, the message went out that Kyle and Ann were in trouble. And after a response time that would make any fire chief proud, Kyle was starting at his two friends.

For months, these men had met weekly, usually on Saturday morning at 6:00 A.M., sharing each other's burdens, talking about financial woes or marital frictions. On any given Saturday, they might be going through a book together, or one man might have a particular verse to share. But always there was a time to pray for each other, to listen, to encourage.

And while they didn't have it written down, in unwritten words their small group provided two essential ingredients that would prove the difference between Kyle and Ann's falling apart or staying together.

First Terry drove over and talked to Kyle, offering emotional support of a close friend. Later, Kyle said that his time with Terry was like having an ice pack and a splint applied to a wrenched ankle. Shortly after that, Mike arrived, providing another dose of encouragement and support.

Since both were joggers, Mike suggested, "Let's talk while we are running around the block." And as Kyle let out built-up physical steam in their four trips around the block, even more importantly, he let go of the dam of emotional pressure that had built up in his life.

His time with Mike was a period of repentance, cleansing, and healing. As they walked and ran together, Kyle finally broke down and began to cry. For the first time in years, he let down all of his burdens.

While Terry and Mike supported Kyle, their wives, Gail and Shirley, were there for Ann. And the result was instead of becoming another single-parent home in the sea of heartache, Kyle and Ann became a shelter from the storm.[2]

In my own experience, small local groups—whether men, women, or couples—that meet regularly, or national groups that meet less frequently, provide at least five key benefits to their members.

• *A release mechanism for pent-up emotions.* To enjoy intimacy with a group of other people is healthy. As the group develops trust and respect for its members, it can become a platform for the release of emotional, mental, physical, marital, parental, social, and professional stress. It becomes the "mass" that protects the "member." When done correctly, over time, you can count on your groupmates for virtually anything.

• *Motivation to do the right things.* Depending on how often you meet, a small group can be the ideal place for you to discover the power to be your best. When you know other group members care deeply for you, without judging you or your actions, and that they may well be working through the same issues themselves, you will feel freer to be authentic. When we bring our small or large problems to others who have been there and messed up, we cut through the pretense and begin the process of changing course. Our resolve is strengthened, our esteem is enhanced, and we make measurable progress in reasonable time.

• *A tender and loving approach to perfecting performance.* When our group began meeting more than two years ago, we were excited about the opportunity of being together although we were still somewhat ill at ease in the beginning. Over time, however, we grew to love each other. Today, we hate to think what it would have been like if we had not made the commitment to meet together. Our love is expressed in hugs, prayer, concern, affirmation, and praise for one another. Simply stated, it just feels good, so we do it and God blesses us for our commitment.

> *If your self-acceptance is high, your self-control will be high. A small group gives you permission to feel good about who you are and what you are becoming.*

• ***Increased discipline.*** To gain and maintain the power to be your best demands a deep inner sense of self-control. A small group can help shape what you do outside the group and give you the necessary self-control that leads you to victory in every area of your life. This intimate fellowship keeps you from succumbing to the temptations you face when away from the group. Knowing you will be held accountable for your actions helps you not to watch movies that take away from your character and self-worth...not to go to a bar and make sexual advances toward another woman or man...not to use your money for things that are frivolous and damaging to the family budget...not to overreact to small problems when you are with your spouse or your kids. Self-control and self-acceptance go hand in hand. If your self-acceptance is high, your self-control will be high. A small group gives you permission to feel good about who you are and what you are becoming.

• ***The "sounding board."*** Small groups provide a great platform to run your ideas about life and business "up the flagpole" before you implement them. This resource reduces the possibility of failing in the major areas of your life. The concept of synergy applies here: Multiple minds working on a single issue will generally produce better results than one mind working alone on the same issue. None of us is as smart as all of us. The small group process fuels confidence and certainty and encourages more purposeful and intentional actions that, in turn, produce purposeful and intentional outcomes.

• **_Increased integrity._** It is difficult to lie to friends—at least it _should_ be. When you enjoy intimacy with a group of people with whom you have developed a trust-based relationship, your integrity will soar, you will be a truth teller, you will be on your way to becoming your best.

Chuck Swindoll provides a wonderful insight on the benefits of a small group when he writes,

> _Being creatures with blind spots and tendencies toward rationalization, we must also be in close touch with a few trustworthy individuals with whom we meet on a regular basis. Knowing that such an encounter is going to happen helps us hold the line morally and ethically. I know of nothing more effective for maintaining a pure heart and keeping one's life balanced and on target than being a part of an accountability group. It is amazing what such a group can provide to help us hold our passions in check._
>
> _Recently I was encouraged to hear about a minister who meets once a week with a small group of men. They are committed to one another's purity. They pray with and for each other. They talk openly and honestly about their struggles, weaknesses, temptations, and trials. In addition to these general things, they look one another in the eye and they ask and answer no less than seven specific questions:_

> The concept of synergy applies here: Multiple minds working on a single issue will generally produce better results than one mind working alone on the same issue. None of us is as smart as all of us.

1. Have you been with a woman this week in such a way that was inappropriate or could have looked to others that you were using poor judgment?
2. Have you been completely above reproach in all your financial dealings this week?
3. Have you exposed yourself to any explicit material this week?
4. Have you spent daily time in prayer and in the Scriptures this week?
5. Have your fulfilled the mandate of your calling this week?
6. Have you taken time off to be with your family this week?
7. Have you just lied to me?[3]

These seven questions pretty much sum it up. After reading them, is an accountability group for you? Do you think this "group mentoring" process would make a positive contribution to your life?

The Value of a Friend

The Book of Ecclesiastes in the Old Testament says, "Again, if two lie down together, they will keep warm; but how can one be warm alone?" (4:11). There is one inherent difference in the mentoring relationship of a small group versus that of a single individual. It is intimacy. Both types of mentoring are necessary. One does not replace the other, but there is a special power in the power of a friend.

I first learned of the power of friendship mentoring when I was fifteen years old. I was a salesperson at a sporting goods store. Over time, I kept seeing two familiar faces that would come into our store repeatedly. Whenever Bob Shank or John Esser came in, I knew they would be buying either running shoes or running gear since they were both avid runners. They were also successful businessmen. John was a dentist, and Bob ran a large heating and air conditioning business. As the weeks passed, they came into the store and

There is one inherent difference in the mentoring relationship of a small group versus that of a single individual. It is intimacy.

THE *POWER!* TO BE YOUR BEST!

asked for me to help them with their purchases. As our relationship grew, my admiration for them also grew. I did not realize it at the time, but our budding friendship was a signal that a mentoring relationship was about to emerge.

Sometime mentors will approach you— as Bob and John approached me and took the time to be my friends. I call these special people angels sent by God.

Throughout the following months, the three of us started doing things together. I was interested in them, and they showed great interest in me. Over the next three years, we developed a friendship that twenty-five years later is still very much alive. Why? Because both John and Bob became my mentors. John first, as he reached out to me and led me through a one-on-one mentoring program called Operation Timothy, a Bible study and sharing time offered by the Christian Businessman's Committee.

Several years later, as I began to become more successful in business—despite my drinking and drug abuse—Bob stepped in and started meeting with me. He helped me set goals and was patient enough to sit with me so he could understand my problem.

Sometime mentors will approach you—as Bob and John approached me and took the time to be my friends. I call these special people angels sent by God. The distinction that made for me was my knowing that when God sends you an angel, that angel is with you often for life. For the next few years, God continued to put Bob in my path. I would run into him at restaurants, pull up alongside him at stoplights, see him at functions. Invariably, each time I saw him I had not performed as I should have in the minutes, hours, or evening before. While I knew Bob loved me, his one simple question was always a judgment on my conduct as he would ask, "Todd, how's your walk?" Oh how that hurt. My walk was pitiful. Lousy. Not worth talking about. I knew it; Bob knew it; and God knew it.

Phil Downer in his book, *Eternal Impact*, says, "One of the things that has become more and more clear to me over time is my walk counts more than my words."[4] Why did I ultimately change for the better? Because I saw the consistency of Bob's life and the way he lived it. To this day, not only does he remain my good friend, but he is also one of three mentors I rely on to help shape my actions.

A Mentor Has X-Ray Eyes

In 1994, when my business was in trouble, I reached out again to a woman who seven years earlier had mentored me into becoming a successful speaker. Glenna Salsbury did more for my speaking career in far less time than any one thing I could have done on my own. I learned from her that a friend and mentor can see into and sometimes through you. If the mentor relationship has matured, a mentor will be able to cut to the chase, put you on the line, and move quickly to the core issues that are messing up your life, but you must be willing to follow your mentor. If you do not, what is the sense in having one?

If the mentor relationship has matured, a mentor will be able to cut to the chase, put you on the line, and move quickly to the core issues that are messing up your life, but you must be willing to follow your mentor. If you do not, what is the sense in having one?

I remember it as if it were yesterday. We were standing by the pool at the 1991 National Speakers Associations Annual Convention in Palm Springs, California, when Glenna said, "Todd, I wouldn't have a partner if I were you. It will only create conflict in the future." She also advised, "Todd, I wouldn't hire a bunch of employees." She also warned, "Todd, I wouldn't get a lot of office space." Okay, so that's two women who knew more about my present and future business than I did. Sheryl had told me the same things. So it would probably be no surprise to you to learn that three years later, in 1994, the first three things Glenna told me to do were the three things three years earlier that she had told me *not* to do.

Listen to your mentors. What they have to say over time may change, even as you change.

I learned my lesson. Over the next two years, Glenna told me twenty-six things to do to help save my business. After reviewing each of her suggestions individually, twenty-one made perfect sense and were implemented. (No partner, less employees, no fancy office were among the top three.)

The Accountability Asset

The two tracks that will make mentoring a valuable experience for you are learning and doing. In some cases you may get both qualities in one mentor, or you may need to get each from two different mentors. For example, John Ross and Daniel Harkavay are not teachers for me, although I have learned a great deal from them, but both are people who have helped me to shape my future actions by holding me accountable for my present behaviors.

Accountability is the most potent fuel you will ever put in your tank on the way to becoming your best... but when it is in sync with your mission and your life purpose, you will settle for nothing else. Go for it!

What I have learned about mentoring and being mentored is that you not only need to ask for accountability, you must demand it. It took me as long as six months to get my two mentors into the habit of holding me accountable. Now, every Friday, these two men ask tough questions of me that are designed to shape how I operate as a human being, a professional, a husband, and a dad. It is the greatest feeling in the world to know that when their questions come, my answers will be ready. I can give my response with integrity and without fear because I live with the daily knowledge that another Friday is around the corner.

Accountability is the most potent fuel you will ever put in your tank on the way to becoming your best. Sure, it takes guts to be held accountable—it also requires a spirit of humility and a desire for excellence—but when it is in sync with your mission and your life purpose, you will settle for nothing else. Go for it!

Plan of Action for Power Mentoring

1. In what areas of your life do you feel it is necessary for you to seek out a mentor?

    _____

    _____

    _____

2. Review the four responsibilities of the one who is being mentored. In what areas of your life could you improve your results by being mentored?

    _____

    _____

    _____

3. Review the job responsibilities of being a mentor. Do you have these qualities now? If so, can you think of a candidate you can begin to mentor?

    _____

    _____

    _____

4. What two steps can you take immediately to enter a relationship with a mentor? Who is that person? When will you pick up the phone and call him or her?

    • _____

    • _____

When you have completed
these four assignments,
go to my website at
www.toddduncan.com
to register for a drawing
for a one-month coaching
relationship with me.
See you on-line. —*TD*

www.toddduncan.com

Action Planner Notes

 TWELVE · From Grave To Glory

---

"Fool! This night your soul will be required
of you; then whose will those things be
which you have provided?" So is he who
lays up treasure for himself, and is not rich
toward God. **Luke 12:20–21**

---

*S*ometimes it happens without warning. At other times, you might get a little lead time. Either way, this life as we know it will end one day. With that as an established fact, that no one gets out of here alive, we need to ask one final question as we come to the last chapter of this book: How do we maintain the power to be our best up to the very end of our life on earth? Do we just fizzle out, or do we make our exit in style? How can we be certain when it is over that our journey will complete itself with glory and fulfillment?

The Pace of Life

It probably is not news to you that the pace of life is increasing. Look back for a moment and review where we have been and then look at where we are today. Twenty-five years ago, copiers were just beginning to appear in the office place.

Fax machines were a distant vision, used by only a few to send urgent messages to the privileged. Today, not only do we have copiers, but these machines also fax, sort, collate, print in any shape and any color, receive e-mail, scan text, and print final pages. These machines are not even called copiers anymore; they are referred to as document communications centers. The pace of life accelerates!

Not only do today's cell phones receive and send calls from anywhere in the world, they also act as pagers, voice mail, and e-mail. Of course, they are digital.

When did you last buy a computer? If you are like me, about six months after you purchased yours, you learned that the latest, greatest, fastest newest computer had just come on the market. Thanks a lot. Not only is the new machine faster and better, it was also less expensive than the one you had purchased. The pace of life accelerates!

We want faster and better and more bells and whistles. Because the industry knows us so well, it commits billions of dollars each year to feed our cyber frenzy. Did you know that the processor chips for the next twenty years are already on the drawing board? The pace of life accelerates!

In 1984 I was the seventh person in Orange County, California, to own a car phone. It was very expensive and it was very slow. It crackled, popped, and sometimes was useless. Fifteen years later, cell phones are free because the profit making is in the service. Not only do today's cell phones receive and send calls from anywhere in the world, they also act as pagers, voice mail, and e-mail. Of course, they are digital. All for the benefit of being available to anyone at any time in any place. The pace of life accelerates!

It was a good idea. The fast food restaurant was designed to do exactly that: serve food fast. Apparently the original *fast!* wasn't fast enough. A few years after fast-food restaurants became national landmarks, the franchises added drive-throughs. People could get their grease and cholesterol while their en-

THE *POWER!* TO BE YOUR BEST!

gines were still running. Fast food is now at your beck and call in most airports and major cities worldwide. Slow food is outdated; fast food is the rage from China to Russia to the tiniest islands in the sea. The pace of life accelerates!

Domino's Pizza figured this out early during the pizza revolution. This food giant became the number-one seller of pizza by guaranteeing delivery in thirty minutes or less. The drivers were under the gun. Any pizza not delivered within the thirty-minute window was free and the price came out of the drivers' pockets. In every city in America where there was a Domino's pizza store, the rate of traffic accidents began to increase. In fact, so prevalent was their message, according to one driver who was interviewed, that cars began pulling over for Domino's delivery vehicles clearly marked with the Domino's logo trailing in the wind. The chief executive officer of Domino's, Thomas S. Monaghan, said that the company was not in the pizza business but the delivery business. Only later, after the hew and cry went up against the danger to which these drivers were exposed was the thirty-minute delivery promise rescinded. Still, if you question that Domino's is not about speedy home delivery, ask yourself, Do I order Domino's because it's haute cuisine, or because it's fast? The pace of life accelerates!

Perhaps it is the old chicken-and-the-egg scenario. Which came first? Do we want more speed, or do the ad agencies and manufacturers create the need for speed and then fill it? Perhaps it is some of both. There is no shortage of claims made for faster and better, which for years promised to give us more time to enjoy ourselves. Yet you may have noticed such refinements in delivery have not given us another second. We still have a shortage of time. We are still racing to the end of our lives at full pace. We have no more time, just more of the same. The pace of life accelerates!

We still have a shortage of time. We are still racing to the end of our lives at full pace. We have no more time, just more of the same. The pace of life accelerates!

Answer the following questions honestly. Are you guilty of any of the following?

Do you ever feel that you are in a hurry?

Do you ever feel that you do not have enough hours in the day?

Do you ever jump a red light or go through the red light while calling it yellow?

At airports, do you walk or stand on the moving sidewalk?

At elevators, do you believe that the speed of the elevator arriving is directly proportional to the number of times you push the button?

At the checkout line at the supermarket, do you crane your neck to count how many items are in the basket of the person in front of you? If he or she has one over the limit, do you feel anxious, like you want to report this violation to the store manager? Do you keep score on which line moves fastest, like it's a race?

The pace of life accelerates. It reminds me of the father who came home from the office every day with his briefcase filled with the work he could not finish during the day.

One evening his son asked, "Dad, how come every day you come home, you always bring your briefcase?"

The father said, "Well son, I can't get all my work done at the office."

The boy replied, "Gee dad, can't they put you in a slower group?"

The truth is that most of us need to slow down and realize that the pace of life is not as important as what we do with our life.

This is what this book is all about—*What we will do with our life to make it the best life possible.* For more than three hundred pages, we have talked about everything from family to parenting to wealth to health. We have also talked about your relationship with God. Every word I have written has been designed to help you experience life to the fullest. As your coach, I have also tried to caution you to make sure that what you are doing, the plans you are making, and the direction in which you are going are in sync with your vision for the future. At the same time, I have tried to help you see that success and significance are not necessarily the same. Listen to what Jesus had to say about these confused priorities as He speaks candidly to a crowd of followers who gathered to hear Him speak:

And He said to them, "Take heed and beware of covetousness, for one's life does not consist in the abundance of the things he possesses." Then He spoke a parable to them, saying: "The ground of a certain rich man yielded plentifully. And he thought within himself, saying, 'What shall I do, since I have no room to store my crops?' So he said, 'I will do this: I will pull down my barns and build greater, and there I will store all my crops and my goods. And I will say to my soul, "Soul, you have many goods laid up for many years; take your ease; eat, drink, and be merry."' But God said to him, 'Fool! This night your soul will be required of you; then whose will those things be which you have provided?' So is he who lays up treasure for himself, and is not rich toward God." **Luke 12:15–21**

> *Get your priorities straight. Pay attention to what is truly important in your life. Do not think you can party forever because the band will finally go home, the liquor will stop flowing, and you will have to meet your Maker.*

What was Jesus' message? Get your priorities straight. Pay attention to what is truly important in your life. Do not think you can party forever because the band will finally go home, the liquor will stop flowing, and you will have to meet your Maker. Jesus is saying: Wake up! Pay attention to what will count long term!

The Bigger Barn

I listened to a tape recently by John Ortberg, an engaging and entertaining speaker. He told the story I have just quoted from the Gospel of Luke, but he changed the context from then to the here and now. His story went something like this:

Once upon a time, there was a bright guy. He worked twelve to fourteen hours a day. There was no question he was on the fast track. His business was growing. He worked every weekend. He joined every professional organization possible so he could network and expand his business development opportunities. When he was not working, he found his thoughts always drifting toward his work. Work was not only his occupation, it was also his preoccupation.

His wife tried to slow him down. She reminded him that he had a family and a home. He was vaguely aware that his kids were growing up and that he was missing out. From time to time they complained, wanting to be together, wanting to play, wanting to have him read them a book, wanting to spend family time together. After a while of not having enough time together, no playing, and no books read, they stopped complaining because they stopped expecting.

Finally, this man said to himself, "Okay, I'll be more available to my spouse. I'll be more available to my kids. I'll come home regularly—as soon as things settle down."

While he was a very bright man, he never seemed to notice that things were not settling down. One morning he felt a twinge in his chest. He told his wife, and they scheduled an appointment with his doctor. The doctor ran the tests, which indicated that the man had heart problems. They told him he had all the symptoms—high cholesterol and elevated blood pressure—and if he did not make some changes fast, he was headed for trouble.

So the man began an exercise program. He cut back on fatty foods. He reduced his drinking, and for a while he made progress. Yet as soon as his symptoms disappeared, his motivation also disappeared as he rationalized he did not have time for this regimen. There would be time for this later—when things settled down.

He recognized that his life was out of balance. His wife tried to get him to go to church. There were many good churches within a few miles of their home. The man intended to go, but when Sunday arrived, he started making excuses: parking was a hassle and the sermon was always too long. Besides, Sundays were the only time he had to recharge his batteries. Nevertheless he promised, "I will start going to church—when things settle down."

One day his chief financial officer came to him with some startling news. He said that the company was on the brink of a major breakthrough. If it all went right, none of them would ever need to work again. They were inches away from the mother lode. To ensure that they caught this wave, he urged that they upgrade all their systems, software, computers, and implement better inventory control, full e-mail accessibility, and total mobile capacity.

So the man became even more consumed. Every waking moment was spent on the opportunity at hand. He said to his wife one night, "Do you know what this means? We are going to be set for life. Our future is assured: financial security, a vacation, and everything we have ever wanted. We are finally going to be able to relax. Finally, things will settle down."

She had heard that before, so she did not get her hopes up.

By 11:00 that night she was exhausted and asked her husband if he was coming to bed. He said to go ahead because he had just a few more things to do on the computer. He would be finished in just a few minutes and would come up then.

At 3:00 A.M., the husband had not yet come to bed, so the wife went downstairs to get him. She went into the library and saw him asleep on his keyboard. She went over and tried to wake him up, but he did not move. She shook him harder. Still no movement. When she felt his hand, it was cold. She called the paramedics, but by the time they arrived, it was confirmed that he had been dead for hours.

His death was a major story in the financial markets. It was covered by *Time, Newsweek, Forbes,* and *Inc.* It was too bad he was dead because he would have loved the things they said about him. Because of his prominence, the entire financial community attended his memorial service. They filed past his casket and made the same inane comment people always make at funerals: "He looks so peaceful." Well, death has a way of doing that to you.

People eulogized him. "He was one of the leading entrepreneurs of his time," said one. Another reflected, "He was an innovator in technology and systems." Another said, "He accomplished so much!" Later, they built a memorial to this man and wrote these words on the headstone: "Pillar, Entrepreneur, Innovator, Success." They came to visit his grave, said their good-byes, and then they all went home.

"Our future is assured: financial security, a vacation, and everything we have ever wanted. We are finally going to be able to relax. Finally, things will settle down." She had heard that before, so she did not get her hopes up.

In the story from the Bible, the word on the man's tombstone needed only four letters: F-o-o-l. As I recounted that story, so aptly reworked by John Ortberg, I found myself reaching deep inside to see if this character sounded like Todd Duncan. Was I going down the same path? Are you going down that path of imagined success while refusing to build significance into your life?

For all this man's success, for all of his plans, for all his noble accomplishments, he neglected to give serious thought to the most obvious event of his life: his death. This was the one scenario he failed to consider. In the biblical story, God calls this the behavior of a fool, not because the man was unloving or mean or lazy—he was probably none of these things—but God called him a fool because he messed up his priorities. He had confused success with significance. For him then, and for you and me now, that is the behavior of a fool.

Two Deadly Illusions

There are two great illusions Ortberg talks about which we must understand clearly. The first can best be described as trading time for results. We often justify being "out of balance" by saying that there will come a time in the future when the insanity will stop and we will be able to enjoy our life in a way we are not enjoying it now. This illusion is referred to as "When life settles down, I'll . . ." The truth, for many, is that the only time life settles down is when we die. The second illusion is referred to as "More is better." This is the fantasy of acquire and accomplish. While there is no fundamental problem in growth, accomplishments, and success, it is how we pursue these objectives that concerns us here.

To better understand this issue, ask yourself, Who do I know who has what I would like to have? Are they really happy? Or ask, Have I ever pursued something only to discover after I received it that it did not bring me the happiness for which I had hoped? Perhaps it was a car, a home, a boat, or more money in the bank, more equity in your portfolio. Once you possessed these things, was your inner joy any greater? Perhaps it was for a while, but things wear out. They lose their luster. In the end, they really do not matter very much. No matter how much you accumulate, if your focus is on accumulation alone, you will continue to experience the same letdown; that is, until you finally discover the one thing that can give you true joy.

These two illusions cause us to miss out on life while we are trying to make a living. They keep us from planning for the most important things because we are so busy planning for that which has no lasting value. As I look at people who continually fall prey to these illusions, I see discontent in their faces. What do people want? Contentment? Happiness? Fulfillment? Respect?

We often justify being "out of balance" by saying that there will come a time in the future when the insanity will stop and we will be able to enjoy our life in a way we are not enjoying it now.

If the God-shaped vacuum in our souls is filled only with horsepower, real estate, and tanned and toned bodies with six-pack abs, there will be no inner peace. The apostle Paul says it like this: "I know how to be abased, and I know how to abound. Everywhere and in all things I have learned both to be full and to be hungry, both to abound and to suffer need. I can do all things through Christ who strengthens me" (Philippians 4:12–13). I think Paul meant that life is to be lived and enjoyed from a position of both success and significance. This is the key to a balanced life, and it will help you be your best until your dying day.

It All Goes Back in the Box

I love the metaphor of "it all goes back in the box." When I first heard Ortberg use it I sensed immediately that this was the best way to approach and live life. Like the story at the beginning of this chapter, putting things back in the box stresses the importance of going through life with the perspective that, when it is all over, the journey will have been fulfilling and your eternity secured.

Let me tell you a story from my childhood. David Stetson, Jeff Youngdale, Jeff Lange, and Gil Grado were my best friends when I was a kid. The street on which I lived had more than twenty-five kids and life was pretty amazing. We grew up together, went to the same schools together, and swam in each other's family pools together. Everything we did, we did together.

Our two favorite games were Risk and Monopoly. As I think back on the hours we spent playing those board games, I recall their central themes: He who acquires the most wins. Our games were intense, sometimes lasting for days—marathons. Buy real estate! Stock up on hotels! Own countries! Cash in big time! I will also never forget that when the game was over, and someone had won, all the pieces went back in the box. No matter how much money you had accumulated, no matter if you owned Park Place and Boardwalk and had hotels all over them, in the end, everything went back in the box. The game was put away. The real estate was left behind. The money went back to the bank. The most telling sign of this truth is when you die, everything you possess today goes back in the box.

The proper accumulation and use of these blessings is not what concerns me, but rather the abandonment of what is truly important to pursue what is ultimately trivial. That is where the tragedy lies because when it's over, it's over.

This is why God calls the man who misunderstands this basic concept of life a fool. He is so busy being a Type A that he gives no thought to the fact that, in the end, it all goes back in the box. You do not even have to believe the Bible to understand this truth. Just look around.

Please do not misunderstand me. We should be thankful indeed to have such great blessings from God in the form of health, homes, autos, clothes, money, and life. The proper accumulation and use of these blessings is not what concerns me, but rather the abandonment of what is truly important to pursue what is ultimately trivial. That is where the tragedy lies because when it's over, it's over.

Most of what we have worked so hard to accomplish will be of no significance in the end. If, however, we are good stewards of all that God has given us, our lives now—until our final breath—will have a significance that brick and mortar, big-screen televisions, larger BMWs, and masses of green folding stuff will never provide. The question that I posed to you in an earlier chapter was, How much is enough, and what will you do with the excess? What was your response then? What is it now? God says, "To whom much is given, much more will be required" (Luke 12:48, paraphrased).

Having Much Land

My friend Matt Gonzales once shared a story with me that marks the final thoughts on the futility of pursuing the two illusions of "When life settles down" and "More is better." It is a tale told by the Russian author Leo Tolstoy and entitled "Having Much Land." The story is about a peasant who, for much of his life, lives a contented life, or so he thinks. Suddenly, it occurs to him that he would be so much happier if he owned much land. He began his quest and discovered a series of opportunities to acquire land. First, he bought a little and then a little more. Later he bought some land with richer soil and then some land with still better soil. With each parcel of land he acquired, he removed himself further and further from his family. He was willing to pay the price because he knew he couldn't be content unless he had enough land.

One day the peasant heard about a village far away where land was being given away. Although to go there and acquire any land would mean a long separation from his wife and children, the man went. He met with the mayor of the village and the town elders, and they said: "You can have as much land as you want. Here is how it works. You start in the morning, and you give us ten thousand rubles. We put it in a hat, and at sunrise you begin to walk. The land you can walk around in a single day will all belong to you. The only rule is this that you must make it back to the hat by nightfall or else you lose the money."

He is so busy being a Type A that he gives no thought to the fact that, in the end, it all goes back in the box.

The peasant was excited, convinced that he could walk around a great deal of land.

The following morning, he gave the mayor the money, and it was placed in the hat. The peasant was then instructed to go to the top of the hill, the place where he was to begin and end his day's journey. As he began to walk up the hill, a strange thing happened to him. He had the entire march mapped out in his mind, but at the summit of the hill he glimpsed the whole countryside. It was all beautiful land, with rich soil and lush green vegetation. He knew his time was limited, but his desire was great. So he walked around plot after plot, determined to own as much land as he could.

While the peasant walked over the land he wanted, the day became warmer. Suddenly, the man noticed that it was almost noon and he had not yet begun his return trip. He walked around one last plot and then turned back. He had to move quickly to return to the top of the hill by sundown.

It was getting hot, he was getting tired, and the sun was setting faster than he could walk. The peasant, however, could not stop or rest. He had to keep going, so he began to run. By then he was so fatigued, he was out of breath. His feet hurt, and it slowly dawned on him that he was not going to make it. His greatest fear was that he was going to die. Yet he could not stop. The peasant said to himself, "If I were to stop now, everyone will think I am a fool."

So he kept going. He finally came into a clearing and saw the hill and the people at the top. As he reached the bottom of the hill, the sun set. The man's heart sank. Then he realized that the people were on the hill and for them the sun had not yet gone down. With one final burst of energy, he raced up the hill. At the very top he reached out to touch the hat with the ten thousand rubles, but as he did he stumbled. Reaching as far as he could, he just barely touched the hat. He had made it.

A man rushed over to help him up, but as he reached out to the peasant he noticed that blood was coming out of the peasant's mouth and that he was not breathing. The peasant was dead.

The mayor laughed, and the people returned to their village. They threw a shovel to the man, who dug a hole in the hill. Yes, the peasant got his land, but it was less than he had hoped for. Instead of hundreds of acres, he ended up with only six feet of soil. It was his reward for losing perspective. In the end, he did not get much land. At the end of our day too, six feet is all we will get—just enough to bury us. How much is enough? To what degree is our quest for accumulation worth the blood, sweat, and tears?

Yes, the peasant got his land, but it was less than he had hoped for. Instead of hundreds of acres, he ended up with only six feet of soil.

In the Blink of an Eye

I opened this chapter with these words: "Sometimes it happens without warning. At other times, you might get a little lead time. Either way, this life as we know it will one day end." What do these statements mean to you?

You probably saw the 1997 movie *Titanic*. The people on that ship died a slow, agonizing death. They had time to think about their fate. They knew they were about to die. As the famous steamship took on water, fifteen hundred people drew closer and closer to death. They had time to review their lives and reflect on the mistakes they had made and the things they wish they had done. I am sure many of those who were about to perish wished they had lived differently, but it was too late. They did not plan to die that night. When they boarded the *Titanic,* they did not plan to make it their last voyage. When the luxury liner sank in the early morning hours of April 15, 1912, this "unsinkable" marvel of engineering that had boasted of nothing but the finest amenities for its passengers had only enough lifeboats for one-third of the people on board. More than 1,500 of the 2,228 people aboard went down with the ship. Among her victims were some of the richest and most powerful men of the day: John Jacob Astor, Isidore Strauss, and Benjamin Guggenheim. Neither the poor in steerage nor the rich and powerful in first class had planned to die that night—but they did.

On July 17, 1996, when TWA Flight 800 exploded at thirteen thousand feet, the scene was much the same. No one boarded that plane expecting to die ten minutes after take off. These passengers were going to Europe for business or vacation, to see family and to have fun. The explosion apparently occurred seconds after a controller at JFK airport had cleared the plane to climb to fifteen thousand feet. At the time of the explosion, the flight's location was pinpointed by the air traffic controllers. Police and emergency medical teams were dispatched to sea.

There were 230 souls on board TWA 800; there were no survivors. While it took the *Titanic* almost two hours to sink, Flight 800 went to its watery grave in minutes. I am sure all the passengers who were on their way to death that night wanted to be saved; however, it was not to be.

As her Mercedes raced into a tunnel that Paris night, Princess Diana was not planning on dying. In the blink of an eye, faster than Flight 800 and infinitely faster than the *Titanic,* she found herself trapped in the rear seat of her luxury automobile with a fatal injury. Perhaps, as she lay there, Diana had only seconds to recall her life. I am sure she did not want to go. I'm sure she wished she could live. It was not her time to die. I am sure she wished she could be saved. Her life was indeed snuffed out like a candle in the wind.

> *Diana had only seconds to recall her life. I am sure she did not want to go. I'm sure she wished she could live. It was not her time to die.*

Every day the story repeats itself with slightly different details across our highways, runways, and living rooms. My family came within inches of death in the car wreck I described earlier. Fortunately, Sheryl and Jonathan were saved. Not everyone can be so lucky. Every day, people are told they have cancer, and they have time to think about it. Every day, thousands die instantly from heart attacks, and they do not have time to think about it. Most would rather choose life than death.

You do not have time to live life over when you receive your "wake up call." Deep within your soul you know where this is impacting you. You know that you need to balance the here and now with what is yet to come—the end of your life. In your heart and in your head you hold more information than you need to live life on earth to the fullest. You have the keys to unlock the power to be your best today and tomorrow—but what about later? In a book that has encouraged you to live a healthy, balanced life, the only thing we have not talked about is the question, Are you prepared to die if, in the blink of an eye, your life is cut short?

As I said at the beginning of this book, choices are the most important thing you can make in life. Your choices today will affect your tomorrows and your eternity. If you were waiting for takeoff on TWA Flight 800 on July 17, 1996, and after buckling your seat belt, a voice came over the intercom saying, "Ladies and gentlemen, this is your Captain speaking. Welcome aboard. We want to inform you there is a possibility that this flight might run into some trouble once in the air. In fact, there is a 10 percent chance that we are going to crash, but a 90 percent chance that we will make it," what would you do? Would you remain on board?

The truth is known by all. The apostle Paul once wrote:

For I am not ashamed of this Good News about Christ. It is God's powerful method of bringing all who believe it to heaven. This message was preached first to the Jews alone, but now everyone is invited to come to God in this same way. This Good News tells us that God makes us ready for heaven—makes us right in God's sight— when we put our faith and trust in Christ to save us. This is accomplished from start to finish by faith. As the Scripture says it, "The man who finds life will find it through trusting God." But God shows His anger from heaven against all sinful, evil men

THE *POWER!* TO BE YOUR BEST!

who push away the truth from them. For the truth about God is known to them instinctively; God has put this knowledge in their hearts. Since earliest times men have seen the earth and sky and all God made, and have known of His existence and great eternal power. So they will have no excuse (when they stand before God at Judgment Day). Yes, they knew about Him all right, but they wouldn't admit it or worship Him or even thank Him for all his daily care. And after awhile they began to think up silly ideas of what God was like and what He wanted them to do. The result was that their foolish minds became dark and confused. Claiming themselves to be wise without God, they became utter fools instead. And then, instead of worshiping the glorious, ever-living God, they took wood and stone and made idols for themselves. **Romans 1:16–23,** TLB

In your heart, you know the truth about life. You know your strongest desire is to be free, truly free—not just free to do anything, but free to do the right thing at the right time. Christ told His disciples what He is telling you and me today, "You shall know the truth, and the truth shall make you free" (John 8:32). You know where your life is out of sync. You know the changes you need to make to turn things around. Part of that discussion must surround what happens to you after you have lived this life. I have done my best to share with you how to live this life to the fullest. Now, if it is at all important to you, I hope you will ask yourself the most important question of all: Where will you go when you die?

I have always been impressed with him. His conviction is unwavering. His integrity is without question. He can counsel presidents and hold his own on *Larry King Live*. Yet, his message could not be simpler. The core of the message of Billy Graham is uncomplicated: "For God so loved the world that He gave His only begotten Son, that whoever believes in Him should not perish [permanent death] but have everlasting life. For God did not send His Son into the world to condemn the world, but that the world through Him might be saved." So here is my question. What if there is only a 10 percent chance that there is really a hell or a heaven? What if there is a 100 percent chance? Which sounds better to you? Because we never know when the game will end, doesn't it make sense to opt for the more attractive of the two options? As you complete your amazing journey on the way to becoming your best in this life, I hope you will also consider the life that is to come.

> *Christ told His disciples what He is telling you and me today, "You shall know the truth, and the truth shall make you free."*

It's a New Beginning

On August 8, 1987, Sheryl and I were married. It was an intimate gathering of about fifty friends on a bluff overlooking the Pacific Ocean. At the reception, my brother Bruce, my best man, offered a toast: "This is a special day. Todd and Sheryl are embarking on a new beginning. My wish for them is that as they experience life, they will see each moment as a fine pearl, that day after day gets added to the one previous. So at the end of their life, they can look back on it, see that fine strand of pearls, and know that it was a life worth living."

Thank you, Bruce. I will never forget your words because they led me to search for a poem on beginnings. What I found I share with you, Bruce, and with you, my faithful reader.

Beginnings

Endings are the seeds to beginnings. Tomorrow will come in time.
Even in hopelessness lies a seed of hope,
and even small seeds can climb.

But the little seed has to give up its past
on its voyage to the sprouting tree.
Didn't you ever transcend your life,
previous visions of who you could be?

Every cloud opens up to the smiling sun,
and the low will soon reach high tide,
Exits and entrances are at the same gate.
Moving through is your ticket to pride.

And two triangles have to surrender themselves to ever become a square.
And every simple discovery in life makes you give up
what you thought was there.

Caterpillars will butterfly off the ground. Give up your past to be king.
Horses run best when not looking back. Let go to reach higher things.

You have to give up your discomforts if you would soar in flight.
But isn't the end of something that's wrong
the beginning of something that's right?

So, you stand at the spot where endings begin,
handcuffed by the past or freed.
One path will take you to where you have been,
the other will set you free.

So pick yourself up like the rising sun, like the wind lifting the silent sea.
Plant a hope in your heart like a seedling in spring and
step forward to your new destiny.

—Anonymous

You Are a Miracle

Before he died, best-selling author and speaker Og Mandino and I talked about my speaking career. He told me the greatest gift I could give other human beings would be ideas that would make a difference in their lives—*a real difference.* I have tried my best to do that in this book. Now, as we come to the end, we have really arrived at the beginning. It is commencement time—the start of the life you desire and the life you deserve. Allow me to say good-bye by sharing with you some of Og's most powerful words from *The Greatest Miracle in the World.*

> *"You are the greatest miracle in the world. And now the laws of happiness and success are three. Count your blessings! Proclaim your rarity! Go another mile!"*

Go another mile! Where is this field from whence you cried there was no opportunity? Look! Look around thee. See, where only yesterday you wallowed on the refuse of self-pity, you now walk tall on a carpet of gold. Nothing has changed . . . except you, but you are everything.

You are my greatest miracle. You are the greatest miracle in the world. And now the laws of happiness and success are three. Count your blessings! Proclaim your rarity! Go another mile!

You are a marvel to behold, and I am pleased. I gave you this world and dominion over it. Then, to enable you to reach your full potential I placed my hand upon you, once more, and

endowed you with the powers unknown to any
other creature in the universe,
even unto this day.
I gave you the power to think.
I gave you the power to love.
I gave you the power to will.
I gave you the power to laugh.
I gave you the power to imagine.
I gave you the power to create.
I gave you the power to plan.
I gave you the power to speak.
I gave you the power to pray.
And, I gave you the power to choose.
Wipe away your tears. Reach out, grasp my
hand, and stand straight.
Let me cut the grave cloths that have bound you.
This day you have been notified, You are the
greatest miracle in the world.[1]

Yet those who wait for the LORD *will gain*
new strength; they will mount up with
wings like eagles, they will run and not get
tired, they will walk and not become weary.
Isaiah 40:31

═══════════════════════════

May you have *The* Power! *to Be Your Best!*

Plan of Action for Securing Your Future!

1. Read the book again.

2. Go back to chapter 2 and revisit your priorities.

3. List below the top ten things you are now motivated to do as a result of reading this book.

- _____

- _____

- _____

- _____

- _____

- _____

- _____

- _____

- _____

- _____

4. Write down the names of five friends you believe should have a copy of this book and call us at 877-833-DOVE.

- _____

- _____

- _____

- _____

- _____

THE *POWER!* TO BE YOUR BEST!

Contact my website to
receive a free twenty-minute
audiocassette on *The* Power! *to
Be Your Best!* if you would like
to hear more about developing a
personal relationship with
God Almighty.
See you on-line. —TD

www.toddduncan.com

Action Planner Notes

References

Read This First
1. Viktor E. Frankl, *Man's Search for Meaning* (New York: Pocket Books, 1980), 104–5.

Chapter 1
1. Bob Buford, *Halftime: Changing Your Game Plan from Success to Significance* (Grand Rapids: Zondervan Publishing House, 1994), 49–51. Used by permission of Zondervan Publishing House.

Chapter 2
1. Zig Ziglar, *See You at the Top,* 52. ©1976. Used by permission of the licensee Pelican Publishing Company, Inc.

Chapter 3
1. Shad Helmstedter, *Choices,* Shad Helmstedter Pocket Books, a division of Simon & Shuster, Inc. ©1989.
2. Norman Vincent Peale, *The Power of Positive Thinking* (New York: Prentice Hall, 1956), 14.
3. Al Ries, *Focus* (New York: Harper Collins, 1996), xi.
4. Peale, *Positive Thinking,* 13.

Chapter 4
1. George Rogers (ed), *Benjamin Franklin's The Art of Virtue* (Eden Prairie, Minn.: Acorn Publishing, 1990), 12–14.
2. Ibid., 48.
3. Peter M. Senge, *The Fifth Discipline: The Art and Practice of the Learning Organization* (New York : Doubleday/Currency, 1990), 13.

Chapter 5
1. Bob Beltz, *Becoming a Man of Prayer* (Colorado Springs: Navpress, 1996), 11. Used by permission of NavPress/Pinion Press. All rights reserved. For copies, call (800) 366-7788.

Chapter 6

1. Richard I. Winwood, *Time Management: An Introduction to the Franklin System* (Salt Lake City: Franklin International Institute, 1990), 10.
2. Charles R. Swindoll, *Intimacy with the Almighty* (Dallas: Word Publishing, 1996), 30. Used by permission. All rights reserved.
3. Benjamin Franklin, *The Works of Benjamin Franklin,* ed. George L. Rogers (Eden Prairie, Minn.: Acorn, 1990), 41.
4. Ibid., 42–43.
5. Ibid., 44–45.

Chapter 7

1. *The Hidden Value of a Man* by Gary Smalley and John Trent, Ph.D., a Focus on the Family book published by Tyndale House. Copyright ©1992, 1994 by Gary Smalley and John Trent, Ph.D. All rights reserved. International copyright secured. Used by permission. 42-44.
2. Ibid., 44.

Chapter 8

1. Steve Farrar, *Point Man* (Sisters, Oreg.: Multnomah Press, 1990), 17–18.
2. Ibid., 24–25.
3. Peter Wyden, *Growing Up Straight* (New York: Stein and Day, 1968), quoted in Farrar, *Point Man,* 202.
4. George Gilder, *Men and Marriage* (Gretna: Pelican Publishing Company, 1986), quoted in Farrar, *Point Man,* 204.
5. Sueann Robinson Ambrom, *Child Development,* 2d ed. (New York: White, Rheinhart and Winston, 1989), quoted in Farrar, *Point Man,* 204.
6. Peter Blitchington, *Sex Roles and the Christian Family* (Wheaton, Ill.: Tyndale House, 1984), 121.
7. *Raising a Modern-Day Knight* by Robert Lewis, a Focus on the Family book published by Tyndale House. Copyright © 1997 by Robert Lewis. All rights reserved. International copyright secured. Used by permission. 135.
8. Ibid., 60.
9. Smalley and Trent, *The Hidden Value of a Man,* 44.
10. Douglas Southall Freeman, *R. E. Lee,* 4 vols. (New York: Macmillan, 1934), 1:178.

Chapter 9

1. Marsha Sinetar, *Do What You Love, The Money Will Follow* (New York: Bantam Doubleday Dell, 1987), 10.
2. Buford, *Halftime*, 71–72
3. David Viscott, *The Language of Feelings: The Time-and-Money Shorthand of Psychotherapy* (New York: Arbor House, 1976), 127.
4. Peggy Anderson, comp., *Great Quotes from Great Women* (Franklin Lakes, N.J.: Career Press, 1997), 30. Copyright 1997 by Successories. Published by Career Press, P.O. Box 687, Franklin Lakes, NJ 07417.
5. Ibid., 86.
6. Denis Waitley, *Empires of the Mind* (New York: Morrow, 1995), 209.

Chapter 10

1. Buford, *Halftime*, 32.

Chapter 11

1. Smalley and Trent, *The Hidden Value of a Man*, 135.
2. Ibid., 133–35.
3. Farrar, *Point Man*, 151–52.
4. Phil Downer, *Eternal Impact* (Eugene, Oreg.: Harvest House, 1997), 65. Copyright 1997 by Phil Downer. Published by Harvest House Publishers, Eugene, Oregon 97402. Used by permission.

Chapter 12

1. Og Mandino, *The Greatest Miracle in the World* (New York: F. Fell, 1975), 111–15.